THE CENTURY

THE CENTURY

Alain Badiou

Translated, with a commentary and notes,
by Alberto Toscano

polity

First published in French in 2005 by Éditions du Seuil as *Le Siècle* and
© Éditions du Seuil, 2005

This English translation © Polity Press, 2007
Reprinted twice in 2008

This book is supported by the French Ministry of Foreign Affairs, as
part of the Burgess programme run by the Cultural Department of the
French Embassy in London (www.frenchbooknews.com)

ïï institut français

Ouvrage publié avec l'aide du Ministère français chargé de la Culture –
Centre national du livre.
Published with the assistance of the French Ministry of Culture –
National Centre for the Book.

Polity Press
65 Bridge Street
Cambridge CB2 1UR, UK

Polity Press
350 Main Street
Malden, MA 02148, USA

ISBN-10: 0-7456-3631-4
ISBN-13: 978-07456-3631-3
ISBN-10: 0-7456-3632-2 (pb)
ISBN-13: 978-07456-3632-0 (pb)

Typeset in 11 on 13 pt Berling
by SNP Best-set Typesetter Ltd, Hong Kong

For further information on Polity, visit our website: www.polity.co.uk

Contents

Translating the century

These thirteen lessons on the twentieth century were originally intended to be accompanied by a facing English translation. Rights and ownership intervened to foreclose that possibility. In the spirit of that original project, and by way of introduction, I would like nevertheless to include in this monolingual edition a reflection born of the initial plan that I shared with Alain Badiou. Since the lectures to follow aim to cleave as stringently as they can to the century's own propositions, it might be pertinent to ask what the century itself has to say about the question of language in general, and of bilingualism in particular.

While in many respects the century's philosophy has been marked, bar a few renegades and 'extremists' (I have in mind especially that brilliant and sombre Neo-Parmenidean from Trieste, Carlo Michaelstadter and his 1910 book *La persuasione e la rettorica*), by something like an apotheosis (if not a proto-theology) of language, an equation of philosophical with linguistic reflection (from the pedestrian propositions favoured in Cambridge to the tellurian homilies of Todtnauberg), the century's wordsmiths have been far more sceptical, experimental, or even despairing about the powers of language, be it ordinary or prophetic.

In concordance with the ever-increasing and often austere attentions that the arts of the century lavished upon 'medium', though perhaps with far more intimate and contorted repercussions, poets and novelists multiplied the ordeals undergone by linguistic material; just to consider the conventional armature of punctuation, so brilliantly explored by Adorno, the century's literature enacted both its suppression (Beckett's *How It Is* comes to mind) and its seemingly erratic, 'agrammatical' proliferation (see, for example, the stories of Arno Schmidt).

However, this endemic manipulation or flaunting of conventions was always accompanied not just by a reflective purification of medium (the belaboured narrative of aesthetic modernism) but by a veritable *hatred* of language. From William Burroughs's disquisitions on the 'word virus' and the prospects of an 'electronic revolution', to the sundry experiments (seldom compelling) in concrete poetry, language was attacked for being the very substance of convention itself, for its complicity with man's enslavement to utility, for its participation in the more or less surreptitious political control of human action and publicity. The twentieth century was also, after all, the century of prodigious, ramified investigations into the complicities between recording and control, inscription and domination.

Part of Samuel Beckett's enduring force lies precisely in the unique and exacting way in which his work combines, on the one hand, a formidable experimentation with syntactical and elocutionary devices and, on the other, a deep-seated, programmatic mistrust of the written word. Beckett channels these seemingly disparate demands through the strategy of bilingualism and self-translation (moving in the inverse linguistic direction, the obvious comparison would be to Nabokov's aristocratic delight in the infinitely layered fashioning and manipulation of linguistic worlds, with its labyrinthine complexity and ludic attention to detail – an aesthetic demeanour mostly untrammelled by the tortures of the Beckettian voice).

One doesn't have to (though one certainly should) frequent *The Unnamable* or the *Texts for Nothing* in order to get a taste of Beckett's intimate hatred of language (a hatred entirely proportionate to, and exacerbated by, his heterodox erudition). Already in his notorious letter to Axel Kaun of 1937, Beckett writes (originally written in German, I give this quotation in Martin Esslin's translation):

It is indeed becoming more and more difficult, even senseless, for me to write an official English. And more and more my own language appears to me like a veil that must be torn apart in order to get at the things (or the Nothingness) behind it. Grammar and style. To me they seem to have become as irrelevant as a Victorian bathing suit or the imperturbability of a true gentleman. A mask. Let us hope the time will come, thank God that in certain circles it has already come, when language is most efficiently used where it is being most efficiently misused. As we cannot eliminate language all at once, we should at least leave nothing undone that might contribute to its falling into disrepute. To bore one hole after another in it, until what lurks behind it – be it something or nothing – begins to seep through; I cannot imagine a higher goal for a writer today. Or is literature alone to remain behind in the old lazy ways that have been so long abandoned by music and painting? Is there something paralysingly holy in the vicious nature of the word that is not found in the elements of the other arts? Is there any reason why that terrible materiality of the word surface should not be capable of being dissolved, like for example the sound surface, torn by enormous pauses, of Beethoven's seventh Symphony, so that through whole pages we can perceive nothing but a path of sounds suspended in giddy heights, linking unfathomable abysses of silence? An answer is requested.

Note the urgency with which Beckett raises the question – which his entire work will endeavour to answer – of the capacity of literature to be as worthy of its time as the other arts (which only intensifies the irony of depicting the task of literature in an anticipation of Lucio Fontana's punctured, 'spatialist' canvases, or even Alberto Burri's burnt plastic openings). It is almost as if the burden of literature were compounded by this 'vicious nature of the word', as if the purification of its material required even riskier operations than those of the other arts (because the writer is ensnared or possessed by his own medium, constitutively incapable of abandoning it). Hence the call for a creative, resourceful hatred, an 'efficient misuse'.

Beckett's much debated bilingualism is part and parcel of this programme, which he brilliantly dubbed as that of 'literature of the unword'. A programme, it should be noted, which he adamantly distanced from that of Joyce. In Joyce's perversely erudite 'corruption' of the English language, the young Beckett (in his single extended essay of 'criticism', 'Dante . . . Bruno. Vico . . . Joyce', from *Disjecta*) already discerned something that would end up serving as the counter to his own linguistic strategies of 'leastening' and 'worsening': a saturation and corporealization of language, the transformation of the store of universal language into an inexhaustible, quasi-somatic reservoir of affective materials, symbolic allusions, delectable opacities.

Now, it is telling that from his beginnings as a writer – the period where he brashly laid down some of the ethical and aesthetic parameters that would later silently guide his punitive regimen of experimentation – Beckett already formulated the question of writing, and of his relationship to Joyce, in terms of what was to be done with the English language. First of all, he saluted Joyce's disdain for the ersatz humanist search after a universal tongue, in terms of his kinship with Dante: 'They both saw how worn out and threadbare was the conventional language of cunning literary artificers, both rejected an approximation to a universal language. If English is not yet so definite a polite necessity as Latin was in the Middle Ages, at least one is justified in declaring that its position in relation to other European languages is to a great extent that of mediaeval Latin to the Italian dialects.' For both there was no access to a universal language, but only a universalizing gesture: the invention of a language bearing a determinate relation to the multiplicity of spoken tongues and the capacity for thought and speech. Beckett paints Joyce in the image of Dante, saying of the latter: 'He wrote a vulgar that could have been spoken by an ideal Italian who had assimilated what was best in all the dialects of his country, but which in fact was certainly not spoken nor ever had been.'

The operation of linguistic universalization in Joyce is therefore not depicted in terms of the idealization of a canon, but rather of an all-embracing impurification: 'Mr. Joyce has desophisticated language. And it is worth remarking that no language is so sophisticated as English. It is abstracted to death.' But, crucially, Joyce's anti-abstractive opting for a full, almost synaesthetic language, which tries to turn 'the terrible materiality of the word surface' into a kind of pulsating flesh in which 'form is content, content is form', a language that is 'not about something [but] that something itself', is ultimately viewed by Beckett as an image of purgatory, a continuous, multi-directional, infinitely variegated space where 'a flood of movement and vitality' drives 'the vicious circle of humanity . . . without culmination'.

In such a domain there is no room for the nihilating desire of the hater of language, holes are not punched in language; on the contrary, language is constantly filled, multiplied, nourished (Joyce's somatic language remains the worthiest rival of Beckett's voices in the dark). Whence the crucial allusion to the subject of purgatory in the closing line of Beckett's 1928 essay: 'And the partially purgatorial agent? The partially purged.' Arguably, it was a dissatisfaction with this partial purging within a joyfully corrupted, garrulous English that partly drew Beckett to the bilingual stratagem, the purification of his thought in the transit between languages, the attempt to stop the vicious and natural adherence of language to speaker. Bilingualism conceived not as a machine for hybridization, but as a way of fighting the intimate compulsion of an irrevocably conventional speech; (self-)translation as a minutely calibrated filter for language, moving against the ease and obviousness of expression – the project to desaturate language is certainly one of Beckett's great contributions to a century that was not averse, especially in its waning years, to think of itself as a purgatory.

Transcriptions, as it were, of public speech, these lessons and their English rendering do not seek to imitate or reproduce the century, or even to be 'that something itself'; rather, as befits a pedagogy of conviction that must of necessity abhor nostalgia, it is a matter of conveying moments and inventions that were simultaneously refractory to interpretation and addressed to everyone, over and above linguistic affiliation. This universal address does not however exempt us from reflecting, in light of the hurdles and spurs that cultural and linguistic particularities presented to the subjects of the century, on the effects of the planetary hegemony of the 'new Latin', whether 'official' or otherwise. The problems that Beckett some seventy years ago discerned in *Finnegans Wake* – What is to be done with the English language? How can it be creatively manipulated, stripped or reconfigured? Can it be universalized *against* its status as the 'common currency' of global transactions (but also without slipping into platitudinous and reactionary jeremiads against 'Americanism' or 'globish')? – are still with us today.

Philosophical soundings of the century's molten subjective core, these lessons wager that the century's wilful compulsion to treat the intractable can be matched, in view of other, future passions, by the lucid transmission of moves and motivations that lay beyond the pale of consensual discourse and conversation; in other words, that philosophy can become a non-autochthonous space where the dark desires of the century can be rendered transparent to thought, or, to invert Beckett, where they may finally be *abstracted to life*.

I am grateful to Roberto Toscano, Lorenzo Chiesa, Peter Hallward, Esther Leslie, Bruno Bosteels, Michael Dutton, Donald Fanger, John Malmstad, Justin Clemens, Michelle Speidel and Sebastian Budgen for their timely help with issues of expression, reference and translation at various junctures during the preparation of this manuscript. Special thanks to Ray Brassier for his thorough examination of an earlier draft and his numerous and vital suggestions, and to Nina Power for her corrections on the final version. I am also grateful to Alice Brett and the staff at Polity for their fine work on this project.

Alberto Toscano

University of Nebraska Press for the extract in chapter 2 from *Mad Love* by André Breton, translated by Ann Caws (1988). First published in French by Éditions Gallimard.

Oxford University Press for the extract on p. 199 from *The Arrivants: A New World Trilogy* by Edward Kamau Brathwaite (Oxford University Press, 1973); and extracts from the poems of Osip Mandelstam, from *Selected Poems*, translated by Clarence Brown and W. S. Merwin (Penguin, 1986).

Persea Books for the extract in chapter 8 from the *Poems of Paul Celan*, translated by Michael Hamburger. Translation copyright © 1972, 1980, 1988, 1994, 2002 by Michael Hamburger. Reprinted by permission of Persea Books, Inc. (New York).

Princeton University Press for the extract on p. 207 from Paul Valéry, 'The Graveyard by the Sea', translated by James R. Lawler, in *The Collected Works of Paul Valéry*, edited by Jackson Mathews (Princeton University Press, 1956–1975).

Simon & Schuster for extracts from the poems of Osip Mandelstam, from *Selected Poems*, translated by Clarence Brown and W. S. Merwin (Penguin, 1986).

Every effort has been made to trace copyright holders, but if any have been inadvertently overlooked, the publisher will be pleased to make suitable arrangements at the first opportunity.

Dedication

The very idea for these texts could only have arisen thanks to Natacha Michel, who one day – against the current of all the anathemas launched at revolutions and militants, and flouting the obliteration of the latter by today's 'democrats' – pronounced the verdict: 'The twentieth century has taken place.'

The matrix for these thirteen lessons derives from a seminar given at the Collège International de Philosophie, during the academic years 1998–9, 1999–2000 and 2000–1.

I therefore thank the Collège, and in particular its president during that period, Jean-Claude Milner, for having hosted the public delivery of these considerations.

I thank the seminar's audience, whose collective support alone could have made the undertaking meaningful.

I thank Isabelle Vodoz, whose excellent notes, catching my improvisations on the wing and later committing them to type, served as the prime material for this small book.

Alain Badiou

1

Search for a method

What is a century? I have in mind Jean Genet's preface to his play *The Blacks*.[1] In it, he asks ironically: 'What is a black man?' Adding at once: 'And first of all, what colour is he?' Likewise, I want to ask: A century, how many years is that? A hundred? This time, it's Bossuet's question that commands our attention: 'What are a hundred years, a thousand years, when a single instant effaces them?'[2] Must we then ask which is the instant of exception that effaces the twentieth century? The fall of the Berlin wall? The mapping of the genome? The launch of the euro?

Even supposing that we could manage to construct the century, to constitute it as an object for thought, would this be a philosophical object, exposed to that singular will which is the will to speculation? Is the century not first and foremost a historical unit?

Let's be tempted by the mistress of the moment: History. History, which is presumed to be the unshakeable support for any politics whatsoever. For instance, I could plausibly make the following claim: the century begins with the war of 1914–18 (a war that includes the revolution of October 1917) and comes to a close with the collapse of the USSR and the end of the Cold War. This is the short century (seventy-five years), a strongly unified century. In a word, the Soviet century. We construct this century with the aid of historical and political parameters that are both thoroughly recognizable and entirely classical: war and revolution. Here, war and revolution are specifically connected to the 'world'. This century is articulated, on the one hand, around two world wars and, on the other, around the inception, deployment and collapse of the so-called 'communist' enterprise, envisaged as a planetary enterprise.

It's true that others, equally obsessed with History (or with what they call 'memory') count the century in an entirely differ- ent fashion. I can easily follow their lead. This time, the century is the site of apocalyptic events – events so ghastly the only cat- egory capable of reckoning with the century's unity is that of crime: the crimes of Stalinist communism and the crimes of Nazism. At the heart of the century lies the Crime which pro- vides the paragon for all the others: the destruction of the Euro- pean Jews. This century is an accursed century. The principal parameters for thinking it are the extermination camps, the gas chambers, massacres, tortures and organized state crime. Number intervenes as an intrinsic qualification. The reason is that once the category of crime is linked to the state, it designates mass murder. The balance sheet of the century immediately raises the question of counting the dead.[3] Why this will to count? Because, in this instance, ethical judgement can only locate its real in the devas- tating excess of the crime, in the counting – by the millions – of the victims. The count is that point at which the industrial dimen- sion of death intersects with the necessity of judgement. The count is the real which is presupposed by the moral imperative. The union of this real with state crime has a name: this century is the totalitarian century.

Note that the totalitarian century is even shorter than the 'com- munist' century. It begins in 1917 with Lenin (some would happily have it begin in 1793, with Robespierre,[4] but then it would grow far too long), reaches its apex in 1937 with Stalin and 1942–5 with Hitler, and to all intents and purposes comes to an end with Mao Tsetung's death in 1976. It lasts about sixty years – provided one ignores exotic survivors like Fidel Castro, or certain marginal and diabolical resurgences, such as Islamic 'extremism'.

Nevertheless, it is possible, for one coldly straddling this short century in all its lethal furore or seeking to turn it into the object of memory or contrite commemoration, to think our epoch his- torically in terms of its result. When all's said and done, the twen- tieth century would be the century of the triumph of capitalism and the global market. Having interred the pathologies of an unbridled will, the happy correlation of a Market without restrictions and a Democracy without shores would finally have established that the meaning of the century lies in pacification, or in the wisdom of mediocrity. The century would thereby express the victory of the economy, in all senses of the term: the victory of Capital, economizing on the unreasonable passions of thought. This is the liberal century. This century – in which parliamentarianism and its support pave the way to the triumph of minuscule ideas – is the shortest of them all. Beginning, at the earliest, after the seventies (the final years of revolutionary fervour), it lasts only thirty years. A happy century, they say. A rump century.

How can we meditate philosophically on all this? What can we say, in accordance with the concept, about the interlacing of the totalitarian century, the Soviet century and the liberal century? It's no use at this point picking some kind of objective or historical unity (the communist epic, radical evil, triumphant democracy . . .). For us philosophers, the question is not what took place in the century, but what was thought in it. What did the men of this century think, over and above merely developing the thought of their predecessors? In other words, what are the century's uninherited thoughts? What was thought in the century that was previously unthought – or even unthinkable?

My method will consist in extracting, from among the century's productions, some documents or traces indicative of how the century thought itself. To be more precise, how the century thought its own thought, how it identified the thinking singularity of the relation it entertained with the historicity of its own thought.

To clarify this issue of method, allow me to raise what nowadays is a provocative, or even forbidden, question: What was the thought of the Nazis? What did the Nazis think? There is a way of always leading everything back to what the Nazis did (they undertook the extermination of the European Jews in gas chambers) that completely precludes any access to what they thought, or imagined they were thinking, in doing what they did. But refusing to think through what the Nazis themselves thought also prevents us from thinking through what they did, and consequently forbids the formulation of any real politics that would prohibit the return of their actions. As long as Nazi thinking is not itself thought through it will continue to dwell among us, unthought and therefore indestructible.

When some say, casually, that what the Nazis did (the extermination) is of the order of the unthinkable, or of the intractable, they forget something crucial: that the Nazis both thought and treated what they did with the greatest care, the greatest determination.

To maintain that Nazism is not a form of thought, or, more generally, that barbarism does not think, is to abet a process of surreptitious absolution. It is one of the guises taken by today's intellectual hegemony, encapsulated in the slogan 'there is no alternative', what the French call *la pensée unique*. This is really nothing but the promotion of a *politics without an alternative*, a *politique unique*. Politics thinks, barbarism does not, ergo no politics can be barbarous. The sole aim of this syllogism is to hide the otherwise evident barbarity of the capitalist parliamentarianism which presides over our current fate. In order to escape this obfuscation we must maintain, in and by the century's testimony, that Nazism itself is both a politics and a thought.

Some will retort: 'You refuse to see that Nazism – and Stalinism by proxy – is above all a figure of Evil.' On the contrary, I maintain that by identifying them as forms of thought (or politics) it is I who finally accord myself the means to judge them, and you who, by hypostasizing judgement, end up protecting their repetition.

In fact, the moral equation that identifies the Nazi (or Stalinist) 'unthinkable' with Evil amounts to nothing more than a feeble theology. We have inherited a long history, after all, that of the theological equation of Evil and non-being. If, in effect, Evil *is* – if Evil enjoys a positive ontological status – it follows that God is its creator, and therefore responsible for it. To absolve God, Evil must be denied any being whatsoever. Those who affirm that Nazism is not a form of thought, or that it is not a politics (unlike their 'democracy'), simply desire the absolution of thinking, or of politics. That is, they wish to conceal the deep and secret bond between the political real of Nazism and what they proclaim to be the innocence of democracy.

One of the century's truths is that the democracies allied in war against Hitler were more or less unconcerned with the extermination. Strategically speaking, they were at war with German expansionism, not at all with the Nazi regime. Tactically speaking (in the timing of the offensives, the choice of bombing targets, the commando operations, and so on), none of their decisions aimed at preventing, or even limiting, the extermination. This was the case even though, from an early date, they were perfectly aware of what was taking place.[5] Today we can say the same thing as we witness our democracies – utterly humanitarian when it comes to bombing Serbia or Iraq – displaying an almost total lack of concern for the extermination of millions of Africans by AIDS, a disease that can and is effectively brought under control in Europe and America. But for reasons of property and economics, reasons stemming from commercial law and the priority of investments – for imperial reasons, reasons that are entirely thinkable and indeed are thought – medication will not be provided for dying Africans. Only for white democrats. In both cases, the century's real problem is to be located in the linkage between 'democracies' and that which, after the fact, they designate as their Other – the barbarism of which they are wholly innocent. What needs to be undone is precisely this discursive procedure of absolution. Only thus will we be able to construct some truths about the matter at hand.

The logic of these truths presupposes that we determine their subject, in other words, that we identify the actual operation at work in the denial of this or that fragment of the real. That is what I will attempt to do with regard to the century.

My idea is that we stick as closely as possible to the subjectivities of the century. Not just to any subjectivity, but precisely to the kind of subjectivity that relates to the century itself. The goal is to try and see if the phrase 'twentieth century' bears a certain pertinence for thinking, in a manner that goes beyond mere empirical calculation. Thus, we will adopt a method of maximal interiority. Our aim is not to judge the century as an objective datum, but rather to ask how it has come to be subjectivated. We wish to grasp the century on the basis of its immanent prescriptions; to grasp 'the century' as a category of the century itself. Our privileged documents will be the texts (or paintings, or sequences . . .) which evoke the meaning that the century held for its own actors; documents which, while the century was still under way, or had only just begun, made 'century' into one of their keywords.

In this way, we might manage to replace the passing of judgements with the resolution of some problems. The current moral inflation means that, on all sides, the century is being judged . . . and condemned. My aim is not to rehabilitate the century, but only to think it, and thus to show how it is thinkable. What should primarily arouse our interest is not the century's 'worth' before a court of human rights whose intellectual mediocrity bears comparison with the juridical and political mediocrity of the International Criminal Tribunal set up by the Americans. Instead, let us attempt to isolate and work through a few enigmas.

To conclude this lesson, I will address one of these enigmas, whose significance is hard to underestimate.

The twentieth century kicks off in an exceptional fashion. Let us take the two great decades between 1890 and 1914 as the century's prologue. In every field of thought these years represent a period of exceptional invention, marked by a polymorphous creativity that can only be compared to the Florentine Renaissance or the century of Pericles. It is a prodigious period of excitement and rupture. Consider just a few of its milestones. In 1898, Mallarmé dies, shortly after having published the manifesto of modern writing, *Un coup de dés jamais* . . . In 1905, Einstein invents special relativity (unless he was anticipated by Poincaré), together with the quantum theory of light. In 1900, Freud publishes *The Interpretation of Dreams*, providing the psychoanalytic revolution with its first systematic masterpiece. Still in Vienna, in 1908, Schoenberg establishes the possibility of an atonal music. In 1902, Lenin creates modern politics, a creation set down in *What is to be Done?* This period also sees the publication of the vast novels of James and Conrad, the writing of the bulk of Proust's *In Search of Lost Time*, and the maturation of Joyce's *Ulysses*. Mathematical logic, inaugurated by Frege, with the contribution, among others, of Russell, Hilbert and the young

Wittgenstein, together with its sister discipline, the philosophy of language, takes hold both on the continent and in the United Kingdom. Now witness, around 1912, how Picasso and Braque undermine the logic of painting. Husserl, with solitary obstinacy, elucidates phenomenological description. In parallel, geniuses such as Poincaré and Hilbert – heirs to Riemann, Dedekind and Cantor – give a new foundation to the very style of mathematics. Just before the war of 1914, in Portugal, Fernando Pessoa sets some Herculean tasks for poetry. Cinema itself, having been invented only recently, finds its first geniuses in Méliès, Griffith and Chaplin. The list of wonders populating this brief period could go on and on.

But this period is immediately followed by something resembling a long tragedy, whose tone is established by the war of 1914–18: the tragedy of the unfeeling manipulation of human material. There is certainly a spirit of the thirties. As we shall see, it is far from being sterile. But it is as violent and monolithic as the spirit of the beginning of the century was unbridled and inventive. The sense of this succession confronts us with an enigma.

Or perhaps a problem. Let's ask ourselves this: The terrible thirties, forties, or even fifties – with their world wars, colonial wars, opaque political constructions, vast massacres, gigantic and precarious undertakings, victories whose costs are so astronomical one is tempted to call them defeats – is all this in relation (or nonrelation) with the luminous, creative, and civilized inception that the first years of the century seem to represent? Between these two periods, there is the war of 1914. So what is the meaning of this war? Of what is it the result, or the symbol?

There is no hope of resolving this problem unless we keep in mind that the blessed period before the war is also that of the apogee of colonial conquest, of Europe's stranglehold over the entirety of the earth, or very nearly. And therefore that elsewhere, far away but also very close to everyone's conscience, in the midst of every family, servitude and massacre are already present. Well before the war of 1914, there is Africa, delivered over to what some rare witnesses and artists will call an upright conquering savagery.[6] I myself gaze with dread upon that Larousse dictionary of 1932, passed on to me by my parents, wherein, under the heading – viewed as universally unproblematic – of the hierarchy of races, the skull of the black man is positioned between that of the gorilla, on the one hand, and the European, on the other.

After two or three centuries of the deportation of human meat for the purpose of slavery, conquest managed to turn Africa into the horrific obverse of European, capitalist, democratic splendour. And this continues to our very day. In the dark fury of the thirties, in the indifference to death, there is something that certainly originates in the Great War and the trenches, but also something that comes – as a sort of infernal return – from the colonies, from the way that the differences within humanity were envisaged down there.

Let us grant that our century is the one – as Malraux put it – in which politics turned into tragedy. What was it at the beginning of the century, during the golden inauguration of the *belle époque*, that prepared this vision of things? Basically, from a certain point onwards, the century was haunted by the idea of changing man, of creating a new man. It's true that this idea circulates between the various fascisms and communisms, that their statues are more or less the same: on the one hand, the proletarian standing at the threshold of an emancipated world, on the other, the exemplary Aryan, Siegfried bringing down the dragons of decadence. Creating a new humanity always comes down to demanding that the old one be destroyed. A violent, unreconciled debate rages about the nature of this old humanity. But each and every time, the project is so radical that in the course of its realization the singularity of human lives is not taken into account. There is nothing there but a *material*. A little like the way in which, for practitioners of modern art, sounds and forms, torn from their tonal or figurative harmony, were nothing but materials whose destination needed to be entirely recast. Or like the way formal signs, divested of any objective idealization, projected mathematics towards an automated completion. In this sense, the project of the new man is a project of rupture and foundation that sustains – within the domain of history and the state – the same subjective tonality as the scientific, artistic and sexual ruptures of the beginning of the century. Hence it is possible to argue that the century has been faithful to its prologue. Ferociously faithful.

What is intriguing is that today these categories are dead and buried, that no one gets involved any more with the political creation of a new man. On the contrary, what we hear from all sides is the demand for the conservation of the old humanity and of all endangered species to boot (our ancient wheat included) – when it is precisely today, with the advent of genetic engineering, that preparations are under way for a real transformation of man, for the modification of the species. What makes all the difference is that genetics is profoundly apolitical. I think I could even say that it is stupid, or at least that it doesn't represent a form of thought, but, at best, a technique. Thus, it is perfectly coherent for the condemnation of the Promethean political project (the new man of the emancipated society) to coincide with the technical (and ultimately financial) possibility of transforming the specificity of man. This is because such a change does not correspond to any kind of project. We learn of its possibility from newspapers; that we could have five limbs, or be immortal. And all this will come to pass precisely because it is not a project. It will happen in accordance with the automatism of things.

In short, we are living through the revenge of what is most blind and objective in the economic appropriation of technics over what is most subjective and voluntary in politics. And even, in a certain sense, the revenge of the scientific problem over the political project. Science – therein lies its grandeur – possesses problems; it does not have a project. 'To change what is deepest in man'[7] was a revolutionary project, doubtless a bad one; it has now become a scientific problem, or perhaps merely a technical problem, in any case a problem that allows for solutions. We know how, or at least we will know.

Of course, we could ask: What is to be done about the fact that we know how? But to reply to this question we require a project. A political project: grandiose, epic and violent. Believe me, inane ethical committees will never provide us with an answer to the following question: 'What is to be done about this fact: that science knows how to make a new man?' And since there is no project, or as long as there is no project, everyone knows there is only one answer: profit will tell us what to do.

Ultimately, and right to its very end, the century will indeed have been the century of the emergence of another humanity, of a radical transformation of what man is. In this respect it will have remained faithful to the extraordinary cognitive ruptures that marked its initial years – though it will have shifted, little by little, from the register of the project to that of the automatisms of profit. The project will have killed many. Automatism likewise, and it will continue to do so, but without anyone being able to name a culprit. Let's agree – so that we may then seek an explanation – that this century has served as the occasion for vast crimes. But let's immediately add that it's not over, now that criminals with names have been replaced by criminals as anonymous as joint-stock companies.

2

The beast

Since our method takes its cue from the ways in which the century relates to itself, the poem entitled *The Age* by the Russian poet Osip Mandelstam is without doubt an exemplary document.* All the more for having been written in the twenties, right after the war of 1914 and during the first years of Bolshevik power.

Mandelstam[8] is now recognized as one of the century's greatest poets. This was certainly not so during the years under consideration. That's not to say he was an obscure writer. Mandelstam traversed the formal frenzy that characterized the poetic schools of the pre-war period. In his own way, he too was a man of the war and the revolution. The violent and unprecedented happenings taking place in his country moved him, eliciting his poetic meditation. In the thirties, he embarked upon an artistic rebellion of sorts against Stalinist despotism, but without either becoming a genuine political opponent or ever imagining that his fate could lie elsewhere than in the USSR. His judgement was always anchored in poetry, or in the very subtle thinking that surrounds it. He was first arrested in 1934 after having written a poem about Stalin,[9] a poem that is less an act of political criticism than a sardonic and bitter warning. Mandelstam, who was an imprudent man, a man possessed with a naive confidence in thought, showed this poem to a dozen people – probably eight or nine too many. Everyone reckoned he was done for, but he was freed following a personal intervention by the Leader himself. It was one of those theatrical effects that despots love to indulge in when dealing with artists. Stalin telephoned Pasternak in the middle of the night to ask him if Mandelstam was really one of the great poets of the

Russian language. On the basis of Pasternak's affirmative response, what would have probably been a fatal deportation was commuted into house arrest. This was but a brief respite. Mandelstam was caught up in the great purges of '37 and perished at the edges of Asia, on his way to the camps.

The poem we are about to study precedes these events by quite some time, dating as it does from 1923. In 1923, while the fate of the USSR remained in suspense, an intense intellectual activity still reigned.[10] Mandelstam was poetically conscious that something fundamental was at stake in the chaotic developments affecting his country. He attempted to elucidate for his own sake the enigma represented by this moment of uncertainty and oscillation, which caused him great disquiet. Let us read the entire poem, in Steven Broyde's translation:*

My age, my beast, who will be able	1
To look into your pupils	2
And with his own blood glue together	3
The vertebrae of two centuries?	4
Blood-the-builder gushes	5
From the throat of earthly things,	6
Only a parasite trembles	7
On the threshold of new days.	8
A creature, as long as it has enough life,	9
Must carry its backbone,	10
And a wave plays	11
With the invisible vertebration.	12
Like a baby's tender cartilage,	13
Oh age of infant earth,	14
Once again the sinciput of life, like a lamb,	15
Has been sacrificed.	16
In order to pull the age out of captivity,	17
In order to begin a new world,	18
The elbows of nodular days	19
Must be bound with a flute.	20
It's the age that rocks the wave	21
With human anguish,	22
And in the grass a viper breathes	23
The golden measure of the age.	24

Buds will again swell,	25
A sprout of green will spurt,	26
But your backbone is broken,	27
My beautiful, pitiful age.	28
And with a senseless smile	29
You look backward, cruel and weak,	30
Like a beast, once supple,	31
At the tracks of your own paws.	32

(1) The poem's central figure, the one that prescribes its meaning, is the figure of the animal or the beast, on which the text begins and ends. This century – which has barely begun but which in Russia has inflicted a break far more radical than elsewhere – is a beast. The poem will X-ray the beast, producing an image of its skeleton, of its bone-structure. At the outset, the beast is alive. By the end, it is looking at its own footprints. In the interim, the decisive question is that of vertebration, of the solidity of the beast's backbone. What is the philosopher to make of all this?

This poem attempts to construct an organic (as opposed to a mechanist) vision of the century. The duty of thought is to subjectivate the century as a living composition. But the whole poem shows that the question of this beast's life remains uncertain. The poem asks: In what sense can a century be regarded as living? What is the life of time? Is our century the century of life or the century of death?

Nietzsche in German and Bergson in French (the latter possessed, in contrast to the madman of Turin, of our national moderation) are the true prophets when it comes to these types of questions. They demand, in effect, the production of a unified and organic representation for every single thing. It is a matter of breaking with the mechanist or thermodynamic models proposed by the scientism of the nineteenth century. The main ontological question that dominates the first years of the twentieth century is: What is life? Knowledge must become the intuition of the organic value of things. This is why the typology of an animal can serve as the metaphor for the century's knowledge. As for the normative question, it is formulated as follows: What is the true life – what is it to truly live – with a life adequate to the organic intensity of living? This question traverses the century, and it is intimately linked to the question of the new man, as prefigured by Nietzsche's overman. The thinking of life interrogates the force of the will-to-live. What is it to live in accordance with a will-to-live? More specifically: What is the century as organism, as animal, as a structured and living power? In part, we still belong to this vital century. We necessarily partake of the life that is its own. As Mandelstam says, in the poem's opening line, the century, considered as a beast, is 'my beast'.

This vital identification commands the movement of the poem: we pass from looking at the beast to the beast's own look; from a face-to-face with the century to the fact that it is the century that looks back upon itself. The poetic thinking of time entails that whilst seeing things with our own eyes, we must also see them through the eyes of the century itself. Here we touch upon the astounding historicism that characterizes the whole of modernity, a historicism that introduces itself even into the vitalism of Mandelstam's poem. This is because Life and History are two different names for the same thing: the movement that wrests us away from death, the becoming of affirmation.

When all's said and done, what is this ontological and narrative problematic that has haunted the century, this problematic of life? To what is it opposed? To the idea that philosophy is a form of individual wisdom. To this idea, the century says 'No!' – at least until the Restoration that began around 1980. No, there is no individual wisdom. Under the twinned words Life and History, thought is always related to far more than the individual. It is related to an animality far more powerful than that of the mere human animal. This relationship demands an organic comprehension of what is, a comprehension for the sake of which it may be just to sacrifice the individual.

In this respect, the century is that of the human animal, viewed as a partial being transcended by Life. What kind of animal is man? What is the vital becoming of this animal? How can it be more profoundly attuned to Life or History? These questions explain the force manifested throughout the century by those categories that exceed singularity – categories such as revolutionary class, proletariat or Communist Party. But they also explain, as we cannot but recognize, the unceasing burden of questions of race.

The poem does not yield to this type of transcendence. But it does firmly tie the century to the image of a beast's vital resources.

(2) 'Who will be able to look into your pupils . . . ?' The question of the face-to-face is the heroic question of the century. Can one stand firmly in the face of historical time? Much more is at stake than simply being *in* the time of History. To stare the beast-century in the face demands a subjective capacity far superior to the one possessed by someone who simply walks in step with his epoch. The man of the century must stand in the face of the magnitude of History; he must uphold the Promethean project of a possible congruence between thought and History. The nineteenth century's Hegelian idea was to rely on the movement of history, 'to surrender to the life of the object'.[11] The twentieth century's idea is to confront History, to master it politically. For, after the war of 1914–18, no longer can anyone trust in History to the point of surrendering to the alleged progress of its movement.

In terms of subjectivity, the figure assumed by the relation to time has become heroic – even if Marxism continues to drag along, without actually making any use of it, the idea of a sense of History. Between the core of the nineteenth century and the beginning of the 'short twentieth century' – so between 1850 and 1920 – we go from historical progressivism to politico-historical heroism. That is because, in what concerns spontaneous historical movement, we pass from trust to distrust. The project of the new man imposes the idea that History will be compelled, that it will be forced. The twentieth century is a voluntaristic century. We could even say that it is the paradoxical century of a historicist voluntarism. History is a huge and powerful beast hanging over us and yet we must endure its leaden gaze, forcing it to serve us.

The problem of the poem, which is also the problem of the century, lies in the link between vitalism and voluntarism, between the evidence of time's bestial power and the heroic norm of the face-to-face. How are the questions of life and of voluntarism connected in the century? Here too, with his notion of 'will to power', Nietzsche is prophetic. He identified the main dialectic between life and will. This dialectic displays a striking tension, symbolized by the fact that its key players always maintained that what took place within the century answered to a vital necessity or historical compulsion, and yet could never have been achieved without the intervention of a strained and abstract will. There is an incompatibility of sorts between the ontology of life (in my view homogeneous with the ontology of History) and the theory of voluntaristic discontinuity. But this incompatibility constitutes the acting subjectivity of the beast-century. It is as though vital continuity could only accomplish its ends through voluntaristic discontinuity. Philosophically, the question is precisely that of the relationship between life and will, the very question that lies at the heart of Nietzsche's thought. Nietzschean overhumanity is the integral affirmation of everything: the Dionysian noon as the pure, affirmative unfolding of life. But at the same time, in an anxiety that gains momentum from 1886–7 onwards, Nietzsche will realize that this total affirmation is also an absolute rupture, that one must, according to his own expression, 'break the history of the world in two'.[12]

The important thing to notice is that the imposition of a heroism of discontinuity onto vital continuity finds its (political) resolution in the necessity of terror. The underlying question is that of the relationship between life and terror. The century unflinchingly maintained that life can only accomplish its positive destiny (and design) through terror. Whence a sort of reversal between life and death, as if death were nothing but the instrument of life. Mandelstam's poem is haunted by this undecidability between life and death.

(3) The great question that the poem poses to the beast-century is that of its vertebration. What is the century's skeletal structure? What holds it together? Vertebra, cartilage, *sinciput* . . . This is the question of the century's consistency, a very sensitive point within Mandelstam's metaphorical apparatus that also plays a central role in another superb poem devoted to time and to the subject of time, entitled *Whoever Finds a Horseshoe*. In *The Age*, Mandelstam

says three apparently contradictory things about the beast's bone structure, about this consistency of historical time:

(a)   The skeleton is heavy, crushing, gnarled (lines 3, 4, 19). Between the lines, the X-ray reveals an essential heaviness. Once the beast was agile (line 31), it is so no longer. In 1923, one is barely emerging from the butchery of 1914–18, and in Russia from something even worse: the civil war and war communism. The essence of the beast-century is life, but a life that gushes out blood and death.

(b)   Inversely: the skeleton is extremely fragile (lines 13–14), something remains to be sedimented; the beast is in its infancy, still nascent.

(c)   And finally: this backbone is already broken (line 27). Before even having begun, the century's spine has already cracked.

These contradictory utterances should be perceived as a subjectivated description of the century: the century begins in heaviness and blood, already crushing us with its funereal weight. Nevertheless, it is on its cusp, and thus harbours something undetermined, a nascent and fragile promise. But something within it is broken, discontinuous, unable to cohere.

The poem can say all these things at the same time, since it is never obliged to be dialectical. We are not dealing here with an objective utterance, but rather with a mental construction, whose name is 'century'. Indeed, long after Mandelstam, this century is haunted by its own horror. It is a century that knows how bloody it is, particularly after the war of '14, which represented an unimaginable trauma. The war of '14 was experienced as something other than a war; the expression 'butchery' was employed to characterize it from quite early on. 'Butchery' means slaughter, the pure and simple consumption of the lives of men – in the millions. But it is equally true that the century thinks of itself as the beginning of a new age, as the infancy of true humanity, as a promise. Even the exterminators presented themselves under the sign of promise and of a new beginning. They promised the golden age, a thousand-year peace.

The century's subjectivity generates an entirely new configuration of the relation between end and beginning. Mandelstam's poem juxtaposes these two ideas:

> In order to pull the age out of captivity,
> In order to begin a new world

The century is simultaneously a prison and a new day, a doomed dinosaur and a newborn beast.

We still need to read the sense of the fracture, of the broken spine:

> But your backbone is broken,
> My beautiful, pitiful age.

This idea has traversed the entire century: that its chance – its moment – has already passed. In other words, that the most it could do is try, pathetically, to mend its own impotence. Precisely because it is vitalist, the century interrogates its own vitality, and frequently casts doubt upon it. Precisely because it is voluntaristic, the century measures the shortcomings of its own volition. It sets itself such grandiose objectives that it's easily persuaded they cannot be attained. It then asks itself if true greatness does not already lie behind it. Nostalgia is always lying in wait, and the century has a tendency to look back. When the century thinks it has already squandered its energy, it represents itself as a broken promise.

Vitalism (the powerful beast), voluntarism (facing up to the beast), nostalgia (everything has already passed, energy is wanting): these are not contradictions; they are what the poem describes – in 1923 – as the subjectivity of the short century that is just beginning. The gnarled skeleton, the infantile cartilage and the broken backbone designate a century respectively doomed, exalted and lamented.

(4) But looking backwards it is the nineteenth century that one sees. A fateful question then arises, a question that is of crucial significance for the identification of the century. This is the question of its relationship to the preceding century. One asks:

> [who will be able to] with his own blood glue together
> The vertebrae of two centuries?

The sense of the phrase 'glue together' is clear if we bear in mind that it is war and massacre that define the threshold between the two centuries. But what is the real meaning of this relationship? This is one of the absolutely fundamental questions of the twentieth century. We could say that the meaning of the twentieth century is determined by the way one thinks through its connection to the nineteenth. Two possible links are immediately apparent, both of them strongly present in the various pronouncements on the century.

(a)   Ideal finality: the twentieth century fulfils the promises of the nineteenth. What the nineteenth century conceived, the twentieth realizes. For instance, the Revolution, as it was dreamt of by the Utopians and the first Marxists. In Lacanian terms, there are two ways of putting this: either the twentieth century is the Real of that for which the nineteenth century was the Imaginary; or it is the Real of that for which the nineteenth was the Symbolic (i.e. what the nineteenth produced in terms of doctrine; what it thought and organized).

(b)   Negative discontinuity: the twentieth century renounces everything that the nineteenth century (the golden age) promised. The twentieth century is a nightmare, the barbarity of a collapsed civilization.

In the first case, the key point is that one is led to accept a certain horror of the real. It has often been remarked that the barbarity of the twentieth century was a consequence of the fact that its main actors – be they revolutionaries or fascists – accepted horror in the name of a promise, in the name of 'glorious tomorrows'. On the contrary, I am convinced that what fascinated the militants of the twentieth century was the real. In this century there is a veritable exaltation of the real, even in its horror. The century's key players were anything but a bunch of simpletons manipulated by illusions. Just think what the endurance, the experience, or even the disenchantment of an agent of the Third International must have been! During the Spanish Civil War, when a Russian communist envoy to the International Brigades was abruptly recalled to Moscow, he was fully aware that he was returning to certain arrest and execution. From an early date, he knew that Stalin – who was not fond of people experiencing anything that might lie beyond his control – had undertaken the liquidation of practically all the veterans of Spain. Was the envoy going to escape, defend himself, remonstrate? Not at all. In this situation, the envoys spent the night getting drunk and returned to Moscow in the morning. Is someone really going to tell us that this was the result of illusions, promises and glorious dawns? No, the fact is that for these subjects the real included that dimension. Horror was nothing but an aspect of the real, and death a part of it.

Lacan correctly perceived that the experience of the real is always in part the experience of horror. The genuine question is in no way that of the imaginary, but rather that of knowing what it is in these radical experiments that assumes the role of the real. Whatever it may be, it's certainly not the promise of better days. Besides, I'm convinced that the subjective capacities of action, courage or even resignation are always in the present tense. Who has ever done anything in the name of an undetermined future?

(5) The importance of Mandelstam's third stanza stems from the fact that it accords a decisive role to both the poem and the poet. Essentially, we are told that if we wish to begin a new world 'a flute' (art) must unite the joints of days, that it must unify the body of time.

We encounter here another of the century's obsessive themes: What is the function of art? What is the common measure between art and the century? As you know, the question already haunted the nineteenth century. It derives from a tension between historicism and the aesthetic absolute. During a whole stretch of the nineteenth century there existed the function of the poet-guide, with whom the absolute of art orientates peoples within time. Hugo was its archetype in France, Whitman in the United States. This is a figure of the avant-garde in the strict sense – the one who marches in front – a figure tied to the awakening of peoples, to progress, to liberation, to an upsurge of energies.

But the imagery of the poet-guide, already obsolete by the end of the nineteenth century, is utterly ruined in the twentieth. As heir to Mallarmé, the twentieth century establishes another figure, that of the poet as secret, active exception, as the custodian of lost thought. The poet is the protector, in language, of a forgotten opening; he is, as Heidegger says, 'the guardian of the Open'.[13] The poet, ignored, stands guard against perdition. We are still immersed in the obsession with the real, since the poet guarantees that language preserves the power to name this real. Such is the poet's 'restricted action', which remains a very elevated function.

In the third stanza of *The Age* it becomes clear that the task of art in the century is to unite – not in the sense of a monolithic unity, but of an intimate fraternity, one hand joining another hand, an elbow touching another elbow. Were it to successfully carry out this task, it would save us from three dramas.

(a)   The drama of heaviness and enclosure. This is the poem's principle of freedom, alone capable of wresting the century away from its prison, that is, from itself. The poem is empowered to wrest the century from the century.

(b)   The drama of passivity, of human sadness. Without the unity prescribed by the poem, we are buffeted by waves of sadness. Thus, there is a principle of joy in the poem, an active principle.

(c)   The drama of treason, of venom and the stinging wound. The century is also, in the figure of the serpent (ubiquitous in Valéry),[14] the temptation of absolute sin: to surrender without resistance to the real of the age. 'Golden measure' means the following: to be tempted by the century itself, by its cadence, and thus to consent without mediation to violence, to the passion for the real.

To counter all this there is only the flute of art. Without doubt this is the principle of courage that underlies any cognitive enterprise: to be of one's time, through an unprecedented manner of not being in one's time. In Nietzsche's terms, to have the courage to be untimely. Every true poem is an 'untimely observation'.

Ultimately, Mandelstam tells us that from 1923 onwards the poem, watching over the century's violence without recoiling, is installed in the wait. Indeed, it is not devoted to time, to the promise of a future, or to pure nostalgia. The poem maintains itself in the wait as such, creating a subjectivity of the wait, of the wait as welcome. Mandelstam can thus say that spring will indeed return, that 'a sprout of green will spurt', but that, with a broken century on our knees, we keep struggling to resist the wave of human anguish.

This century has been the century of a poetics of the wait, a poetics of the threshold. The threshold will not have been crossed, but its maintenance will have constituted the power of the poem.

I would like to end this lesson by presenting three very different inflections of this theme, in André Breton, Heidegger and Yves Bonnefoy.

(a)   André Breton, Mad Love (1937)

In the century, 1937 is a date of no little importance. It is a metonymical year in which something essential unfolds; an absolute distillate of the essence – of the excess in the essence – of the Stalinist terror, the year of what is called the 'Great Terror'. Things begin to take a wrong turn in the Spanish Civil War, which is like an internal miniature of the entire century, since all of the century's principal actors are present within it (communists, fascists, internationalist workers, farmers in revolt, mercenaries, colonial armies, fascist states, 'democracies', etc.). It is the year in which Nazi Germany enters irreversibly into the preparations for total war. It also represents the major turning point in China. In France, it becomes evident that the Popular Front has failed. Let's not forget that the parliamentarians of 1937 are those who two years later will hand plenary powers over to Pétain.

It is, after all, also the year of my birth.

What does André Breton offer us in 1937? A potent variant of the poetics of the wait: the poetics of the watchman. Here is the beginning of chapter 3 of *Mad Love*, as translated by Mary Ann Caws:

> At the forefront of discovery, from the moment when, for the first navigators, a new land was in sight to the moment when they set foot on the shore, from the moment when a certain learned man became convinced that he had witnessed a phenomenon, hitherto unknown, to the time when he began to measure the import of his

observation – all feeling of duration abolished by the intoxicating atmosphere of chance – a very delicate flame highlights or perfects life's meaning as nothing else can. It is to the recreation of this particular state of mind that surrealism has always aspired, disdaining in the last analysis the prey and the shadow for what is already no longer the shadow and not yet the prey: the shadow and the prey mingled into a unique flash. Behind ourselves, we must *not let the paths of desire become overgrown.* Nothing retains less of desire in art, in science, than this will to industry, booty, possession. A pox on all captivity, even should it be in the interest of the universal good, even in Montezuma's gardens of precious stones! Still today I am only counting on what comes of my own openness, my eagerness to wander *in search* of everything, which, I am confident, keeps me in mysterious communication with other open beings, as if we were suddenly called to assemble. I would like my life to leave after it no other murmur than that of a watchman's song, of a song to while away the waiting. Independent of what happens and what does not happen, the wait itself is magnificent.

The figure of the watchman or the stalker is one of the great artistic figures of the century. The stalker is the one for whom nothing exists but the stalk, the one for whom shadow and prey are confused in a single flash. The thesis of the stalk, or the wait, says that one can only keep hold of the real by remaining indifferent to what may or may not happen. This is one of the major theses of the century: the wait is a cardinal virtue, because it is the only existing form of intense indifference.

(b) Heidegger

Here is an extract from '. . . Poetically Man Dwells . . .', a lecture given in 1951, now in the collection *Poetry, Language, Thought*, in Albert Hofstadter's translation:

> The statement, *Man dwells in that he builds* [*baut*], has now been given its proper sense. Man does not dwell in that he merely establishes his stay on the earth beneath the sky, by raising growing things and simultaneously raising buildings. Man is capable of such building only if he already builds [*baut*] in the sense of the poetic

taking of measure. Authentic building [*Bauen*] occurs so far as there are poets, such poets as take the measure for architecture, the structure of dwelling.

In the poetics of the century we frequently encounter this contempt for everything that represents an installation, a harvest, a prey. It's a matter of keeping up the wait, the pure vigilance of the wait.

Everything is referred back to a preliminary condition, to a measurement that always ends up presenting itself in the figure of the stalk or the guard. The poetic as such is defined as a guarding of the threshold, marked by the reversibility of crossing and not crossing. To be able to look ahead and behind at the same time. The century of the poets is the threshold-century, a century without a crossing.

The same theme inhabits the final stanza of Mandelstam's poem. There is indeed a kind of novelty – it will flower and be reborn – but there is also a break, the broken stone of the threshold, from whence the backward glance, the obsession with traces, is born. Ahead, there is a promise that cannot be kept (which, incidentally, is Claudel's definition of woman);[15] behind, only your own tracks. Poetically, the century has viewed itself as both the impossibility of a crossing and as the tracks leading to it, as the in-between of trace and destination.

(c) Yves Bonnefoy, 'Out by Where the Earth Ends', from In the Shadow's Light *(1987)*

Since it is at nightfall that Minerva's owl takes flight, the moment has come to speak of you, paths that disappear from this victim earth.

Once there was no doubt about you, now you are nothing but enigma. Once you inscribed time in eternity, now you are only the past, out by where the earth ends, there, before us, like a sheer drop of cliff.

As you can see, Yves Bonnefoy says more or less the same thing as Mandelstam. The century is the transit, the mobility of the threshold, but never its crossing. Incidentally, Bonnefoy has also written another collection entitled *The Lure of the Threshold*. We find ourselves between a path that effaces itself (Heidegger's *Holzwege*, translated as *Off the Beaten Track*) and an earth that comes to an end. The poet's meditation takes place between the two.

More than half a century later, the figure remains the same, that of a poem installed between the trace that effaces itself and the feeling of a finished world. There are no entrances. What occurrence has led to this transport of the threshold? The poem is the thin blade between trace and completion.

Mandelstam tells us that – subjectively speaking – we stand on the threshold with a 'senseless smile'. 'Smile' because we are on the threshold, 'senseless' because, since the threshold is impassable, why smile? We go from life, from hope (the smile), to the absence of sense in the (senseless) real. Is this not the century's subjective maxim?

3

The unreconciled

What are we to call the last twenty years of the century, if not the second Restoration? In any case, we should note this period's obsession with number. Since a restoration is never anything other than a moment in history that declares revolutions to be both abominable and impossible, and the superiority of the rich both natural and excellent, it comes as no surprise that it adores number, which is above all the number of dollars or euros. The extent of this adoration is manifest in the immense novels of Balzac, the great artist of the first Restoration, the one that followed the French Revolution of 1792–4.

More importantly, every restoration is horrified by thought and loves only opinions; especially the dominant opinion, as summarized once and for all in François Guizot's imperative: 'Enrich yourselves!' The real, as the obligatory correlate of thought, is considered by the ideologues of restorations – and not entirely without reason – as always liable to give rise to political iconoclasm, and hence Terror. A restoration is above all an assertion regarding the real; to wit, that it is always preferable to have no relation to it whatsoever.

If number (polls, accounts, audience ratings, budgets, credits, stock market trends, print runs, salaries, stock-options . . .) is today's fetish, it's because at the place where the real comes to falter, there stands blind number.

This very blindness is what singles out the bad number, in the sense that Hegel speaks of the bad infinite. The distinction between number as a form of being, on the one hand, and number as a stopgap for the failure of the real, on the other, is so important for me that I have devoted an entire book to it.[16] Let's make do here with a counter-example: Mallarmé is a thinker of number in the guise of the dice-throw. But for Mallarmé number is anything but the material of opinion. It is 'the unique number that cannot be another', the moment in which chance is fixed – by the intermediation of the dice-throw – as necessity. There is an indissoluble link between chance, which is not abolished by a dice-throw, and numerical necessity. Number is the cipher of the concept. That is why, as Mallarmé concludes, 'Every thought emits a dice-throw.'

Today number is consigned to the indefinitely numerable. Unlike Mallarmé's number, the main characteristic of the Restoration's number is that it may be substituted by any other number, without the slightest drawback. Its essence is arbitrary variability; it is the floating number. That is because behind this number lie the fluctuations of the stock market.

The trajectory that goes from Mallarmé's number to the number of the polls transforms the cipher of the concept into an indifferent variation.

Why this long preamble? Precisely in order to introduce another preamble, which, to all intents and purposes, stands apart from what will follow it. In the very midst of the Restoration, I too have my own numbers. I take them from some serious publications,[17] which themselves take them from even more serious official reports.

The significance of these numbers may be grasped on the basis of two themes whose main features these lessons on the century will have sought to convey:

(a)   The obscure (almost ontological) tie that binds a satisfied Europe to a crucified Africa. Africa as the secret blackness at the heart of the white man's moral detergent.

(b)   The question of what is once again being labelled – as in the golden age of bourgeois dictatorships – 'the egalitarian utopia'.

Here then, as matter-of-factly as possible, are my figures for the day.

1   Today there are more or less 500,000 people infected with AIDS in Europe. With the implementation of tritherapy, mortality rates are decreasing rapidly. The great majority of these

500,000 people will live, albeit paying the costs of a burdensome and chronic treatment.

In Africa there are 22 million people infected with AIDS. Pharmaceuticals are practically absent. A staggering majority of these people will die; in some countries, this will mean one child in four or even one in three.

The distribution of the needed medications to all African sufferers of AIDS is perfectly possible. All that is required is for the governments of those countries in possession of the appropriate industrial means to decide to produce generic drugs and provide them to the populations in question. This amounts to a minimal financial effort, much lower in cost than any supposedly 'humanitarian' military expedition.

A government that decides not to act towards this end effectively decides to be co-responsible for the death of tens of millions of people.

2   The richest three people in the world possess a combined fortune greater than the total GDP of the forty-eight poorest countries in the world put together.

3   Let's suppose we want to provide the world's total population with a quantifiable access to nutrition, say 2,700 calories a day, as well as access to drinkable water and basic health resources. This will add up, more or less, to the amount of money that the inhabitants of Europe and the United States spend every year on perfumes.

4   Take the poorest 20 per cent of the global population and the richest 20 per cent. In 1960, the upper section had an income thirty times greater than the lower section. In 1995, this income was eighty-two times greater.

5   In seventy countries (= 40 per cent of countries in the world) the per capita income is inferior in real currency to what it was twenty years ago.

End of my preamble.

Today, I will begin with the second stanza of Mandelstam's poem, which last time served as our textual support. What is at issue is the inception of the century as the site of a sacrifice:

Like a baby's tender cartilage,
Oh age of infant earth,
Once again the sinciput of life, like a lamb,
Has been sacrificed.

This is manifestly a Christian metaphor, the metaphor of a link between novelty, annunciation and promise, on the one hand, and the death of the innocent and sacrifice, on the other. We should not forget the perseverance, and even the renewal, of Christian thought throughout the century. Nietzsche's antichrist gave rise to its own anti-antichrist. The twenties and thirties, for instance, were marked by a certain vogue for Christianity. And from Claudel to Pasolini – and by way of Mandelstam – the century also saw a number of great Christian poets, or poets engaged in an intimate dialectic with Christianity. We should also not forget the perseverance of a Christian philosophy, and in particular the almost total absorption of phenomenology by Christian moralism.[18] We can even register the ample development of a Christian psychoanalysis, which certainly suggests that when it comes to digesting poisons, the body of religion is blessed with an iron constitution.

An essential thesis of established Christianity – of Christianity as state power – is that the new world is born under the sign of the torment and death of the innocent. The new alliance of God and men, as incarnated in the Son, begins with the crucifixion. How can we recover from such an inception? How can we move beyond the absolute violence of that commencement? This has always been one of the great problems faced by official Christianity. But, all things considered, it was also one of the problems that occupied the beginning of the twentieth century. This is because of the war of 1914, the revolution of 1917, and also – in the background, as it were – because of the unnameable practices of colonialism. The question is that of knowing how one harmonizes the atrocities of the inception with the promise of a new man. What horror haunts this promise? How can the inaugural sacrifice be redressed?

There have always been two orientations of thought when it comes to this type of problem.

First orientation: Since that is how things began, we are in the time of death, in the endtime. This is what the first Christians thought: since Christ is dead, the end of the world is imminent. Right after the 1914–18 war, the dominant idea, especially in France, was that such butchery could only lead to the end of all wars, to a definitive peace. This position was articulated in the slogan 'peace at all costs', and in the enormous strength of the pacifist current. The thesis proper to this orientation is that what begins in blood is also what declares that this blood shall be the last – 'the last of the last' (*la der des ders*), as the war of 1914 was referred to back then.

Second orientation: Because it all began in violence and destruction, this violence and destruction must be brought to an end by a superior destruction, by an essential violence. Bad violence must be followed by good violence, which is legitimated by the former. What is proposed is a bellicose foundation for peace; the good war will put an end to the bad war.

These two paths intertwine and confront one another, especially between 1918 and 1939. What dialectic is instituted by a bellicose inception? Is it the war/peace dialectic or the dialectic of good war/bad war, just war/unjust war?

Such questions encapsulate the history of French pacifism in the interwar period. Pacifism was principally a 'left-wing' current, and paradoxically – in terms of opinion – one of the ingredients in the ferment of Pétainism. That is because Pétainism gave political shape to the taste for capitulation: anything but the war. This is the path of the 'never again'.

The problem is that the Nazis upheld the other orientation: To go back over the bad war – which moreover they'd lost – by means of a good war; an imperial, national and racial war. This was to be a decisive war, the foundation for a thousand-year Reich. All of a sudden, for the French, peace at all costs meant making peace with total war, peace with the Nazis, and therefore being passively included in an 'absolute' war, a war that lays claim to the right of extermination. This is the essence of Pétainism: To make peace with the war of extermination, thereby becoming its abject accomplice – all the more abject in being passive, preoccupied only with its own survival.

It is telling that De Gaulle, in 1940, simply had to say that the war was continuing. In short, De Gaulle and the fighters of the resistance had to re-open the war, to re-install it. But they were nonetheless faced with a paradox: How could the century, which had begun with an atrocious war, continue with an even worse one? In this historical sequence, what had become of the 'Christly' promise of new man?

A paradoxical subjectivity subtends what I am saying here about war, a subjectivity whose inclinations we have begun to describe with respect to Mandelstam. The century thought itself simultaneously as end, exhaustion, decadence *and* as absolute commencement. Part of the century's problem is the conjunction of these two convictions. In other words, the century conceived of itself as nihilism, but equally as Dionysian affirmation. Depending on what moment we examine, the century appears to act according to either of two maxims: one (operative today, for example) calls for renunciation, resignation, the lesser evil, together with moderation, the end of humanity as a spiritual force, and the critique of 'grand narratives'.[19] The other – which dominated the 'short century' between 1917 and the 1980s – inherits from Nietzsche the will to 'break the history of the world in two', and seeks a radical commencement that would bear within it the foundation of a reconciled humanity.

The relationship between these two approaches is not at all straightforward. It does not constitute a dialectical correlation, but an entanglement. The century is haunted by a non-dialectical relation between necessity and will. This is manifest in Nietzsche, who in this regard is a prophet of the century. Nietzsche carries out an extremely detailed diagnosis of nihilism, devoted to the genealogy of negative affects (guilt, *ressentiment*, and so on). But at the same time he voices the voluntaristic certainty of a Great Noon, a certainty bearing no relation to the domination of nihilism, whether as its result or as its dialectical sublation. No theory of negativity can guarantee this passage, and Deleuze is completely right to name this relation which is not a relation a 'disjunctive synthesis'.[20]

In the register of History, and of its voluntaristic submission to politics, this disjunction constitutes a problem. It is because of this disjunction that the century is marked through and through by a singular violence. This violence is not simply objective, it amounts to a subjective claim that may attain the characteristics of a cult. Violence takes place at the point of disjunction; it substitutes itself for a missing conjunction, like a dialectical link forced into being at the very point of the anti-dialectical.

Violence is legitimated by the creation of the new man. Needless to say, this theme only makes sense within the horizon of the death of God. A godless humanity must be recreated, so as to replace the humanity that was subject to the gods. In this sense, the new man is what holds together the fragments of the disjunctive synthesis. He is at once a destiny (the destiny of humanity in the epoch of the death of gods) and a will (the will to overcome the man of the past). If we can say that the century is tremendously ideological, it is because it gives shape to the disjunctive synthesis that both generates and elaborates its orientations of thought. The famous 'end of ideologies', which supposedly defines our present modesty, our humanitarian compassion, represents nothing less than the forsaking of any novelty that could be ascribed to man. And this, as I already said, is happening at the very moment when a total transformation of humanity – realized through blind manipulations and financial transactions – is in the offing.

Truth be told, it is not the ideological dimension of the theme of the new man that is operant in the twentieth century. What impassions subjects and militants is the *historicity* of the new man. For we find ourselves in the real moment of commencement. The nineteenth century announced, dreamed, and promised; the twentieth century declared it would make man, here and now.

This is what I propose to call the *passion for the real.** I'm convinced it provides the key to understanding the century. There is a conviction, laden with pathos, that we are being summoned to the real of a beginning.

The real, as all key players of the century recognize, is the source of both horror and enthusiasm, simultaneously lethal and creative. What is certain is that it is – as Nietzsche splendidly put it – 'Beyond Good and Evil'. Any conviction about the real advent of a new man is characterized by a steadfast indifference to its cost; this indifference legitimates the most violent means. If what is at stake is the new man, the man of the past may very well turn out to be nothing but disposable material.

For today's well-tempered moralism, which is nothing but the endorsement of aseptic crimes – backing virtuous wars or decorous profits – the short century, the century of revolutionary politics assembled under the equivocal name of 'communism', was barbarous because its passion for the real placed it beyond good and evil. For example, in a stark opposition between politics and morality. But from the inside, the century was lived as epic and heroic.

Reading the *Iliad*, we are forced to acknowledge that it consists of an uninterrupted succession of massacres. But in its movement as a poem this is not presented as barbarous, but instead as epic and heroic. The century has been a subjective *Iliad* – even if barbarity has often been acknowledged and condemned, usually by the other camp. Whence a certain indifference with regard to the objective signs of cruelty. It is the same indifference that we inhabit when reading the *Iliad*, because the force of the action overrides in its intensity any moral squeamishness.

Some famous literary examples testify to this subjective relation vis-à-vis the most barbarous episodes of the century, a relation which is aestheticized by epic feeling. As regards the war of 1914, we can refer to the way T. E. Lawrence, in *The Seven Pillars of Wisdom* (1922), describes the horrific scenes, not just in the opposing camp (the Turks massacring all the villagers), but also in his own, when the cry of 'no quarter' rises to his own lips, and no prisoners will be taken, all the wounded will be finished off. Nothing in these acts is justified – on the contrary – but they belong to the epic flow of the Arab war. On the side of revolutions, we can cite Malraux's *Man's Hope* (1937), in particular those passages when, discussing the Spanish war, Malraux recounts and comments upon the practice of torture and summary executions, not only in Franco's camp but also among the Republican forces. Once again, everything is carried away by the popular, epic greatness of the resistance. Using his own categories, Malraux treats the disjunctive synthesis in terms of its most opaque aspect: the figure of History as destiny. If the atrocities themselves cannot provide the situation with a 'moral' meaning it's because, as in the *fatum* Nietzsche borrowed from the Stoics, we've moved beyond all considerations of this kind. The idea is that in intense situations everyone must meet their fate and face up to it, just as one must face up to the beast-century in Mandelstam's poem. For, as Malraux says, Spain, bled white by the war, becomes conscious of itself, in such a way that every actor in the drama partakes in this consciousness. Atrocities are only a feature of this revelation, to the extent that what reveals History as destiny is almost invariably the experience of war.

This brings me to what, after the passion for the real, is without doubt the principal characterization of the century: the century of war. This does not simply mean that the century is full – up to the present day – of brutal wars, but that it has unfolded *under the paradigm of war*.

The fundamental concepts through which the century has come to think itself or its own creative energy have all been subordinated to the semantics of war. Note that we are not dealing with war in Hegel's sense, i.e. the Napoleonic war. For Hegel, war is a constitutive moment in the self-consciousness of a people. War creates consciousness, national consciousness in particular. Twentieth-century warfare is not of this type; the twentieth century's idea of war is that of the decisive war, of the *last war*. For the whole world, the war of 1914–18 is the bad war, the heinous war that must never again take place – whence the expression 'the last of the last'. It is absolutely imperative that 1914–18 be the last war of this bad type. The question has become that of putting an end to the world that brought forth the heinous war. The only thing that can put an end to war is war, but it will have to be another type of war. The reason for this is that between 1918 and 1939 peace is the same thing as war. No one believes in this peace. Another war is necessary, a war that will truly be the last.

Mao Tsetung is a typical bearer of this conviction. He led a war for more than twenty years, from 1925 to 1949. He renewed entirely the thinking of the relationship between war and politics. In a text from 1936, *Strategic Problems of Revolutionary War in China*, he develops the notion that in order to obtain perpetual peace a new war must be invented. Ordinary war, the kind of war that pits the current holders of power against one another, must be countered by a new war, organized by proletarians and farmers, a war that Mao precisely calls 'revolutionary war'.

Prior to Mao, and even in Lenin's thought, war and revolution were contrary terms, making a complex dialectical situation. As Sylvain Lazarus has exhaustively shown, it is with reference to the question of war that Lenin separates political subjectivity from historical consciousness, remarking, in the spring of 1917, that war is a clear given, while politics remains obscure.[21] The Maoist theme of revolutionary war establishes an entirely different distinction, juxtaposing two different kinds of war, which are linked organically to two different politics. On this basis, it is up to (the politically just) war to put an end to (politically unjust) wars. Consider the following text from 1936, taken from *Strategic Problems of Revolutionary War in China*:

> War, this monster that makes men kill one another, will finally be eliminated by the development of human society, and this will happen in a future that is not remote. But in order to suppress war there is only one path: To oppose war to war, to oppose revolutionary war to counter-revolutionary war [...]. Once human society will attain the suppression of classes and the suppression of the State, there will be no more wars – neither revolutionary nor counter-revolutionary, neither just nor unjust. This will be the era of perpetual peace for humanity. By studying the laws of revolutionary war, we start from the aspiration to suppress all wars; here lies the difference between us communists and the representatives of all the exploitative classes.

And again two years later, in *Problems of War and Strategy*:

> We are for the abolition of wars; we do not want war. But war can only be abolished by war. In order that there be no more rifles, we must take up rifles.

This theme of a total and final war to end all wars underlies all those moments, which punctuate the century, in which the 'definitive' settlement of a given problem is an object of conviction. The dark form, the atrocious and extremist form taken by this conviction is doubtless to be found in the 'final solution' of the supposed 'Jewish problem', decided by the Nazis at the Wannsee conference. This murderous extremism cannot be entirely separated from the idea – widely held in all domains of thought and action – that problems allow for an 'absolute' solution.

One of the century's obsessions was that of obtaining something definitive. One can observe this obsession at work even in the most abstract regions of science. Just think of the mathematical endeavour that goes by the name of *Bourbaki*, which seeks to build a mathematical monument that will be integrally formalized, complete and definitive. In art, it is thought that by putting an end to the relativity of imitations and representations absolute art will be attained, the art that shows itself integrally as art; an art that – taking its own process as its object – is the exposition of what is artistic in art; the articulation, within art, of the end of art itself. In short: the last work of art, in the form of art un-worked.

In every instance we can see that this longing for the definitive is realized as the beyond of a destruction. The new man is the destruction of the old man. Perpetual peace is achieved through the destruction of the old wars by total war. By means of an integral formalization, the monument of completed science destroys the old scientific intuitions. Modern art brings the relative universe of representation to ruin. A fundamental couple is at work here, that of destruction and the definitive. Once again, this is a non-dialectical couple, a disjunctive synthesis. That is because destruction does not produce the definitive, which means that we are faced with two very distinct tasks: to destroy the old, and to create the new. War itself is a non-dialectical juxtaposition of appalling destruction, on the one hand, and the beauty of victorious heroism, on the other.

Ultimately, the problem of the century is to exist in the non-dialectical conjunction of the theme of the end and that of beginning. 'Ending' and 'beginning' are two terms that, within the century, remain unreconciled.

The model for the non-reconciliation is war – total and definitive war, which displays three main features:

(a) It puts an end to the possibility of the bad war, the useless or conservative war whose model is the war of 1914–18.

(b) It must uproot nihilism, because it advocates a radical commitment, a cause, a true face-to-face with history.

(c) It will lay the foundations for a new historical and planetary order.

Unlike the war of '14, this war is not a simple operation of the State; it is a subjective entailment. This war is an absolute cause that generates a new type of subject; a war that is also the creation of its combatant. In the end, war becomes a subjective paradigm. The century has borne a combative conception of existence, meaning that the totality itself – in each of its real fragments – must be represented as conflict. Whatever its scale, private or planetary, every real situation is a scission, a confrontation, a war.

In the twentieth century, the shared law of the world is neither the One nor the Multiple: it is the Two. It is not the One, because there is no harmony, no hegemony of the simple, no unified power of God. It is not the Multiple, because it is not a question of obtaining a balance of powers or a harmony of faculties. It is the Two, and the world represented by the modality of the Two excludes the possibility of both unanimous submission and combinatory equilibrium. One simply must decide.

The whole world thinks that the century will decide, that it will make a break. This is the key to the century's subjectivity. As the century shows, men possess a considerable capacity to invent the Two. War is the Two's resolute visibility, opposed to any combinatory equilibrium. It is in this respect that war is omnipresent. But the Two is anti-dialectical. It harbours a non-dialectical disjunction, without synthesis. We need to investigate how this paradigm is present in aesthetics, in the relation of the sexes, in technical aggressiveness.

The century's 'beast', invoked by Mandelstam, is nothing other than the omnipresence of scission. The passion of the century is the real, but the real is antagonism. That is why the passion of the century – whether it be a question of empires, revolutions, the arts, the sciences, or private life – is nothing other than war. 'What is the century?', the century asks itself. And it replies: 'The final struggle.'

4

A new world. Yes, but when?

To summarize: the century's subjectivity, prey to the passion for the real and placed under the paradigm of definitive war, stages a non-dialectical confrontation between destruction and foundation, for the sake of which it thinks both totality and the slightest of its fragments in the image of antagonism, and posits that the cipher of the real is the Two.

Today we will filter this phrase, so to speak, through a text by Brecht, so that it may take on its full force and colour.

Whether we think of him as a writer, playwright, Marxist dialectician, fellow traveller of the Party or ladies' man, Brecht is an emblematic figure of the twentieth century. There are a number of reasons for this, four of which I'll foreground here: Brecht is German, a theatre director, a communist and a contemporary of Nazism.

(1) Brecht is a German who begins writing in the immediate postwar period, in that astonishing Weimar Germany which is all the more creative in that it endures the German trauma, the trauma which, alas, will reveal itself to go far deeper than mere defeat. Brecht is one of the artists who best capture Germany's identity crisis. He will settle his score with the Germany that has just emerged from the war of '14 in a kind of frenzied trance.

In fact, Brecht is one of those Germans desperately striving to produce a thinking of Germany that would be entirely purged of romanticism and wholly withdrawn from the grip of Wagnerian mythology (which has less to do with Wagner's genius than with

its appropriation by petit bourgeois *ressentiment*: the bankrupt
shopkeeper in rags mistaking himself for Siegfried in a Kaiser
helmet). The quarrel with romanticism, sometimes pushed to the
extremes of neo-classicist zeal, is one of the century's central
motifs. In this context, Brecht often turns towards France. One of
the decisive figures for the young Brecht is Rimbaud. In *Baal* and
In the Jungle of Cities one finds lines by Rimbaud directly incorporated into the text. This is because, according to Brecht, the
misfortune of the Germans lies in having to wrestle with the
density of a language perennially turned towards the bass drums
of the sublime. Brecht's ideal is eighteenth-century French, a language at once fast and sensuous – Diderot's French, for example.
On this point, as on many others, Brecht is a closer descendant of
Nietzsche than of Marx. Nietzsche too wanted to impart a French
levity upon the German tongue, much in the way that he mis-
chievously claimed to opt for Bizet against Wagner. All this excru-
ciating work of Germany upon herself – against herself – is pivotal
to the century's disasters.

(2) Brecht's fate is tied above all to the theatre. Throughout his
life he was a writer and practitioner of the theatre, proposing and
experimenting fundamental reforms in dramaturgy, both in his
writing and in what concerns acting and *mise en scène*. Now, it can
be argued (and this is an important symptom) that the twentieth
century is the century of the theatre as art. It is the twentieth
century that invented the notion of the *mise en scène*. It transformed the thinking of representation into an art in its own right.
Copeau, Stanislavski, Meyerhold, Craig, Appia, Jouvet and Brecht
– and then Vilar, Vitez, Wilson and many others – turned what
was merely the placement of representation into an independent
art. These men brought to the fore a type of artist whose art
belongs neither to that of the writer nor to that of the performer,
but who creates instead, in both thought and space, a mediation
between the two. The theatre director is something like a thinker
of representation as such, who carries out a very complex inves-
tigation into the relationships between text, acting, space and
public.

Why does this invention of the theatrical *mise en scène* take place in our century? Brecht, one of the theatre's great artists, displaying a rare preoccupation with both text and acting, was also committed to a reflection upon the contemporariness of the theatre. For instance, he interrogated himself about the theatricality of politics, about the role of representation, of staging, in the construction of political consciousness. What are the manifest figures of politics? Debate on this point is very lively in the period between the two wars, especially apropos of fascism. Walter Benjamin's emphatic theses are well known: The (fascist) aestheticization of politics must be opposed by the (revolutionary) politicization of art. Brecht goes even further, doubling theoretical reflection with effective experimentation, with an artistic invention. But he shares the conviction that a singular bond exists between theatrics and politics.

What is this theatrics linked to? Probably to the new role accorded to the masses within historical action following the Russian Revolution of 1917. Consider Trotsky's formula,[22] according to which what characterizes our epoch is 'the irruption of the masses onto the stage of History'. The image of the stage is very striking. The categories of revolution, proletariat and fascism all refer to figures of massive irruption, to potent collective representations, to scenes that have been rendered immortal – whether we're talking about the taking of the Winter Palace or the March on Rome. The same question is repeatedly brandished: What is the relationship between the fate of the individual and the historical irruption of the masses? But the question can also be rephrased as follows: Who is the actor of which play, and on what stage?

Brecht asks himself how the relationship between personal fate (the character) and impersonal historical development (the massive irruption) can be represented, depicted and theatrically deployed. It is here that the twentieth century returns to the question of the chorus and the protagonist, showing that its theatre is more Greek than Romantic. The inventiveness and progress in the *mise en scène* are spurred on by this Greek inspiration. In the twentieth century, theatre is more than just putting on plays. For better or worse, its stakes seem to have changed: it is now a question of collective historical elucidation.

Lacking a conviction of this calibre, the *mise en scène* may find itself doomed in the present day, as the old ways make their return to the stage: a good text, some good actors – that's enough! Please stop boring us with political consciousness or the Greeks.

Regardless of the play – whether it be ancient or modern – for Brecht it must always be interrogated about the relationship between character and historical destiny. How can one represent the development of a subject while at the same time elucidating the play of forces that constitutes it, but which is also the space of its volition and its choices? Brecht is certain that the theatre must change, that it must be something besides the self-celebration of a spectating bourgeoisie.

Today too there is a widespread belief that the theatre must change: it must become the celebration of moral and democratic consensus, a sort of morose chorus chanting the world's unhappiness and its humanitarian remedy. No hero, no conflict of types, no thought – nothing but unanimous bodily emotion.

Brecht and his contemporaries pondered the nature of acting and character. They reflected on how the character – who does not pre-exist theatrical circumstances – is constructed in the play, which is above all a play of forces. We are neither in the realm of psychology nor in that of the hermeneutics of meaning, neither amid language games nor within the Parousia of the body. The theatre is a device for the construction of truths.

(3) Brecht adhered to the communist movement, even though, like many men of the theatre (I have in mind the singular communism of Antoine Vitez or Bernard Sobel), he always found ways of making this commitment a little tangential or diagonal. These people of the theatre were friends of the Party in a manner that was simultaneously very sincere and not very sincere at all. The theatre is a good place wherein to practise these acrobatics. What is both certain and sincere is that Brecht makes Marxism or communism into a condition for the question of the being of art: 'What is a didactic art, an art at the service of popular lucidity, a proletarian art, etc.?' Brecht is surely a pivotal figure in these

debates. But he is also a great artist, whose works are still performed everywhere today, when debates about the dialectic between theatre and politics have withered away. Without doubt, Brecht is the most universal and most indisputable among those artists who explicitly linked their existence and creativity to so-called communist politics.

(4) Brecht encountered the problem of Nazism in Germany. He was struck with full force by the question of the possibility of Nazism, the possibility of its success. He addressed this question in numerous essays and plays, such as *Arturo Ui*, from whence comes the famous (and dubious) formula: 'The bitch that bore him is in heat again.' I say dubious because it treats the Nazi singularity as a structural consequence of a state of affairs and of subjects – not the most promising way of genuinely thinking through this singularity. Even so, with the means at his disposal and facing it directly, Brecht ultimately tried to produce a refined theatrical didactics that could address Hitler's rise to power. By way of consequence, he lived through the Second World War as an exile. Again, this is one of those points where Brecht adheres strongly to the century – this century for which the figure of the exile is essential, as revealed by its novels, and especially by the works of Erich Maria Remarque.[23] There is an entirely specific subjectivity of exile. This is particularly true of the exile to the United States, where numerous German intellectuals banished by Nazism resided. These artists, writers, musicians and scientists made up a small world, which was extremely active but also divided and uncertain. As far as Brecht is concerned, we should note that America had long been a source of amusement, fascinating him with its flashy modernity, its pragmatism and its technological vitality. Among other things, Brecht was also a good European witness of the United States. Finally, we should recall that he was a man who in the German Democratic Republic experienced socialist realism at its most voluntaristic and inflexible. There he became an official figure of sorts, but not without rifts, tortuous disavowals and veiled actions. A fundamental episode of Brecht's last years (he died rather young, in 1956) was the workers' insurrection of 1953, suppressed in Berlin by the Soviet army. Brecht

wrote a letter to the communist state authorities, part of which (the only section made public) approved of the repression, while the other, which remained 'private', raised burdensome questions about the crushing of a workers' revolt by the 'Workers' and Farmers' State'. How Brecht could be the subject of these obliquities of circumstance can be discerned behind the successive revisions of his indisputable masterpiece, *The Life of Galileo*, one of whose themes is the duplicity of the scientist in the face of political authority (in his period of exile, during what have been called the years of McCarthyism,[24] Brecht, suspected of communist activities, had already been questioned by the American police and judiciary).

As you can see, there are numerous reasons for summoning Brecht as a witness to the century, as a legitimate document for the immanent method I am advocating, which is an examination of what the century meant for the people of the century.

The text by Brecht I have chosen is entitled: *The Proletariat Wasn't Born in a White Vest* (*Das Proletariat ist nicht in einer weien Weste geboren*). This text is directly connected to one of our central hypotheses: That, under the paradigm of war, the century strove to think the enigmatic link between destruction and commencement. The text is from 1934. As you'll see, what is immediately at stake in this passage is culture, or to be more precise, the subjective categories of culture. The text recognizes that great bourgeois culture is no more, but that the new culture is not yet with us. Brecht asks himself a question typical of the century: When will the new finally come? Is the new already at work, can we already discern its development? Or are we still spellbound by what is merely an old form of the new, a 'new' that is all too ancient because it is still prisoner to destruction? Consequently, the question is 'When?' I will extract from the text a sort of central litany, punctuated by this 'when'.

> Briefly: when culture, in the midst of its collapse, will be coated with stains, almost a constellation of stains, a veritable deposit of garbage;
> when the ideologues will have become too abject to attack property relations, but also too abject to defend them, and the masters

they championed, but were not able to serve, will banish them;

when words and concepts, no longer bearing almost any relation to the things, acts and relations they designate, will allow one either to change the latter without changing the former, or to change words while leaving things, acts and relations intact;

when one will need to be prepared to kill in order to get away with one's life;

when intellectual activity will be so restricted that the very process of exploitation will suffer;

when great figures will no longer be given the time needed to repent;

when treason will have stopped being useful, abjection profitable, or stupidity advisable;

when even the unquenchable blood-thirst of the clergy will no longer suffice and they will have to be cast out;

when there will be nothing left to unmask, because oppression will advance without the mask of democracy, war without the mask of pacifism, and exploitation without the mask of the voluntary consent of the exploited;

when the bloodiest censorship of all thinking will reign supreme, but redundant, all thought having already disappeared;

oh, on that day the proletariat will be able to take charge of a culture reduced to the same state in which it found production: in ruins.

The text is perfectly clear, so I'll simply call attention to five points.

(a)   The essential thematic: the new can only come about as the seizure of ruin. Novelty will only take place in the element of a fully accomplished destruction. Brecht does not say that destruction by itself will engender the new. His dialectic is not simply Hegelian. Rather, he says that destruction is the terrain upon which novelty can seize the world. Note that this logic is not exactly that of a play of forces. We cannot predict that the new will carry the day by becoming stronger than the old. As regards the old culture, what is both required and conceivable as a space for possible novelty is not its weakening, but something like a rotting on the spot, a nourishing decomposition.

(b)   Besides, the adversary is not really represented as a force. It's no longer a force. Rather, it is a sort of neutral abjection or plasma – in any case not a form of thought. This rotting neutrality could never be dialectically sublated. If the paradigm of war is drawn from the definitive (or final) war, it is because the protagonists of that war are not commensurable; they do not belong to the same type of force. This obviously brings to mind the Nietzschean opposition between active and reactive forces, Dionysus and the Crucified – a further indicator of what I argued earlier: Brecht is often closer to Nietzsche than to Marx.

(c)   A very important point for the artist is that one of the symptoms of decomposition is the ruin of language. The power of words to name is affected; the relation between words and things comes undone. One recognizes (and this is one of the foremost truths of the present day) that a central component of any oppression nearing its end is this ruin of language – a contempt for any rigorous and inventive nomination, the dominion of a language which is at once facile and corrupt, the language of journalism.

(d)   What Brecht ultimately says is that the end is only attained when we're faced with the alternative: kill or be killed. This is another sign of the century's violence. Murder functions as a kind of central icon. In murder, we can make out a metonymy of History. Once again, we encounter the stigmata of the passion for the real, all the more terrible in that this passion now arises within a language, a medium, that has become incapable of naming. The century as the thought of the end (of the end of the old culture) is death in the guise of the unnameable murder.

What strikes me is that this category has well and truly become a fundamental category of the contemporary spectacle. The most represented character ends up being that of the serial killer, who universally doles out a death stripped of any symbolization, a death which in this respect fails to be tragic.

The thesis of a conjunction between murder and the failure of language is a powerful one. In any case, it is a spectacular emblem of the century's ending. Brecht sensed the association between the flight of words and something touching on death, something touching on a body which, with the disappearance of symbolization, is no more than a residue.

(e)   The question of the mask. Brecht says that the end is with us when the figures of oppression no longer need masks, because the thing itself has taken root. It is necessary here to think the relation between violence and the mask, a relation that Marxist thinkers in the century, up to and including Althusser, called the question of ideology. We will come back to this point.

What is it to 'unmask' an instance of oppression? What is the exact function of the mask? Brecht is a thinker of the theatre conceived as a capacity to unmask the real, precisely because theatre is above all the art of the mask, the art of semblance. The theatrical mask is the symbol of a question that is often designated, quite erroneously, as that of the importance in the century of the lie. This question is better formulated as follows: What is the relationship between the passion for the real and the necessity of semblance?

5

The passion for the real and the montage of semblance

What is this 'distancing' that Brecht turned into a maxim for the actor's performance? It is the display – within the play – of the gap between the play and the real. More profoundly, it is a technique that dismantles the intimate and necessary links joining the real to semblance, links resulting from the fact that semblance is the true situating principle of the real, that which localizes and renders visible the brutal effects of the real's contingency.

Much of the century's greatness lay in its commitment to thinking the relationship – often obscure at first – between real violence and semblance, between face and mask, between nudity and disguise. This point can be encountered in the most varied registers, from political theory to artistic practice.

Let's start with the Marxists, or Marxians. Those among them who lived in the century ascribed extraordinary importance to the notion of ideology, a notion designating the dissimulating power of false consciousness with regard to a decentred real that is neither grasped nor localized. Ideology is a discursive figure whereby the representation of social relations is effectuated, an imaginary montage that nevertheless re-presents a real. In this sense there is indeed something almost theatrical about ideology. Ideology stages figures of representation that mask the primordial violence of social relations (exploitation, oppression, anti-egalitarian cynicism). As in the Brechtian theatre of distancing, ideology organizes a consciousness separated from the real that it nevertheless expresses. For Brecht the theatre is the didactic exposition of this separation; it shows how the violence of the real is only effective in the gap between the real effect and its dominant representation. The very concept of ideology is the crystallization of the 'scientific' certainty whereby representations and discourses must be read as masks of a real that they both denote and conceal. As Althusser observed,[25] we are in the presence of a symptomal set-up; representation is a symptom (to be read or deciphered) of a real that it subjectively localizes in the guise of misrecognition. The power of ideology is nothing other than the power of the real inasmuch as the latter is conveyed by this misrecognition.

The word 'symptom' obviously indicates, when it comes to this power of misrecognition, that the century's Marxism and its psychoanalysis have something in common. Lacan made this point especially clear when he demonstrated that the Ego is an imaginary construct. Within this construct, the real system of drives is only legible by means of all sorts of decentrings and transformations. The word 'unconscious' precisely designates the set of operations whereby the real of a subject is only consciously accessible via the intimate and imaginary construction of the Ego. In this sense, the psychology of consciousness is a personal ideology, what Lacan calls 'the individual myth of the neurotic'. There exists a function of misrecognition which makes the abruptness of the real operate only through fictions, montages and masks.

Where the positivism of the nineteenth century affirmed the power of knowledge, the twentieth century deploys the theme of the efficacy of misrecognition. Against the cognitive optimism that characterized positivism, the twentieth century both discovers and stages the extraordinary power of ignorance, of what Lacan rightly calls 'the passion of ignorance'.

Distancing – conceived as the way that semblance works out its proper distance from the real – can be taken as an axiom of the century's art, and of 'avant-garde' art especially. What is at stake is the fictionalization of the very power of fiction, in other words, the fact of regarding the efficacy of semblance as real. This is one of the reasons why the art of the twentieth century is a reflexive art, an art that wants to exhibit its own process, an art that wants to visibly idealize its own materiality. Showing the gap between the factitious and the real becomes the principal concern of facticity. For the Marxists, it is clear that a dominant class needs an ideology of domination, and not just domination alone. If art is an encounter with the real channelled through the exhibited means of the factitious, then art is everywhere, since every human experience is traversed by the gap between domination and the dominant ideology, between the real and its semblance. We find the exercise and experience of this gap everywhere. This is why the twentieth century proposes artistic gestures that were previously impossible, or presents as art what used to be nothing but waste matter. These gestures and presentations testify to the omnipresence of art, inasmuch as the artistic gesture ultimately comes down to an intrusion into semblance – exposing, in its brute state, the gap of the real.

Pirandello is a great inventor in this regard – all the more so in that he is entirely alien to Marxism, and even reliant on the worst bourgeois representations (cloistered families, affairs, salons). Pirandello's essential thesis is that the reversibility between the real and semblance is the only artistic path for accessing the real. Pirandello presents the entirety of his theatre under a particularly suggestive title: 'Naked Masks'. The real, or the naked, is what gives itself only by adhering to the mask, adhering to semblance.

What makes the theatrical incarnation of this thesis so forceful is that it takes place in an unusually violent subjective context. An exemplary passage can be found in the conclusion to *Henry IV*, in my view one of Pirandello's strongest works, together with *As You Desire Me, The Pleasure of Honesty* and *Madame Morlì, One and Two*. The Henry IV in question is a German sovereign of the thirteenth century. The hero of the piece is a present-day man who declares throughout that he is Henry IV, surrounding himself with a court of people who, for various reasons, agree to be the conscious accomplices of this fable. In the end, he carries out a murder. This murder can be understood in a 'historical' register, on the basis of the character traits and existential circumstances that one presumes would pertain to the 'real' Henry IV. It can also be understood in a subjective register, on the basis of the life and passions of the hero of the piece who, perhaps, exploits the historical mask of Henry IV. Throughout the bulk of the play, the thesis of reversibility, set forth with amazing virtuosity, stems from our inability to decide whether the hero 'really' does take himself for Henry IV – which would mean that he's mad (in the ordinary sense of the term) – or whether, for complicated reasons to do with the context of his private life, he's only playing at being Henry IV, and thus 'making it seem' (the verb is here particularly apposite) that he is mad. Once the murder is committed, however, things change. From that moment on, lest he be condemned for murder, the hero is definitively forced to make others believe that he's mad and that he killed because he took himself for Henry IV. Beyond semblance there is a *necessity* of semblance, which has perhaps always constituted its real. At this juncture Pirandello introduces a remarkable stage direction: 'Henry IV is to remain on stage with eyes wide open, terrified by the living force of his own fiction, which in the flash of an instant has led him to crime.' Though it reckons with the living force of fiction – and therefore with what makes fiction into a real power – this stage direction is not entirely decidable. It only says that a force must pass through a fiction. But a fiction is a form. One will therefore conclude that every force is only localizable, or effective, through a form that nevertheless cannot decide upon meaning. This is why one must maintain that it is precisely the energy of the real that presents itself as mask.

Within the century, there has been no shortage of terrifying manifestations of this thesis. First and foremost, we must recall the *mise en scène* by Stalin and his entourage of the Moscow trials at the end of the thirties. After all, in these trials it is purely and simply a matter of killing people, of liquidating a significant part of the communist establishment. We are in the realm of pure, real violence. The 'Bolshevik Old Guard', as it was called by Trotsky (its supposed linchpin and himself the victim of assassination), must be annihilated.

Why then stage trials in which pre-designated and most often resigned victims will be forced to recount utterly far-fetched things? Who would ever believe that throughout their whole lives people like Zinoviev and Bukharin were Japanese spies, Hitler's puppets, hirelings of the counter-revolution, and so forth? What is the point of this gigantic sham? Of course, rational hypotheses can be formulated about the need, in Stalin's eyes, to eliminate all these people. One can also try to reconstruct the political land-scape during the great purges.[26] But it is far more difficult to estab-lish the necessity of the trials, especially since a large number of high-ranking officials, particularly among the military, were elim-inated in the basements of the secret service without the slight-est public performance. For these trials are pure theatrical fictions. The accused themselves, who had been carefully prepared, by torture if necessary, had to conform to a role whose performance had been rehearsed and pretty much scripted in the punitive cor-ridors of the regime. In this regard it is very instructive to read the transcript of Bukharin's trial,[27] in which a significant slip momentarily unsettled the entire *mise en scène*, as though the real of semblance had come to perturb its functioning.

It seems that the absolute violence of the real (here, the ter-rorist Party-State) is indeed obliged to go through a representa-tion which nevertheless is only capable of convincing those people (numerous, it's true) who've already decided to be convinced. But on the whole, these people – the convinced communists – would just as easily have sanctioned the straightforward liquidation of the 'enemies of the people'. They didn't need a trial to offer their endorsement. Their passion for the real, it seems, would have saved them this laborious semblance, especially since most found it quite difficult to explain to sceptics the mechanism of the trials. We are therefore left with the following enigma, which touches upon one of the great questions of the century: What is the func-tion of semblance in the passion for the real, this passion that places politics beyond Good and Evil?

I think the crucial point (as Hegel grasped long ago with regard to the revolutionary Terror)[28] is this: the real, conceived in its con-tingent absoluteness, is never real enough not to be suspected of semblance. The passion for the real is also, of necessity, suspicion. Nothing can attest that the real is the real, nothing but the system of fictions wherein it plays the role of the real. All the subjective categories of revolutionary, or absolute, politics – 'conviction', 'loyalty', 'virtue', 'class position', 'obeying the Party', 'revolutionary zeal', and so on – are tainted by the suspicion that the supposedly real point of the category is actually nothing but semblance. Therefore, the correlation between a category and its referent must always be publicly *purged*, purified. This means purging subjects among those who lay claim to the category in question, that is, purging the revolutionary personnel itself. Furthermore, this must be carried out in accordance with a ritual that teaches everyone a lesson about the uncertainties of the real. Purging is one of the great slogans of the century. Stalin said it loud and clear: 'A party becomes stronger by purging itself.'

I would not want you to take these somewhat bitter reflections as yet more grist to the mill of the feeble moralizing that typifies the contemporary critique of absolute politics or 'totalitarianism'. I am undertaking the exegesis of a singularity and of the greatness that belongs it, even if the other side of this greatness, when grasped in terms of its conception of the real, encompasses acts of extraordinary violence.

To cut short any anti-political interpretation of these dark deeds, bear in mind that, among other things, purging, or purification, was also an essential slogan for artistic activity. There was a desire for pure art, an art in which the only role of semblance would be to indicate the rawness of the real. There was also a call to purify – through axiomatics and formalism – the mathematical real, to purge it of the entire spatial or numerical imaginary of intuitions. And so forth. The idea that force is attained through the purging of form was by no means monopolized by Stalin. Or by Pirandello. What all these attempts have in common, I repeat, is the passion for the real.

Let's go back for a moment to the Hegelian anticipation of this theme. In the *Phenomenology*, Hegel tries to explain why the French Revolution was terroristic. His thesis is that the Revolution presents the subjective figure of absolute freedom. But absolute freedom is a freedom that is not bound by any objective representation of the Good. Therefore, it is a freedom without criterion, a freedom whose efficacy nothing can ever attest to. One is always justified in thinking that such and such a subject is about to betray it. Ultimately, the essence of absolute freedom within concrete experience is given only as freedom-that-must-be-betrayed. The subjective name of true freedom is Virtue. But it is impossible to put forward a shared and reliable criterion of virtue. Everything suggests that what reigns is the opposite of virtue, the name of which is 'corruption'.[29] In the end, the essence of real freedom is the struggle against corruption. And since corruption is the 'natural' state of affairs, everybody is a possible target of this struggle, which means: everybody is *suspect*. Freedom is thus enacted, in an entirely logical manner, both as the 'law of suspects' and as a chronic purge.

What matters for us is the following: we are in the realm of suspicion when a formal criterion is lacking to distinguish the real from semblance. In the absence of such a criterion, the logic that imposes itself is that the more a subjective conviction presents itself as real, the more it must be suspected. It is thus at the summit of the revolutionary state, where the ardent desire of freedom is incessantly declared, that the greatest number of traitors is to be found. The traitor is both the leader and, ultimately, oneself. In these conditions, what is the only certainty? Nothingness. Only the nothing is not suspect, because the nothing does not lay claim to any real. The logic of purification, as Hegel astutely remarks, amounts to bringing about the nothing. Ultimately, death is the sole possible name of pure freedom, and 'dying well' the only thing that escapes suspicion. The maxim – all in all a rather simple one – is that strictly speaking, and despite the theatre proceeding *a contrario*, it is impossible to seem to die.

This why our century, aroused by the passion for the real, has in all sorts of ways – and not just in politics – been the century of destruction.

Yet we must immediately distinguish two orientations. The first assumes destruction as such and undertakes the indefinite task of purification. The second attempts to *measure* the ineluctable negativity; this is what I will call the 'subtractive' orientation. Destruction or subtraction? This is one of the century's central debates. What is the active figure taken by the negative side of the passion for the real? I'm particularly sensitive to the conflict between these two orientations since it has played a decisive role in my own philosophical trajectory. An important section of my *Theory of the Subject* (1982) bears the title 'Lack and Destruction'. At that time, an altogether prophetic phrase of Mallarmé served as my banner: 'Destruction was my Beatrice.' In *Being and Event* (1988), I formulated an explicit self-critique on this point, showing that a subtractive thinking of negativity can overcome the blind imperative of destruction and purification.

Art provides the first guiding thread for our attempt to think the couple 'destruction/subtraction'. The century experienced itself as artistic negativity, in the sense that one of its themes, anticipated in the nineteenth century by a number of texts (for example, Mallarmé's *Verse in Crisis*, or farther back still, Hegel's *Aesthetics*), is that of the end of art, of representation, of the painting, and, finally, of the work as such. Behind this theme of the end there obviously lies, once again, the question of knowing what relationship art entertains with the real, or what the real of art is.

It is with regard to this point that I would like to call on Malevich. Malevich is born in Kiev in 1878. He arrives in Paris in 1911. By then, his painting is already organized geometrically. Then, around 1912–13, with Mayakovsky's collaboration, he moves to another doctrine, suprematism.

Malevich affirms the Bolshevik revolution. He returns to Moscow in 1917, and is appointed professor at the University of Moscow in 1919. In 1918, he paints the very famous *White on White*, now at MoMA in New York. In the twenties, as the situation for artists and intellectuals becomes increasingly tense, he is relocated to Leningrad and more or less forbidden from exhibiting his work. In 1926 he publishes, in German, an essay that bears a decisive title: *Die gegenstandlose Welt* (The World of Non-Representation). He dies in 1935.

White on White is – within the field of painting – the epitome of purification. Colour and form are eliminated and only a geometrical allusion is retained. This allusion is the support for a minimal difference, the abstract difference of ground and form, and above all, the null difference between white and white, the difference of the Same – what we could call the vanishing difference.

We find here the origin of a subtractive protocol of thought that differs from the protocol of destruction. We must beware of interpreting *White on White* as a symbol of the destruction of painting. On the contrary, what we are dealing with is a subtractive assumption. The gesture is very close to the one that Mallarmé makes within poetry: the staging of a minimal, albeit absolute, difference; the difference between the place and what takes place in the place, the difference between place and taking-place. Captured in whiteness, this difference is constituted through the erasure of every content, every upsurge.

Why is this something other than destruction? Because, instead of treating the real as identity, it is treated right away as a gap. The question of the real/semblance relation will not be resolved by a purification that would isolate the real, but by understanding that the gap is itself real. The white square is the moment when the minimal gap is fabricated.

There exists a passion for the real that is obsessed with identity: to grasp real identity, to unmask its copies, to discredit fakes. It is a passion for the authentic, and authenticity is in fact a category that belongs to Heidegger as well as to Sartre. This passion can only be fulfilled as destruction. Herein lies its strength – after all, many things deserve to be destroyed. But this is also its limit, because purification is a process doomed to incompletion, a figure of the bad infinite.

There is another passion for the real, a differential and differentiating passion devoted to the construction of a minimal difference, to the delineation of its axiomatic. *White on White* is a proposition in thought that opposes minimal difference to maximal destruction.

This opposition within art relates to a conviction about beginning. The passion for the real is always the passion for the new – but what is the new? And, as Brecht asked, when will it come, and at what price?

To end on this question of the new, I would like to quote for you a poem by Malevich, written immediately prior to the composition of *White on White*:

Try never to repeat yourself – not in the icon, not on the
     canvas, not in the word;
if something in its act recalls an ancient deed,
     then, the voice of the new birth tells me:
Erase, be quiet, stifle the fire if fire it be,
so that the corset of your thoughts may be lighter
     and not rust,
so that you may hear the breath of a new day in the desert.
Cleanse your hearing, erase the bygone days, only thus
     will you be more sensitive and more white,
     for like a dark stain these days sagely
     lie upon your vestments, and in the breath of the wave
     you will find the furrow of the new.
Your thought will find the contours and stamp them with the seal
     of your advance.

We have done enough work for you to be able to grasp immediately two things that this poem intertwines.

The first, typical of the century's prophetic stance towards the
real, is that thought must interrupt repetition. There must be, and
there will be, a new act, a 'new birth' which it is the century's
task to invent. It is a question of responding, once and for all, to
the imperative: 'Erase the bygone days.'

The second concerns the hearing that must be cleansed in order
to find the contours. Attentiveness is realized as the invention of
an outline, the seal of an advance, and not by grasping a pre-existing ideality.

Finally, Malevich tells us what the act of subtraction is: to invent
content at the very place of the minimal difference, where there
is almost nothing. The act is 'a new day in the desert'.

6

One divides into two

So the century is in no way the century of 'ideologies', in the sense of the imaginary and the utopian. Its major subjective trait is the passion for the real, for what is immediately practicable, here and now. We have shown that the importance of semblance is simply a consequence of this passion.

What does the century have to say about itself? At any rate, that it is not the century of promise, but that of realization. It is the century of the act, of the effective, of the absolute present, and not the century of portent, of the future. The century experiences itself as the century of victories, after millennia of attempts and failures. The cult of the vain and sublime attempt, and the ideological enslavement it entails, is ascribed by the actors of the twentieth century to the unhappy Romanticism of the nineteenth century. The twentieth century declares: no more failures, the time of victories has come! This victorious subjectivity outlasts all apparent defeats because it is not empirical but constitutive. Victory is the transcendental theme that determines failure itself. 'Revolution' is one of the names for this theme. The October revolution of 1917, followed by the Chinese and Cuban revolutions, as well as the victories of the Algerians and the Vietnamese in their wars of national liberation – they add up to an empirical validation of the theme and to the defeat of defeats, redressing the massacres of June 1848 or of the Paris Commune.

The instrument of victory is theoretical and practical lucidity in preparation for a decisive conflict, a total and final war. Only a total war will lead to a victory that is truly victorious. In this respect, as we have said, the century is the century of war. But this statement ties together several ideas, all of which turn around the question of the Two, or of antagonistic scission. The century declared that its law was the Two, antagonism; in this respect, the end of the cold war (American imperialism versus the socialist camp), as the last total figure of the Two, also signals the end of the century. However, the Two is conjugated in three different ways:

1   There exists a central antagonism, two subjectivities organized on a planetary scale in mortal combat. The century is the stage for this combat.

2   There is an equally violent antagonism between two ways of considering and thinking antagonism. This is the very essence of the confrontation between communism and fascism. For the communists, the planetary confrontation is in the last instance the confrontation between classes. For the radical fascists it is instead the confrontation between nations and races. Here the Two itself divides into two. There is an entanglement between an antagonistic thesis, on the one hand, and antagonistic theses about antagonism, on the other. This second division is essential, perhaps more than the first. All things considered, there were more anti-fascists than communists, and it is characteristic that the Second World War was fought in accordance with this secondary split, and not on the basis of a unified conception of antagonism. The latter gave rise only to a 'cold' war, except on the periphery (the Korean and Vietnam wars).

3   The century is summoned as the century of the production – through war – of a definitive unity. Antagonism will be overtaken by the victory of one camp over the other. Therefore we can also say that, in this respect, the century of the Two is animated by the radical desire for the One. What names the articulation of antagonism with the violence of the One is victory, which testifies for the real.

Note that we are not dealing with a dialectical schema. Nothing allows us to foresee a synthesis, an *internal* overcoming of contradiction. On the contrary, everything points to the suppression of one of the two terms. The century is a figure of the non-dialectical juxtaposition of the Two and the One. Our question is that of the century's assessment of dialectical thinking. Is the motor of the victorious outcome antagonism itself or is it instead the desire for the One?

In connection with this question, I would like to invoke an episode – renowned in its time yet largely forgotten today – of the Chinese revolutions.[30] Around 1965 there begins in China what the local press – ever inventive when it came to the designation of conflicts – calls 'a great class struggle in the field of philosophy'. On one side stand those who think that the essence of dialectics is the genesis of antagonism, and that it is given in the formula 'one divides into two'; on the other, those who argue that the essence of dialectics is the synthesis of contradictory terms, and that consequently the right formula is 'two fuse into one'. The apparent scholasticism harbours an essential truth. For what is really at stake is the identification of revolutionary subjectivity, of its constituent desire. Is it a desire for division, for war, or is it instead a desire for fusion, for unity, for peace? In any case, in China at that time those who espouse the maxim 'one divides into two' are declared 'leftists', while those who advocate 'two fuse into one' are called 'rightists'. Why?

Taken as a subjective formula, as desire for the One, the maxim of synthesis (two fuse into one) is declared rightist because in the eyes of the Chinese revolutionaries it is entirely premature. The subject of this maxim is yet to fully traverse the Two to its end, and does not yet know what a fully victorious class war is. It follows that the One it covets is not even yet thinkable, which means that *under the cover of synthesis, this desire is calling for the old One*. This interpretation of dialectics is restorative. In order not to be a conservative, in order to be a revolutionary activist in the present, it is instead obligatory to desire division. The question of novelty immediately becomes that of the creative scission within the singularity of the situation.

In China, particularly during 1966 and 1967, and in the midst of unimaginable fury and confusion, the Cultural Revolution pits the partisans of these two versions of the dialectical schema against one other. When it comes down to it, there are those who follow Mao – at the time practically in a minority among the Party leadership – and think that the socialist state must not be the policed and police-like end of mass politics, but, on the contrary, that it must act as a stimulus for the unleashing of politics, under the banner of the march towards real communism. And then there are those who, following Liu Shaoqi but especially Deng Xiaoping, think that – since economic management is the principal aspect of things – popular mobilizations are more nefarious than necessary. The educated youth will spearhead the Maoist line. The Party cadres and a great number of intellectual cadres will put up a more or less overt opposition. The peasants will cautiously bide their time. Last but not least, the workers, the decisive force, will be so torn between rival organizations that in the end, from 1967–8 onward, with the State at risk of being swept away in the whirlwind, the Army will be forced to intervene. What ensues is a long period of extremely violent and complex bureaucratic confrontations, not without a number of popular irruptions, right up to the death of Mao (1976), which is swiftly followed by the Thermidorian coup that brings Deng to power.

As far as its stakes are concerned, this political hurricane is so novel but at the same time so obscure that many of the lessons it no doubt harbours for the future of the politics of emancipation have yet to be drawn. This is in spite of the fact that it provided a decisive inspiration for French Maoism between 1967 and 1975, the only innovative and consequential political current of post-May 1968. In any case, the Cultural Revolution undeniably signals the closure of an entire sequence, whose central 'object' is the Party, and whose main political concept is that of proletariat.

By the way, it is fashionable nowadays, among the restorers of imperial and capitalist servility, to describe this unprecedented episode as a feral and bloody 'power struggle', with Mao, in a minority position within the Chinese politburo, attempting, by any means necessary, to climb his way back up to the top. First of all, one will reply that to affix the epithet 'power struggle' on a political episode of this type is to invite ridicule by busting down a wide-open door. The militants of the Cultural Revolution never stopped quoting Lenin's declaration (perhaps not his best, but that's another matter) according to which in the final analysis 'the problem is that of power'. As Mao himself officially indicated, his threatened position was one of the explicit stakes of the conflict.

The 'findings' unearthed by our sinologist interpreters[31] are nothing but immanent and public themes of the quasi-civil war that took place in China between 1965 and 1976; a war whose authentically revolutionary sequence (in the sense of the existence of a new thinking of politics) is to be found only in its initial segment (1965–8). Besides, since when are our political philosophers outraged by a threatened leader who tries to regain his influence? Is this not what they spend all their time commenting on, deeming it to be the delectable, democratic essence of parliamentary politics? Furthermore, we can observe that the meaning and importance of a power struggle is judged according to the stakes involved. Especially when the weapons in the struggle are classically revolutionary, in the sense that led Mao famously to remark that the revolution 'is not a dinner party': the unprecedented mobilization of millions of workers and youths, a truly unparalleled freedom of expression and organization, gigantic demonstrations, political assemblies in all places of work or study, brutal and schematic debates, public denunciations, the recurrent and anarchic use of violence including armed violence, and so on. Now, who today can dispute that Deng Xiaoping – portrayed by the activists of the Cultural Revolution as the 'number-two capitalist roader in the party' – did in fact endorse a programme of development and social construction diametrically opposed to Mao's innovative, collectivist project? After seizing power in a bureaucratic coup following Mao's death, did we not witness Deng, throughout the eighties and right up to his death, unleashing an utterly savage and corrupt variety of neo-capitalism, all the more illegitimate in that it prolonged the despotism of the Party? When it comes to these questions, and especially the most important (relations between town and country, between intellectual work and manual work, between the Party and the masses, and so on), we can indeed say that what the Chinese, in their delightful tongue, call a 'struggle between two classes, two paths and two lines' really did take place.

What about the violence, often so extreme? The hundreds of thousands of dead? The persecutions, especially against intellectuals? One will say the same thing about them as about all those acts of violence that, to this very day, have marked the History of every somewhat expansive attempt to practise a free politics, to radically subvert the eternal order that subjects society to wealth and the wealthy, to power and the powerful, to science and scientists, to capital and its servants, and considers worthless what people think, worthless, the collective intelligence of workers, worthless, to tell the truth, any thought that is not homogeneous to the order in which the ignoble rule of profit is perpetuated. The theme of total emancipation, practised in the present, in the enthusiasm of the absolute present, is always situated beyond Good and Evil. This is because in the circumstances of action, the only known Good is the one that the status quo turns into the precious name for its own subsistence. Extreme violence is therefore the correlate of extreme enthusiasm, because it is in effect a question of the transvaluation of all values. The passion for the real is devoid of morality. Morality's status, as Nietzsche observed, is merely genealogical. Morality is a residue of the old world. As a result, the century's threshold of tolerance for that which, from the vantage point of our weary, pacified present, constitutes the worst, was incredibly high – regardless of which camp one pledged allegiance to. This is obviously what leads some today to speak of the century's 'barbarity'. Nevertheless, it is entirely unjust to isolate this dimension of the passion for the real. Even when what is at stake is the persecution of intellectuals, disastrous as its spectacle and effects may be, it is important to recall that what makes it possible is the conviction that what permits political access to the real is not knowledge and its privileges. As Fouquier-Tinville had already declared during the French Revolution, when he judged and condemned Lavoisier, the creator of modern chemistry, to death: 'The Republic does not need scientists.' Barbarous words if there ever were, totally extremist and unreasonable – but they must be understood, beyond themselves, in their abridged, axiomatic form: 'The Republic does not need.' It is not from need or interest – or from the correlate of interest, privileged knowledge – that originates the political capture of a fragment of the real, but from the occurrence of a collectivizable thought, and from it alone. This can also be stated as follows: politics, when it exists, grounds its own principle regarding the real, and is thus in need of nothing, save itself.

But perhaps it's the case that today every attempt to submit thought to the test of the real – political or otherwise – is regarded as barbarous. The passion for the real, much cooled, cedes its place (provisionally?) to the acceptance – sometimes enjoyable, sometimes grim – of reality.

It is true that the passion for the real is accompanied by a proliferation of semblance, and that the purification and stripping bare of the real must always begin again. I believe I've already elucidated what drives this process.

What I would like to underscore today is that to purify the real is to extract it from the reality that envelops and conceals it. Whence the violent taste for surface and transparency. The century attempts to react against depth. It carries out a fierce critique of foundations and of the beyond; it promotes the immediate, as well as the surface of sensation. As an heir to Nietzsche, it proposes the abandonment of all 'otherworlds' and posits that the real is identical to appearance. Precisely because what drives it is not the ideal but the real, thought must seize hold of appearance as appearance – or of the real as the pure event of its own appearance. To achieve this, it is necessary to destroy every density, every claim to substantiality, and every assertion of reality. It is reality that constitutes an obstacle to the uncovering of the real as pure surface. Here lies the struggle against semblance. But since the semblance-of-reality adheres to the real, the destruction of semblance is identified with destruction pure and simple. At the end of its purification, the real, as total absence of reality, is the nothing. We can call this path, taken up by innumerable ventures within the century – whether political, artistic or scientific – the path of terroristic nihilism. Since its subjective motivation is the passion for the real, it does not represent a *consent* to the nothing; it is a creation, and in it one should recognize the lineaments of an active nihilism.

How do we stand today with regard to these questions? The figure of active nihilism is regarded as completely obsolete. Every reasonable activity is limited and limiting, hemmed in by the burdens of reality. The best one can do is to avoid evil and to do this the shortest path is to avoid any contact with the real.

Eventually, one meets up once again with the nothing, the nothing-real, and in this sense one is still within nihilism. But since the element of terrorism, the desire to purify the real, has been suppressed, nihilism is deactivated. It has become passive, or reactive, nihilism – that is, a nihilism hostile to every action as well as every thought.

The other path that the century sketched out – the one that attempts to hold onto the passion for the real without falling for the paroxysmal charms of terror – is what I call the subtractive path: to exhibit as a real point, not the destruction of reality, but minimal difference. To purify reality, not in order to annihilate it at its surface, but to subtract it from its apparent unity so as to detect within it the minuscule difference, the vanishing term that constitutes it. What takes place *barely* differs from the place where it takes place. It is in this 'barely', in this immanent exception, that all the affect lies.

For both paths the key question is that of the new. What is the new? The century is obsessed with this question, because ever since its inception the century has summoned itself as a figure of commencement. And first of all as the (re)commencement of Man: the new man.

This phrase has two opposite meanings.

For a whole host of thinkers, particularly in the area of fascist thought (and without excepting Heidegger), 'the new man' is in part the restitution of the man of old, of the man who had been eradicated, had disappeared, had been corrupted. Purification is actually the more or less violent process of the return of a vanished origin. The new is a production of authenticity. In the final analysis, the task of the century is viewed here as restitution (of the origin) through destruction (of the inauthentic).

For another cluster of thinkers, particularly in the area of marxisant communism, the new man is a real creation, something that has never existed before, because he emerges from the destruction of historical antagonisms. The new man of communism is beyond classes and beyond the state.

The new man is thereby either restored or produced.

In the first case, the definition of the new man is rooted in mythic totalities such as race, nation, earth, blood and soil. The new man is a collection of predicates (Nordic, Aryan, warrior, and so on).

In the second case, on the other hand, the new man is envisioned in opposition to all enveloping forms as well as to all predicates, in particular against family, property and the nation-state. This is the project of *The Origin of the Family, Private Property, and the State* by Engels. Marx had already underscored that the universal singularity of the proletariat derives from its bearing no predicate, possessing nothing, and in particular not having, in the strong sense of the term, any 'fatherland'. This anti-predicative, negative and universal conception of the new man traverses the century. A very important point in this respect is the hostility towards the family as the primordial nucleus of egoism, rooted particularity, tradition and origin. Gide's cry – 'Families, I hate you' – partakes in the apologetics of the new man thus conceived.

It's very striking to see that, as the century draws to a close, the family has once more become a consensual and practically unassailable value. The young love the family, in which, moreover, they now dwell until later and later. The German Green Party, allegedly a protest party (everything's relative – they're now in government . . .), at one time contemplated calling itself the 'party of the family'. Even homosexuals, who during the century, as we've just seen with Gide, played their part in the protest, nowadays demand their insertion within the framework of the family, inheritance and 'citizenship'. How far we have come. In the real present of the century, the new man primarily stood – if one was progressive – for the escape from family, property and state despotism. Today, it seems that 'modernization', as our masters like to call it, amounts to being a good little dad, a good little mum, a good little son, to becoming an efficient employee, enriching oneself as much as possible, and playing at the responsible citizen. This is the new motto: 'Money, Family, Elections.'

The century concludes on the motif of the impossibility of subjective novelty and the comfort of repetition. This motif has a categorical name: obsession. The century ends with the obsession of security, under the dominance of the following, rather abject maxim: It's really not that bad being where you are already; it is, and has been, worse elsewhere. Yet precisely what was most alive in these last hundred years placed itself, in the wake of Freud, under the sign of a devastating hysteria: What novelty have you to show us? Of what are you the creator?

Which is why it's not a bad idea to also enter the century via psychoanalysis.

7

Sex in crisis

Talk about psychoanalysis? Again? Everything's been said already – and besides, one always arrives too late, since psychoanalysts already exist and talk. What's more, my question is far more indistinct than those philosophy customarily addresses to a psychoanalysis which it always seems to find in a bad mood. When Mallarmé tries to take stock of the nineteenth century – which is to say, to take stock of its poetry – he suggests this formula: 'One has touched on Verse.' For my part, I will try to assess whether, in the twentieth century, one has touched on sex. I call on psychoanalysis to ask it whether, in our century, it bears witness to the claim that human sexuality has been thought and transformed in such a way that a new promise of existence opens up before us. I summon psychoanalysis to tell us what has happened to us in terms of sex.

I believe that on this point we must take our cue from Freud. With respect to the relations between thought and sex – to what one must indeed call the ineluctable sexuation of the desire to think – there is a genuine Freudian inauguration, a founding personal courage exhibited by Freud himself. We will apply to him our immanent method. To what does Freud hold himself accountable with regard to sexuality? Over and above the mere transgression of a few moral and religious taboos, does Freud think of himself as the agent of a break into the real of sex? Does he entertain the tremulous conviction of having touched on sex in the way that, in the wake of Hugo, poetry has touched on verse?

I will inquire into this question by commenting on four texts taken from Freud's five major case histories. These texts were composed between 1905 and 1918.

In my eyes these case histories make up one of the main works of the century. They are masterpieces in every respect: invention, daring, literary verve, bewildering intelligence. These texts can be read as magisterial products of the human mind, creations whose degree of evidence is magnificent, irrespective of the interest one may otherwise take in psychoanalytic ratiocination. What's more, it is especially remarkable that despite thousands of attempts, some of them by people of great talent, no case history, no transmission of a unique analytic procedure has ever managed even to be in the same league as one of Freud's five studies. One could say that we have already before us the definitive cases, whether it be Dora's hysteria, the Rat-Man's obsession, Little Hans's phobia, Judge Schreber's paranoia, or the borders between neurosis and psychosis with the Wolf-Man. These five studies, extracted from the generally dismal material of unconscious formations, and in a sense inexplicable, constitute, to quote Thucydides, 'a possession forever'. To elevate the miserable tribulations of human character to eternity required uncommon genius and endurance.

Thus it is perfectly legitimate to ask how, in these case histories, Freud approaches the question of his own audacity with regard to the real of sex, or to the mental genealogy of sexuality; or again, how he tackles the instauration – of which he is the first subject – of a confrontation between thought and sex. For not only does this confrontation refuse to take the form of a moral inquisition, but, rather than merely resting content with measuring thought's greater or lesser capacity for mastering the sexual impulse, it examines the determining power of the real avatars of sex upon the constitution of thought.

Let's begin with a text taken from the prologue to the case of Dora. Like the first Russian revolution, which the Bolsheviks retrospectively qualified as the 'dress-rehearsal' (for the revolution of October 1917), it dates from 1905. I quote the texts in the standard edition, edited by James Strachey. Here then are Freud's avowals and defensive precautions:

> Now in this case history – the only one which I have hitherto succeeded in forcing through the limitations imposed by medical discretion and unfavourable circumstances – sexual questions will be

discussed with all possible frankness, the organs and functions of
sexual life will be called by their proper names, and the pure-
minded reader can convince himself from my description that I
have not hesitated to converse upon such subjects in such language
even with a young woman. Am I, then, to defend myself upon
this score as well? I will simply claim for myself the rights of the
gynaecologist – or rather, much more modest ones – and add that
it would be the mark of a singular and perverse prurience to
suppose that conversations of this kind are a good means of excit-
ing or of gratifying sexual desires.

Considered in terms of the question that preoccupies us here, this
text is remarkably dense. In it, Freud manifests an acute awareness of the modifications he is introducing into the question of
sex and of the sexual. At the same time, a defensive worry – seemingly 'social' in character and no doubt combined with unconscious resistances – leads him to an unanalysed disavowal which,
had it been exhibited by someone else, would surely not have
escaped his notice. A whole host of signs tells us that part of
Freud's greatness lay in having to work against himself (the same
can be said of Cantor, who perhaps provides the third of the
twentieth century's intellectual sources – with Lenin and, precisely, Freud himself). Freud had to grant the sexual, in terms of
its effects for thought, an extension which he was in no way prepared for – one for which he even harboured a spontaneous
antipathy. Similarly, it was by touching on the infinite and rescind-
ing its sublime link to the One that Cantor eventually upset his
own theological convictions.

If we move from the explicit towards the implicit, or from conscious theses towards unconscious operations, Freud's text tells us
four things:

(1) 'I merely name the sexual as it is, I call sexual things by their
names, I speak frankly.' This declaration seems very simple, or even
self-evident. In actual fact, in terms of the conditions dictated by
the epoch, it is absolutely fundamental. Of course, the psychoanalytic invention consists in confronting thought with the sexual
as such. But the important thing is that we're not dealing with a
simple relation of knowledge. As Foucault unrelentingly declared,

the will to 'know sex' has never been lacking, linked as it has always been to the power-effects of a control over bodies, and particularly over the bonds between bodies. The singularity of Freud's approach is that the face-to-face with the sexual is not of the order of knowledge, but of the order of naming or intervention – to 'be discussed with all possible frankness'. Such a discussion seeks precisely to separate the effects of the sexual from any purely cognitive comprehension and thus from any subordination to the power of the norm. From this point of view, the attestation of an 'ontology' of the sexual (the sexual such as it is, with its 'organs and functions') serves indeed to support an emancipation of judgement. Little by little, whether it wants to or not, psychoanalysis will accompany the withering away of the explicit norms which had hitherto organized the knowledge of sexuality. By thinking the face-to-face with sexuality as the un-known of every form of thought, psychoanalysis accorded it a status, we might even say a nobility, which none of the ancient norms could countenance.

On this point, Freud is aware of his own originality, of his courage, and he assumes the face-to-face between thought and sexuality as a genuine break.

(2) 'I do not hesitate to discuss it with a young woman.' The question of femininity – of the autonomy of feminine sexuality and its effects – is one of the principal upheavals that psychoanalysis simultaneously provokes, accompanies, and ends up following from a certain distance. In the case of Dora, however, it is more a question of listening to (of following *to the letter*) what a young girl has to say about sex than of 'discussing' it with her. That is because this nascent psychoanalysis is above all the decision to listen to what the hysteric says without immediately turning it into some sort of sorcery, the kind that oscillates between mere anecdote and witch-burnings. Freud seeks to abide in the harrowing labyrinth of this hysteric speech, even venturing into the arcana of a founding sexuality and thereby creating a new region of thought. That women need not be sheltered from this form of thought – quite the contrary – is attested to by the sheer number of female psychoanalysts, from the dawn of the discipline onwards. Thus begins the long history, within the century, of the metamorphosis of sexuality. This metamorphosis is mainly brought about by the explicit integration

of thought's feminine dimension, and, some time later, of what is properly creative in the expression of its homosexual component. Of course, psychoanalysis was not alone in bringing this about. But it is enough to read the case of Dora to see how, in 1905, Freud was by no means lagging behind.

(3) The formula with which Freud declares his claim to have a more modest role than that of the gynaecologist introduces us to the defensive strategy. The gynaecologist is the one who sustains the theme of a purely objective relation to the avatars of sex. Not for nothing is the State today pushing for his disappearance. Sheltered by the objectivity of the gynaecologist's relation to sex, millions of women have found ways of secretly defending certain bodily zones of their subjectivation. This is what the modern economy cannot abide, according to its incontrovertible rationale: If it's objective, its measure is cost, and the specialization is too costly. Go see your general practitioner. If it's subjective, it doesn't exist, and, more to the point, should not cost anything. Do without it. Or consider it a luxury. Take the plane and have your consultation in Los Angeles.

This is the law of our world, which decrees that what is objective must align its costs with the market, whilst what is subjective must not exist as anything other than an unattainable luxury.

Be that as it may, when Freud lays claims to the role of gynaecologist, he strongly de-subjectivates the entanglement that binds his thought to the sexualized speech of the young hysteric. Anyway, what exactly does he mean by 'more modest' rights? That Dora shouldn't strip? Freud knows perfectly well that to consider sexuality from the side of its efficacy in the constitution of a subject involves a (temporary) nudity that medical undressing could never match.

At the dawn of these transformations, we can indeed witness Freud hesitating about which version of them he intends to make public. Should he adopt the model of medical objectivity, which has always registered both body and sex? Or is it a question of a subversive subjectivation, bearing on the sexual narrative and its effects, from which nothing – not femininity as it is ordinarily understood, not the unnameable pleasure, and especially not the elucidation of the desire to think – will come out unscathed? It's all too clear that in the grip of this hesitation the ideal of science, with the gynaecologist as its placeholder, serves to quell the anxiety of the new.

(4) As Freud ultimately assures us, no desire circulates in this affair, and it would be 'perversely prurient' to think otherwise. Thus, the paragraph concludes with what could easily function as a textbook case of disavowal. For we know (and just reading the case, we know it from a very good source) that desire did indeed circulate in a particularly intense manner between the young hysteric and her analyst, to the point that Freud literally ran away, leaving the 'case of Dora' – and this is one of its literary charms – largely undecided. So that Freud bequeathed to his disciples, as well as to himself, a paradigm of what will come to be known as counter-transference, in which the seductive analysand overtakes the master who is analysing her.

It is not the least of the century's contributions to have finally thought through – admittedly in the long wake of Plato's *Symposium* – the massive importance of transferential and counter-transferential operations in everything that concerns both the transmission of knowledges and the agglomeration of human groups around some obscure fetish. As is often the case with the inaugural Master, Freud practises this intellectual incursion into the regions where truth depends on the bar imposed on sex, but also recoils slightly when confronted by the explicit naming of his own practice. Notwithstanding this ambivalence, Freud will have touched upon the desirous disturbance to which is exposed anyone who seeks to elucidate a truth's grip upon the singularity of a subject.

What novel things does the case of little Hans – a text from 1909 – have to tell us about the sexual? I've extracted from the text a pertinent fragment:

> But even a psychoanalyst must confess to the wish for a more direct and less roundabout proof of these fundamental theorems. Surely there must be a possibility of observing in children at first hand and in all the freshness of life the sexual impulses and wishes which

we dig out so laboriously in adults from among their own debris – especially as it is also our belief that they are the common property of all men, a part of the human constitution, and merely exaggerated or distorted in the case of neurotics.

With this end in view I have for many years been urging my pupils and my friends to collect observations of the sexual life of children – the existence of which has as a rule been cleverly overlooked or deliberately denied.

It is a question here of what effectively aroused, and continues to arouse (consider the sometimes strictly nonsensical declarations elicited by paedophilic practices), the most violent reactions – that is, the assertion that a vigorous sexuality is at work in the infant, a sexuality that constitutes the scene wherein the future of a subject is constructed. Moreover, for Freud this sexuality is so insistently marked by its polymorphous perversity that any idea according to which sex is regulated by nature is immediately exposed as inconsistent. Freud is perfectly aware of his doctrine's disruptive potential, which is why he urges his pupils to accumulate their direct observations, so that in the coming controversies they will be armed with a vast empirical arsenal.

Let me say it again: it is far from certain that we have no use for Freud's courage today.

The century has undoubtedly put to rest one of the classical theses about childhood, to be found in Descartes for example, which claims that the child represents no more than a sort of intermediary stage between the dog and the adult, an intermediary which, if it is to attain the rank of man, must be drilled and punished without the slightest hesitation. Today, we have the universal declaration of the rights of the child, and trials based on neighbours' denunciations, notably in Scandinavia, for those parents who still deem it possible to hit their kids. Considered in isolation, who will fail to rejoice at this transformation? It would surely be anachronistic to defend the old English boarding school and its corporal punishment. Yet when it comes to the definition of man, the question is always that of knowing the price to be paid for every extension of his rights. For every equality is reversible. If the child has the same rights as a man, this could mean that the child is a man, but it could also be predicated on man's acceptance that he is no more than a child. Similarly, if even macaques and trout enjoy inalienable rights, this might be an index of refined compassion. Or it could mean that we are asked not to think of ourselves as very different from the monkey or the pig.

Herein lies the significance of the question famously raised by Rousseau: 'What is childhood?' Freud replies that childhood is the scene of the constitution of the subject in and by desire, in and by the exercise of the pleasure linked to the representations of objects. Childhood sets the sexual frame within which all our thinking – sublime as its operations may be – must henceforth dwell.

What to this very day endows this thesis with its subversive dimension is not the objections raised against it in terms of the animality of the child and the necessity of its training. Far from it. *A contrario*, the obstacle currently before us is the idea that the child is an innocent, a little angel, the depository for all our saccharine daydreams, the tiny receptacle for all the world's sentiment. This is evident in the repeated calls for denunciation, the death penalty and immediate lynching that greet any indication that a sexual relation with a child has taken place. In these violent outcries, before which the authorities can hardly retain their impartial composure, it is never a matter of what Freud, with his customary courage, proposed: That, at a far remove from any 'innocence' whatsoever, childhood is a golden age for sexual experimentation in all its forms.

Granted, the law must say who is and who is not a child; at what age one can freely make use of one's body; and how those who transgress these decrees are to be punished. As for murders, as ever, they must be punished with the greatest justice and severity. Having said that, in doling out these punishments it is not only useless but also deeply reactionary and pernicious to invoke archaic representations of childhood and the mendacious morality of a pre-Freudian era, forgetting that every childhood is structured by powerful drives and an ever-alert sexual curiosity. This means that measuring a child's degree of complicity with those endeavouring to sexually seduce him or her is invariably a delicate matter, even if one rightly argues that the existence of this complicity cannot be used to absolve the adult who exploits it.

Let us add that those who organize petitions, denunciations, Internet sites and rampant lynch mobs against paedophiles would do well to examine the pathogenic structure of the family, including its sexual aspects. The overwhelming majority of child murders are carried out, not by sleazy unmarried paedophiles, but by parents, especially mothers. And the overwhelming majority of sexual abuse is incestuous, in this instance courtesy of fathers or stepfathers. But about this, seal your lips! Murderous mothers and incestuous fathers, who are infinitely more widespread than paedophile killers, are an unsettling intrusion into the idyllic portrait of the family, which depicts the delightful relationship between our citizen parents and their angelic offspring.

For his part, Freud refused any fetters, whatever his own bourgeois reticence may have been. He explained human thought on the basis of child sexuality, and gave us the means with which to reflect on what is makeshift, neurotic, or maddening in the familial universe. He also anticipated something patently evident today: the creative resource constituted by the homosexuality – whether latent or explicit – of every human subject. Consider, for example, this fragment from the analysis of Judge Schreber, a text from 1911:

> We shall therefore, I think, raise no further objections to the hypothesis that the exciting cause of the illness was the appearance in him of a feminine (that is, a passive homosexual) wishful phantasy, which took as its object the figure of the doctor. An intense resistance to this phantasy arose on the part of Schreber's personality, and the ensuing defensive struggle, which might perhaps just as well have assumed some other shape. It took on, for reasons unknown to us, that of a delusion of persecution.

Freud boldly maintains that homosexuality is only one of the components of generic sexuality. There is nothing either natural or obvious about the fact that the object of desire for a subject is borne by the opposite sex. Rather, it is the result of a long and fortuitous construction. Note that what leads to delirium in the case of Schreber is in no way the homosexual drive, but the conditions of the conflict into which the subject is dragged by the repression of this drive. Schreber's phantasy is a 'feminine' desire, not because of its pure passive form, but because it is a question, as the final metamorphoses of this phantasy reveal, of conquering the place of the Father's woman (becoming the sexual object of God). Taken on its own, this phantasy simply testifies to the universal ambivalence of drives, to their versatility when it comes to the object upon which they happen to affix themselves. The unconscious repression of the phantasy is itself nothing but the effect of social regulations, familial schemas, the law of the father, and so on. There is nothing natural about it. As for the psychotic outcome, though Freud teases out its logic with considerable virtuosity, he is at pains to state that its cause is purely and simply unknown. In other words, though the link between the homosexual phantasy and madness may be intelligible it nevertheless remains totally contingent. The libidinal forces at play could have assembled themselves into 'some other shape'. Thus, homosexuality is assumed by Freud as one possibility among others, a potential resource for the course taken by the drives. Its universality derives from the fact that it is impossible to isolate pure figures of desire. Every object-fixation is contaminated by its opposite; every desire contains the desire of being 'in the place of' the other sex.

The century was the stage for a subversion of the relation between universality and the resource of sexual desire. That subversion doubtless goes well beyond what Freud himself had envisaged, but which he was able to announce with the implacable vigour of the logician of drives.

Consequently, we should not be surprised that this man, inflexible when the obligations of thought were at stake, swiftly became aware of the menace posed to his endeavour by the resistances of 'normality'. The following passage, from the case of the Wolf-Man (1918), testifies to that awareness:

In the present phase of the battle which is raging around psycho-analysis the resistance to its findings has, as we know, taken on a new form. People were content formerly to dispute the reality of the facts which are asserted by analysis and for this purpose the best technique seemed to be to avoid examining them. That procedure appears to be slowly exhausting itself, and people are now adopting another plan – of recognising the facts, but of eliminating, by means of twisted interpretations, the consequences that follow from them, so that the critics can still ward off the objectionable novelties as efficiently as ever. The study of children's neuroses exposes the complete inadequacy of these shallow or high-handed attempts at reinterpretation. It shows the predominant part that is played in the formation of the neuroses by those libidinal motive forces which are so eagerly disavowed, and reveals the absence of any aspirations toward remote cultural aims, of which the child still knows nothing, and which cannot therefore be of any significance for him.

In this text, Freud analyses a second wave of resistance to psychoanalysis. Whereas the initial cause of scandal was thought's confrontation with the sexual injunction, now there is an attempt to 'spiritualize' this injunction, to turn it into a cultural phenomenon. Obviously, one thinks here of Jung's archetypes, in which the sexual element finds itself immediately formalized within Culture. Freud denounces this cultural sublimation as nothing but a slightly subtler resistance. It is absolutely necessary to abide in the face-to-face with the sexual, and to reconstruct, without fear or subterfuge, the stage upon which 'libidinal forces' play.

By 1918, as we can see, Freud had already clearly identified a ploy that has been operative ever since, which consists in referring the articulation of desire and its object back to a meaning that is pre-constituted in culture, mythology, or religion. The enduring aim of this ploy is to reintroduce meaning into the place of, and instead of, truth, thereby injecting the 'cultural' into libido. This is the hermeneutic ploy, and Freud immediately saw it as an insidious negation of his discovery. Briefly, it was necessary to come back to bare sex and to its radical absence of meaning.

That what was also at stake was the struggle against religion – in its modern form, the form demanded by our century – was something that Freud, being the great materialist mind that he was, also knew. What frightens religion is not the importance of sex, quite the contrary. The Church fathers knew quite a bit about sex, its perversions, its effects, and they were the last to underestimate its importance. No, what frightened them is the fact that sex can command a conception of truth separate from meaning. The terrifying thing is that sex may repel any donation of meaning, whereas the very existence of religion depends on its capacity to spiritualize the sexual relation, thereby forcing it to signify.

Freud enlisted the century in a great battle about sex, meaning and truth, a battle that Lacan depicted as a great confrontation between religion and psychoanalysis. What is at stake in this conflict is the question of knowing whether sex has a meaning, or, to put it like Lacan, whether there is something reasonably connected in sex, something like a sexual 'relation'; or whether the subjective destiny of sexuation submits the subject to a senseless truth, the truth that, in Lacan's words once more, there is no sexual relation.

Briefly, the anti-religious function of the thought/sex face-to-face under the aegis of truth consists in separating the saying of sex from the claims of morality.

This separation entails a revolution of such amplitude that it remains unclear if the century has really succeeded in carrying it out. Of course, the century has wrested sex away from the most conspicuous figures of morality. But has it thereby de-moralized it? Morality can hide behind hedonism. The imperative 'Enjoy!', which we see plastered all over teen magazines today, both retains and aggravates the structures synthesized by the imperative 'Don't enjoy!' The Freudian revolution, which accompanied the century through the intimate struggle with the religious structuring of meaning, is today in abeyance. It finds itself challenged by new modalities of sexualized subjectivation; ones for which apparent form (hetero- or homo-sexual, feminine or masculine, active or passive, neurotic or depressive, and so on) is less important than the anxiety elicited by the unnameable thing hiding beneath every enjoyment, and especially beneath every mandatory enjoyment.

Ever since the days of the Roman Empire, we know that when enjoyment is what every life tries to guarantee for itself, when it takes the place of the imperative, what one inevitably ends up enjoying is atrocity. Enter the time of general obscenity, of gladiators, of real-time torture, a time that might even make us nostalgic for the political slaughters of the dead century.

No doubt, it is on this point that Freud's courage continues to be an inspiration. Freud was exemplary in knowing how to elevate thought and make logic rear up in the face of that which, supporting itself upon the unnameable alone, is nonetheless an inevitable ingredient of our truth.

To have known how to address the real of sex, rather than its meaning, makes Freud one of this century's great heroes, one of those figures who permit us to say that these years, so often devoted to the vain and horrible indifference of particularisms, were not without use for what is universal in thought.

8

Anabasis

How did the century envisage its own movement, its trajectory? As a re-ascent towards the source, an arduous construction of novelty, an exiled experience of beginning. These meanings, together with a few others, are conjoined in a Greek word: 'anabasis'. More particularly, *Anabasis* is the title of a narrative by Xenophon that tells the story of a troop of about 10,000 Greek mercenaries enlisted by one of the warring camps in a Persian dynastic quarrel.

It is worth noting that the Greeks were appreciated by the 'barbarians' not so much for their refined civilization as for their military qualities. And what constituted the hard core of the Greek (later Macedonian, then Roman) military force, which established its superiority over the enormous conglomerates of warriors gathered together by the Persians or the Egyptians? Discipline. It is not for nothing that the first article of the military regulations specifies that 'discipline constitutes the principal force of an army'. The conquering hegemony of what we customarily refer to as the West rests fundamentally on discipline. This is a discipline of thought, the compact force of certainty, a political patriotism ultimately concentrated in military cohesion. Similarly, when Lenin wants an 'iron discipline' to rule within the proletarian party, it is because he knows that the proletarians, deprived of everything, will not have the slightest chance of prevailing unless they can impose upon themselves – as a consequence and material figure of their political consistency – an unparalleled organizational discipline.

It can be said, therefore, that every anabasis requires that thinking accept a discipline. Without this discipline, it is not possible
to 're-ascend the slope' – one of the possible meanings of 'anabasis'. Xenophon and his 10,000 companions will experience this at
first hand. In the battle of Cunaxa, their Persian employer is killed,
and the Greek mercenaries are left alone in the heart of an
unknown country, bereft of any local support or pre-established
destination. 'Anabasis' will be the name for their 'homeward'
movement, the movement of lost men, out of place and outside
the law.

We can extract three points concerning what, at a first glance,
characterizes the movement named 'anabasis':

(a)   Xenophon describes the collapse of the order that gave
meaning to the collective presence of the Greeks at the heart of
Persia. After Cunaxa, the Greeks find themselves brutally deprived
of any reason for being where they are. They are nothing now but
foreigners in a hostile country. At the root of anabasis lies something like a principle of lostness.

(b)   The Greeks have only themselves, their own will and discipline, to rely on. Having gone there at another's behest, in a position of obedience and paid service, they suddenly find themselves
left to their own devices, forced, as it were, to invent their destiny.

(c)   It is imperative that the Greeks find something new. Their
march through Persia, towards the sea, follows no pre-existing
path and corresponds to no previous orientation. It cannot even
be a straightforward return home, since it invents its path without
knowing whether it really is the path of return. Anabasis is thus
the free invention of a wandering that *will have been* a return, a
return that did not exist as a return-route prior to the wandering.

One of the best known episodes of the anabasis is the one in
which the Greeks climb a hill and, at last laying eyes on the sea,
cry out: θάλασσα, θάλασσα! – 'The sea! The sea!' This goes to
show that for a Greek the sea is already a legible fragment of the
homeland. The sight of the sea is a sign that the invented wandering has probably traced the curve of a return. An unprecedented return.

We are beginning to glimpse how the word 'anabasis' may serve
as a possible support for a meditation on our century. In the tra-

jectory it names, anabasis leaves undecided the parts respectively allotted to disciplined invention and uncertain wandering. In so doing, it constitutes a disjunctive synthesis of will and wandering. After all, the Greek word already attests to this undecidability, since the verb αναβανειν ('to anabase', as it were) means both 'to embark' and 'to return'. There is no doubt that this semantic pairing suits a century that ceaselessly asks itself whether it is an end or a beginning.

And in effect, framing the hard core of the century – the thirties and forties – we find two poets, separated by four decades, writing under the aegis of this same signifier: 'Anabasis'. First, in the twenties, Alexis Leger, a.k.a. Saint-John Perse. Then, at the beginning of the sixties, Paul Ancell, or Antschel, a.k.a. Paul Celan. By contrasting these two anabases we will try to glean the century's awareness of its own movement, its precarious belief that it represented a re-ascent towards a properly human home, the anabasis of a lofty signification.

These two poets could hardly be more different. Allow me to stress this difference, because it makes sense for this century to have poetically welcomed under the same 'Anabasis' such violently contrasting types of existence.

Alexis Saint-Leger Leger, a.k.a. Saint-John Perse (1887–1975), was born in Guadeloupe. He was a white West Indian, a man of colonial descent from a family of planters that had been settled in Guadeloupe for two centuries. In his own eyes, he was born in a paradise, the paradise that the colonies have always been for the colonizers, however progressive and well-intentioned the latter may be. I sympathize – in the etymological sense – with Saint-John Perse when I think of my own childhood in Morocco among my veiled and sumptuous nurses. I remember Fatima, whom we actually used to call 'Fatma'. Since for the colonists the 'natives' (another crucial category of this sort of paradise) form a species whose individuals are difficult to discern, every Arab woman became a 'fatma'. I can still picture my father, effectively a mere maths teacher, as I could see him from the heights of our white villa, under the violet of the bougainvilleas, returning from the hunt accompanied by dogs and servants, bent under the weight of the game that he had just shot. I'm not at all surprised then that for the poet this was a dazzling childhood. It affects the tone of his first collection, *Éloges* (In Praise) (1907–11), one section of which is entitled 'Pour fêter une enfance' (To celebrate a childhood). In that section, Perse poses a genuine question concerning memory, a question worthy of Proust: 'What was there then, save for childhood, that is no longer?' Today we know what the answer is: the obscene and more than succulent colonial nirvana.

Alexis Leger leaves the islands in 1899. He sits the Foreign Affairs exam and becomes a diplomat. He spends the war of 1914 in the ministries, leaves for China as embassy attaché and travels in central Asia, as one can readily imagine reading *Anabasis*, published in 1924. From the middle of the twenties, he's the very image of the high-level civil servant. For almost twenty years Perse does not publish any further poems. He will be Secretary-General (a paramount appointment) at the French Ministry of Foreign Affairs from 1933 to 1939. In 1940 he exiles himself to the United States and is stripped of his French citizenship by Pétain. His American contacts help him to become director of the Library of Congress. He is an American by adoption, and is also estranged from France because of his sincere dislike of de Gaulle. He inscribes his situation in what is probably the most personal of all his poems, *Exil* (Exile), and then celebrates the epic saga of the great Western plains in *Vents* (Winds). He travels and continues to write, this time a canticle to love, *Amers* (Seamarks). He is awarded the Nobel Prize.

Basically, from the fifties onward, Saint-John Perse occupies the post left vacant by Valéry, that of official poet of the Republic. He is a man fulfilled: an Edenic childhood, a distinguished career in the State, a noble exile, serene loves, major honours. He seems beyond the reach of the century's violence. In this regard, continuing and consolidating the Claudelian figure of the poet-diplomat, with a mandarin-like aspect (as if to say: 'I write stanzas on exile and the impermanence of human things, but I allow no one to ignore that I am under-secretary to the Emperor'), Saint-John Perse embodies a figure who manages to perpetuate nineteenth-century conditions in the very midst of the twentieth. He is truly a man of the Third Republic, a man who belongs to the era of tranquil imperialism and the benevolent State; the man of a civilized, sated class society, a society lulled to sleep by its own power and whose dominant literary genre is the award ceremony speech. One only has to read Saint-John Perse's Nobel Prize lecture to sense his familiarity with this exercise, and his ability to rival Valéry (an acknowledged master of academic ceremonies) when it comes to the elegant manipulation of pompous generalities in a manner pleasing to the ear – which is no mean feat.

What can such a man possibly retain from the century and its passion for the real? Why call on him? Precisely because, from the recesses of his gilded armchair in a waning republic, Saint-John Perse clearly perceived – as one does a distant murmur whose cause is either unknown or disregarded – the century's epic dimension. Perhaps his haughty distance, his secret disengagement – all the more radical in that he occupied a key post within the State – even allowed him to grasp more readily than others that this epic was essentially an epic for nothing. The disjunctive synthesis borne by the poetry of Saint-John Perse is that of spiritual vacancy and epic affirmation. The image of the century he endorses, without ever discussing it directly, conforms to an imperative which is well and truly of its time and which can be stated thus: may your force be nihilistic, but your form epic. Saint-John Perse will praise what there is precisely to the extent that it is, without attempting to link it to any meaning whatsoever. His anabasis is the pure movement of the epic, but it is a movement that takes place against an indifferent background. The poem thinks the very deep bond that existed between violence and absence in the course of the century. Let's now read section VIII of *Anabasis*, which illustrates this bond. I quote from T. S. Eliot's translation:*

> Laws concerning the sale of mares. Nomad laws. And
> ourselves. (Man colour.)
>   Our companions these high waterspouts on the march,
> clepsydrae travelling over the earth,
>   and the solemn rains, of a marvellous substance, woven
> of powders and insects, pursuing our folk in the sands like a headtax.
>   (To the scale of our hearts was such vacance completed!)

Not that this stage was in vain: to the pace of the eremite
beasts (our pure bred horses with eyes of elders) many things
undertaken on the darkness of the spirit – infinity of things at
leisure on the marches of the spirit – great seleucid histories to
the whistling of slings and the earth given over to explanations . . .

And again: these shadows – the prevarications of the
sky against the earth . . .
Cavaliers, across such human families, in whom hatreds
sang now and then like tomtits, shall we raise our whip over
the gelded words of happiness? – Man, weigh your weight
measured in wheat. A country here, not mine. What has the
world given me but this swaying of grass? . . .

To the place called the Place of the Dry Tree:
and the starved levin allots me these provinces in the
West.
But beyond are greater leisures, and in a great
land of grass without memory, the unconfined unreckoned
year, seasoned with dawns and heavenly fires. (Matutinal
sacrifice of the heart of a black sheep.)

Roads of the world, we follow you. Authority over all
the signs of the earth.
O Traveller in the yellow wind, lust of the soul! . . .
and the seed (so you say) of the Indian cocculus possesses (if you
mash it!) intoxicating properties.

A great principle of violence dictated our fashions.

With Paul Celan, or Paul Ancell (1920–70), it is instead the real
of the century at its rawest that makes its irruption. No dynasty,
no official comfort, was to protect his person. He is born in
Czernowitz, Romania, in the province of Bukovina. So he is born
around the same time that the diplomat Saint-John Perse, thirty-
three years old, is busy writing *Anabasis*. Celan is from a Jewish
family. His childhood immerses him in a linguistic multiplicity:
German, Yiddish, Romanian. He studies medicine in France in
1938–9. In 1940, after the German–Soviet pact, Bukovina is
annexed by the USSR. Celan begins studying Russian. He will
remain a translator throughout his life, and one of his collections

is dedicated to Mandelstam. In 1941, following a Nazi offensive, the Russians retreat. A ghetto is created, his parents are deported. His father will die of typhus and his mother will be executed. In 1942, Celan is placed in a forced labour camp for the young. In 1944, the region is liberated by the Soviets. Celan resumes his study of English. Between 1945 and 1947 he translates, among other things, some of Chekhov's short stories from Russian into Romanian. He writes his first poems and adopts his pseudonym, Celan. In 1948 he leaves for Paris, where he studies German. His nomadic image is visibly taking shape. He gives several readings of his poems in Germany – readings will always mean a lot to him. In 1958, he is appointed reader in German at the École Normale Supérieure in Paris (before the war, Samuel Beckett had been reader in English at the same institution). At the heart of his work lie the poems from the beginning of the sixties. In 1967, that famous episode takes place, the meeting with Heidegger – a meeting that has given rise to multiple interpretations, as well as to an exceedingly enigmatic poem by Celan himself.[32] Three years later, Paul Celan commits suicide. A significant part of his work is composed of posthumous collections.

If we inspect what I've called the 'short century', the one preceding the Restoration of the last twenty years, Celan can be legitimately considered as the poet who brings this century to a close.

I've never been able to see anything more than a kind of sensationalist journalism in the interminably reiterated motif of philosophy's radical impotence when it comes to confronting the crimes of this century. Philosophy has endured this question just as well, and just as poorly, as every other thought procedure. Better in any case than all those who raise this objection against it. Nor have I ever believed that there is any sense in saying, as Adorno pretends to postulate, that it has become impossible, after Auschwitz, to write a poem. Consequently, as far as I'm concerned, there is no paradox in the fact that Celan, for whom Auschwitz was a particularly intense question – a sort of black consuming fire, a referent at once universal and grimly intimate – never ceased inventing a poetry capable of reckoning with what men underwent during the thirties and forties, and (with supreme defiance) forcing the German language, that of the murderers, to carry this inventiveness. As the poet-witness of those years, Celan closes the period – inaugurated by Trakl, Pessoa and Mandelstam – in which poetry was put in charge of naming the century. After Celan there are certainly many more poems,[33] but there are no more poems of the century. The century, thought as a meditation on itself, is poetically complete.

Celan's poem *Anabasis* is part of the collection *Die Niemands-rose* (The No-one's-Rose), published in 1963, forty years after the poem *The Age* by Mandelstam, Celan's favourite poet. And also forty years after Saint-John Perse's *Anabasis*.

This is how Celan phrases his anabasis, as rendered in Michael Hamburger's translation:

> This
> narrow sign between walls
> the impassable-true
> Upward and Back
> to the heart-bright future.
>
> There.
>
> Syllable-
> mole, sea-
> coloured, far out
> into the unnavigated.
>
> Then:
> buoys,
> espalier of sorrow-buoys
> with those
> breath reflexes leaping and
> lovely for seconds only –: light-
> bellsounds (dum-
> dun-, un-,
> *unde suspirat*
> *cor*),
> re-
> leased, re-
> deemed, ours

Visible, audible thing, the
tent-
word growing free:

Together.

There is more than a simple difference in style between the two
poets and their respective anabases. It is the very conception of
the poetic that differs. We could say that a certain figure of eloquence is terminated herein. I call 'eloquence' the conviction that
language is endowed with resources and cadences that demand
to be exploited. If Celan's poem is not eloquent, it is because it
exposes an uncertainty concerning language itself – to the extent
of presenting language only in its cut, in its section, in its perilous
reparation, and practically never in the shared glory of its resource.
The truth is that, for Celan, although the forties in no way made
poetry impossible, they did render eloquence obscene. Consequently, it is necessary to propose a poetry without eloquence,
because the truth of the century is linguistically impassable so long
as one claims to speak it through those figures and ornaments still
abundantly employed by Saint-John Perse.

Anabasis, Celan says, carries with it the 'impassable-true'. Once
again we encounter a strong disjunctive synthesis. The poem must
install time's truth within the impassibility of the inherited language. This is a measure of the kind of forcing that is required
here – in contrast to Saint-John Perse, who installs his poem in a
true-ease symbolized by the rhythmic arch and the chromatic evidence of his images. The same word, 'anabasis', presides over two
orientations which are almost diametrically opposed to one
another as to the chances and duties of poetry. The interesting
question becomes: Why, then, this same word? What does an
anabasis, conceived as a poetic sign for the century, signify?

The gap is akin to the one that separates the bare and cruel
twentieth century from that which, in the midst of it, prolongs
the nineteenth; that which prolongs an imperial dream whose
horror is distant and discreet, whilst its Edenic and wayfaring force
is nonetheless omnipresent. Having departed for the anabasis in
Saint-John Perse's sense, the century foundered upon a darkness

so real that it was forced to change the *direction* of the movement, as well as the resonance of the words that could articulate it.

Indeed, it is in the initial heterogeneity between the height of inherited rhetoric (rather like Hugo) and the least conventional poetry imaginable (rather like Nerval) that we must construct the eventual univocity of anabasis as the key signifier of the century's trajectory.

I will proceed by thematic samplings. Beginning with the text by Saint-John Perse and echoing our reflections on the century, I shall make some remarks concerning the subject, absence, and happiness.

(1) Any poetic or narrative text poses a question about the subject. This question is: Who speaks? We owe to Natacha Michel an entire logic of the 'who speaks', a logic out of which she has fashioned a wholly new theory of the *incipit* of the novel.[34] In Perse's poem, we find, by way of a response to this question, a near-equivalence between an 'I' and a 'we'. In fact, this equivalence is established from the very beginning of *Anabasis* (let us recall that we are reading only section VIII here), a beginning in which we find, carried by the same movement, verses such as 'it promises well, the soil whereon I have established my Law' and 'Beautiful are bright weapons in the morning and behind us the sea is fair'. As we shall see, this equivalence of first persons, naturally inscribed in the poem's usage of the vocative case, loses all its self-evidence in Celan, not to mention any possibility of being reconstructed. In Perse's *Anabasis*, fraternity, which is what makes the 'I' reciprocal with the 'we', is a precondition of the adventure, its subjective substance. In Celan's anabasis what must be brought about – in a tremulous uncertainty – is the word 'together', which is thus never a condition but only ever a hard-won result.

We can reasonably name 'axiom of fraternity' the conviction that any collective undertaking supposes the identification of an 'I' as a 'we', or the internalization, within action, of a 'we' as the elevating substance of the 'I'. In *Anabasis*, Perse creates a way-faring fraternity, stressing the poetic identity between 'ourselves (Man colour)' and 'the starved levin allots me these provinces in the West'. He can move freely between the exclamation 'To the scale of our hearts was such vacance completed!' and the interrogation 'What has the world given me but this swaying of grass?' 'Fraternity' designates the subjective equivalence between the singular and the plural. And it is beyond doubt that the century's most fervent desire, before it ran aground on the shores of competitive individualism, was fraternity.

Through his poetic fiction, Saint-John Perse stages the idea that the axiom of fraternity is only valid for a real adventure, for a historic exploit that creates its subject precisely as a fraternal subject, as a subject that emerges from the pluralization of the 'I' and the singularization of the 'we'. That is why *Anabasis* recounts a conquering cavalcade on the high plateaus of legend.

But, all of a sudden, the notion of fraternity becomes more complex. What is the protocol whereby the 'we' is delimited? The cavalcade through this imaginary Mongolia must obviously cut through adversity; it must invent its enemy. The 'I' only expands into a 'we' at the approach of war, and that is why the journey is not enough. The praise of the 'Traveller in the yellow wind' only becomes meaningful in the formula that closes the text: 'A great principle of violence dictated our fashions.' Violence is the horizon required by wandering. For wandering to be the equivalent of the 'great seleucid histories' one must come to the 'whistling of slings'. Or, better still: the principle of knowledge and litigation ('the earth given over to explanations') is worthless unless it is accompanied by the praise of hostility ('in whom hatreds sang now and then like tomtits'). By the same token, the 'roads of the world' and the 'land of grass without memory' – indices of the most total freedom – are accompanied by a sort of grandiose despotism ('authority over all the signs of the earth'). Moreover, the fact that atrocity is one of the resources of the journey, an obligatory episode of the anabasis, is emphasized in several of the poem's images – for example: 'And the linen exposed to dry scatters! like a priest torn to pieces . . .'

Fraternity as equivalence of the 'I' and the 'we'; the inherent violence of the journey; the reciprocity between wandering and command: these are the dominant motifs of a century spurred by anabasis.

(2) All this is accompanied by an interrogation regarding finality, by a doubt about meaning, in short, by a kind of nihilism that strives to remain serene. What is explicit is that there is a vacant consciousness at work in these adventures: 'To the scale of our hearts was such vacance completed!' The destination of the anabasis is nothing but a sort of negative fiction. The quest is for a place where the signs of space and time have been abolished, a 'great land of grass without memory', on the one hand, 'the unconfined unreckoned year', on the other.

It is this nihilism that brings Perse's solemn poetry into dialogue with the century's awareness of itself as a pure and violent movement, a movement whose outcome is uncertain. The subject represents itself as a kind of wandering, and represents this wandering as valid in and of itself. That nomadic wandering, as Perse says, should be the principle at the heart of man, even in its absence, is an apt geographic and wayfaring metaphor for an epoch proud of being *without security*.

We must understand why, at the heart of the century, repeated disappointments did not in any way undermine the commandeering power of movement. This is particularly hard to understand today, when everyone is signing up to a costly insurance policy against any potential disappointment, even the kind that results from a few drops of rain during the summer vacation. That is because the century's militants, whether in politics, science, the arts or any other passion, think that man is realized not as a fulfilment, or as an outcome, but as absent to himself, torn away from what he is, and that it is this tearing away which is the basis of every adventurous greatness. If Perse belongs to the century it is because he gives poetic form to the link between the obligation of greatness and the 'vacance' of wandering.

The twentieth century is not a programmatic century like the nineteenth. It is not a century of promise. Within it, one accepts in advance that a promise may not be kept, that a programme may not be actualized in any way, because movement alone is the source of greatness. Saint-John Perse identifies the noble figures of what consigns the heart of man to the victorious denial of what is. Perse establishes the poetic value of the absence to self, independently of any destination. It is a matter of conquering unbinding, the end of bonds, the absence to self of the unbound.

It is in this direction that the century was more deeply Marxist than it imagined, faithful to a Marx related to Nietzsche, the Marx who announces in the *Manifesto* the end of the old customs, that is, the end of the old ties of allegiance and stability. Capital's formidable force lies in its dissolution of the most sacred contracts and the most immemorial alliances 'in the icy water of egotistical calculation'. Capital declares the end of a civilization founded on the bond. And it is true that the twentieth century sought – beyond the purely negative force of Capital – an order without bonds, an unbound collective power, so as to restore humanity to its veritable creative power. Whence its watchwords, which are also those of Perse: violence, absence, wandering.

Through learned privative expressions, the poet captured this nihilistic but creative wish for a purely wayfaring order, a fraternity without destination, a pure movement. Hence the 'eremite beasts' (*bêtes sans alliances*), or 'the prevarications of the sky against the earth'. The only companions of the man of greatness are 'these high waterspouts on the march'. All this desire is recapitulated in the admirable oxymoron: 'nomad laws'.

(3) Lastly, we encounter in Perse an assertion that seems especially obscure today: that of the superiority of nomad greatness over happiness. This is pushed so far as to cast doubt on the very value of happiness. The expression 'the gelded words of happiness' (recall that a gelder is a specialist in the castration of horses) seems to indicate that for the man of anabasis, even where language is concerned, the obsession with happiness constitutes a mutilation. This is why the poet demands that we 'raise our whip' against the words of happiness. For us, tired hedonists of this end of the century, which all greatness seems to shun, this is indeed a provocative stance.

The active, violent, or even terroristic nihilism of the century, which makes itself heard even in the high poetry of our ambassador, is far closer to Kant than the contemporary dyad of satisfaction and charity. For it holds that the desire for happiness is what prohibits greatness. And, in a word, that in order to

undertake the nomad adventure woven 'with dawns and heavenly
fires', to shed some clarity on 'the darkness of the spirit', one must
learn to be content with a 'swaying of grass' and meditate upon
absence. Perhaps then, in the evening, one will consent to be
seized by the illegal intoxication procured by 'the seed of the
Indian cocculus'.

Forty years on, where do we stand regarding anabasis? What does
Paul Celan have to say to us, in the wake of Nazism and the war?

To the question 'Who speaks?', the poem answers: 'No one.'
There is just a voice, an anonymous voice the poem tunes into.
Almost contemporaneously, Beckett, in *Company*, begins with 'A
voice comes to one in the dark'. Perse made the 'I' and the 'we'
equivalent, but in Celan's poem, as in Beckett's prose, there is no
longer either an 'I' or a 'we'. There is just a voice trying to trace
a way. In the brief, almost silent lines of the poem, as distant as
possible from Perse's ample verse, this voice, which is the trace of
a way, will murmur what the anabasis – the 'Upward and Back',
an altogether exact translation of the verb αναβανειν – is. It does
so right at the beginning of the poem, with three fragile and
almost improbable connections: 'narrow sign', 'impassable-true',
'to the heart-bright future'.

What is thus murmured is the possibility of a path, the path of
a sensible clearing ('heart-bright'). For Saint-John Perse, the path
is the open in space; as he says at the beginning of *Anabasis*, it is
'given over to our horses this seedless earth'. There is no *problem*
of the path. Instead, Celan asks himself: Is there a path? His reply
will be that yes, there undoubtedly is a path – 'narrow between
walls' – but that, true as this may be, and, indeed, to the degree
that it is true, it is impassable.

We are on the other side of the century. The only thing that
epic nihilism, in its Nazi figure, has been able to create is a slaugh-
terhouse. From now on it is impossible to dwell *naturally* in the
epic element, as if nothing had happened. But if there is no immediate epic interpretation, what is anabasis? How can we practise
the 'Upward and Back'?

On this point, Celan brings the maritime dimension into play:
the Greeks' 'The sea! The sea!' The anabasis begins with a mar-

itime call. In some ports, there are beacons that emit a sound when the tide goes out. The sound of these beacons, these 'light-bellsounds', the sad sounds of the 'sorrow-buoys', together compose a littoral moment of signal, a call. For anabasis, this is the moment of peril and beauty.

The meaning of this image is that anabasis requires the other, the voice of the other. Assuming the call – its enigma – Celan breaks with the theme of an empty and self-sufficient wandering. Something must be encountered. The maritime images function as indices of alterity. We could say that the theme of alterity replaces the theme of fraternity. Where fraternal violence was once the supreme value, we now have the minimal difference of the breath of the other, the call of the buoy, the 'dum-, dun-, un-' which evokes one of Mozart's motets (*unde suspirat cor*), as if to prove that the nigh imperceptible poverty of the call can carry the highest signification.

Everything is constructed so as to arrive, in and through these 're-leased, re-deemed' sounds of a call, to this 'ours' that is no longer the 'we' of the epic. How are we to make alterity ours? That is Celan's question. A difference makes itself heard, and the problem is to make it ours. It is only to the extent that we succeed in doing this that an anabasis will have taken place. There is neither internalization nor appropriation. There is no substantialization of the 'we' into an 'I'. There is a pure call, an almost imperceptible difference that must be made our own, simply because we have encountered it.

The difficulty – present, it is true, in every anabasis – is that nothing pre-exists this attempt, that nothing has prepared the ground for it. We are neither at home nor have we embarked on a path that has already been explored. We are, in what constitutes an admirable nomination of the anabasis as well as of the entire century: 'far out / into the unnavigated'. And it is precisely here, at the point of unknowing and bewilderment, that the 'Upward and Back' must be undertaken; it is here that we stake our claim of one day being able to turn towards 'the heart-bright future'. It is here that the anabasis is invented.

What is thereby created in the movement of anabasis is not a we-subject, it is the 'tent- / word growing free: / Together.' A tent-word is a sheltering word. One can hold fast in the shelter of being-together, but there is no fraternal fusion: Celan's 'we' is not an 'I'.

Through the becoming-ours of an almost imperceptible call, the anabasis is the advent as togetherness of a 'we' that is not an 'I'.

Thus the century is witness to a profound mutation of the question of the 'we'. There was the 'we' of fraternity, the 'we' that in the *Critique of Dialectical Reason* (published, let us note, at the time that Celan was writing *Anabasis*) Sartre characterized as terror-fraternity. This is a 'we' that has the 'I' as its ideal and for which there is no other alterity than that of the adversary. The world is given over to this errant and victorious 'we'. Adorned by sumptuous rhetoric, this figure is at work in Saint-John Perse's nomad adventurer. This 'we-I' is valid as such; it does not need to receive its destination from elsewhere. In Celan, the 'we' is not subject to the ideal of the 'I', because the difference is included within it, as the almost imperceptible call. The 'we' enjoys an aleatory dependence on an anabasis that reascends – outside of any pre-existing path – towards this 'together' that still harbours alterity.

From the end of the seventies onwards, the century has bequeathed to us the following question: What is a 'we' that is not subject to the ideal of an 'I', a 'we' that does not pretend to be a subject? The problem is not to conclude from this that every living collective is over, that the 'we' has purely and simply disappeared. We refuse to join the agents of the Restoration in saying that all there is are individuals in competition for happiness, and that all active fraternity is suspect.

Celan, for his part, holds onto the notion of togetherness. 'Together', let us note, was the main, strange slogan of the demonstrations of December 1995 in France. There really was no other, or at least none that constituted an invention, that had the power to give a name to the anabasis of the demonstrators. And it was not a word used in vain. In quiet little towns like Roanne, on several occasions more than half the population joined in the demonstrations simply to say: 'All together, all together, yeah' (*Tous ensemble, tous ensemble, ouais*). That is because today, everything that is not already mired in corruption raises the question of where a 'we' could originate that would not be prey to the ideal of the fusional, quasi-military 'I' that dominated the century's adventure; a 'we' that would freely convey its own immanent disparity without thereby dissolving itself. What does 'we' mean in times of peace rather than war? How are we to move from the fraternal 'we' of the epic to the disparate 'we' of togetherness, of the set, without ever giving up on the demand that there be a 'we'? I too exist within this question.

9

Seven variations

Today, we endure the dominance of an artificial individualism. In 1995, in France, millions of demonstrators rallied behind one slogan: 'Together!' – Celan's own tent-word; propaganda responds with the 'evidence' of the individual in the competitive search for success and happiness. Even in the literary world, the joint production of biographies and autobiographies saturates the market. Nothing is considered to be worthy of interest except what the Chinese, who adore lists, would have called 'the three relations': the relation to money, the relation to economic and social success, and the relation to sex. The rest is nothing but archaic abstraction, and most likely totalitarian. What is 'modern' is the generalization of the aforementioned three relations into fully fledged Ego-ideals. Behold then not what is, but what – with a sort of vindictive obstinacy – they are trying to impose upon us as what must be.

We should at least beware that, far from pertaining, as it claims, to a nature of things and subjects democratically inscribed in the *media*, this propaganda represents an act of forcing brought about through the extraordinarily brutal inversion of everything that the century desired and invented. Whatever its often violently opposing variants may have been, the current of thought that effectively stamped its seal on the epoch now coming to a close maintained that every authentic subjectivation is collective, and that every vigorous intellectuality implies the construction of a 'we'. That is because it deemed that a subject is necessarily measured by its historicity. In other words, the subject is what resonates, in its composition, with the power of an event. This is one of the forms taken by what I've called the passion for the real: the certainty that, issuing from an event, the subjective will can realize, in the world, unheard-of possibilities; that very far from being a power-less fiction, the will intimately touches on the real.

What is being inflicted on us today, on the contrary, is the con-viction that the will, dominated by a suffocating reality principle whose distillate is the economy, should behave with extraordinary circumspection – lest it expose the world to grave disasters. There is a 'nature of things' and violence must not be done to it. Basi-cally, the spontaneous philosophy of our 'modernizing' propa-ganda is Aristotelian: Let the nature of things manifest its proper ends. We must not do, but let be: laissez-faire. Just imagine the gap between such a stance and the conscience of all those who sang, beneath red banners, 'the earth shall rise on new foundations'.*

If you think the world can and must change absolutely; that there is neither a nature of things to be respected nor pre-formed subjects to be maintained, you thereby admit that the individual may be sacrificable. Meaning that the individual is not indepen-dently endowed with any intrinsic nature that would deserve our striving to perpetuate it.

It is by taking my cue from this theme of the non-naturalness of the human subject – more, of the inexistence of 'man' and hence the vacuity of the notion of 'human rights' – that today I would like to propose some variations.

First variation: philosophical

In varying guises, philosophers between the thirties and sixties worked with the idea that the real of an individual, his constitu-tion as a subject, is entirely modifiable. Obviously, this amounted to a kind of philosophical accompaniment for the theme of the new man. For example, one of Sartre's first texts – *The Transcen-dence of the Ego* – develops the intuition of an open constitutive consciousness whose concrete manifestations as 'Me' or as 'Ego', and therefore as an identifiable individual, are nothing but transi-tory exteriorities. The immanent being of consciousness cannot be grasped through the transcendence or identifiable objectivity of the Me. Later, Sartre would draw the rigorous ontological consequences of this intuition by positing that the being of consciousness is nothingness, which is to say absolute freedom, thus rendering any idea of a subjective 'nature' impossible. In psychoanalysis, and especially in its recasting by Lacan, the Ego* is an imaginary instance and the subject as such can no longer be either a nature or a being because it is ex-centric with respect to its own determination (this is what 'unconscious' means).[35] Lacan names this point of eccentricity the Other, meaning that every subject is something like an Alteration of itself. As Rimbaud had anticipated: 'I is an other'. Once again, it is impossible to think the individual as an objective nature.

To the extent that the century has brought innovations to the theory of the subject, it has conceived the subject at a remove from itself, as an interior transcendence. In my own doctrine, the subject is dependent on an event and only comes to be constituted as a capacity for truth. Since its 'material' is a truth procedure, or generic procedure, the subject cannot be naturalized in any way. Adopting Sartre's terminology, we will say that the subject has no essence (this is the meaning of the notorious formula 'Existence precedes essence'). Adopting Lacan's, we will say that a subject is only identified at the point of lack, as void or lack-of-being.

If the subject is constituted as lack-of-being, the question of its real remains open, since this real is neither an essence nor a nature. It is then possible to maintain that a subject is not, but rather comes to be, under certain determinate conditions, in the place where, as Lacan would say, 'it is lacking'. Nietzsche's imperative – 'Become who you are' – finds here a worthy echo. If one must become a subject, it is because one is not yet a subject. 'Who you are' as a subject is nothing but the decision to become this subject.

You can observe here the emergence of a link between the thesis that a subject is of the order not of what is but of what happens – of the order of the event – and the idea that the individual can be sacrificed to a historical cause that exceeds him. Since the being of the subject is the lack-of-being, it is only by dissolving itself into a project that exceeds him that an individual can hope to attain some subjective real. Thenceforth, the 'we' constructed in and by this project is the only thing that is truly real – subjectively real for the individual who supports it. The individual, truth be told, is nothing. The subject is the new man, emerging at the point of self-lack. The individual is thus, in its very essence, the nothing that must be dissolved into a we-subject.

The affirmative reverse of this sacrificial evidence of the individual is that the 'we' constructed by a truth – whose stakes as well as support is the new man – is immortal. It is immortal by virtue of the fact that it exists not as a perishable nature but as an eternal occurrence; an occurrence as eternal as Mallarmé's dice-throw.

Second variation: ideological

How did the century reorganize the three great signifiers of the French Revolution: liberty, equality, fraternity? Today's dominant thesis, under the imposed name of 'democracy', is that the only thing that counts is liberty. A liberty, moreover, so affected by the contempt in which the other two terms are held (equality is utopian and anti-natural, fraternity leads to the despotism of the 'we') that it becomes purely juridical or regulative: the 'liberty' for all to do the same things, under the same rules.

This idea of liberty (or freedom) was constantly reviled during the short twentieth century, the one that goes from 1917 to 1980. It bore the name of 'formal freedom', and was opposed to 'real freedom' – note the pertinence of the adjective. 'Formal freedom' means a freedom that is neither articulated to a global egalitarian project nor practised subjectively as fraternity.

Throughout the century, equality is the strategic goal: politically, under the name of communism; scientifically, under the name of the axiomatic; artistically, under the imperative of the fusion of art and life; sexually, as 'mad love'. Freedom, as the unlimited power of the negative, is presupposed, but not thematized. As for fraternity, it is the real itself pure and simple, the sole subjective guarantee of the novelty of experiences, since equality remains programmatic and liberty instrumental.

I insist: fraternity is the real manifestation of the new world, and hence of the new man. What is experienced here – in the Party, in action, in the subversive artistic group, in the egalitarian couple – is the real violence of fraternity. And what is the content of fraternity, if not the acceptance that the infinite 'we' prevails over the finitude of the individual? This is what is named by the word 'comrade', now largely fallen into desuetude. My comrade is one who, like myself, is only a subject by belonging to a process of truth that authorizes him to say 'we'.

This is why I argue that in this whole matter it is not in the slightest a question of utopia or illusion. The set-up for the emergence of the subject is, quite simply, complete. In Lacanian terms, equality is the Imaginary (since it cannot come about as an objective figure, even though it is the ultimate reason for everything), freedom is the Symbolic (since it is the presupposed instrument, the fecund negative), and fraternity is the Real (that which is sometimes encountered, in the here and now).

Third variation: critical

The risk that is involved in always articulating the constitution of the subject onto a collective and thus universalizable transcendence is that of transferring to the collective those 'natural', or at least objective, properties that liberals presume to be the prerogative of the human individual. This deviation has not been in short supply throughout the century. Fascisms invariably replaced the subjective universality of truth procedures (political invention, artistic creation, and so on), which they detested, with the designation of great referential collectives: the nation, the race, the West. We can give the name 'Stalinism' to the substitution of such entities (Working Class, Party, Socialist Camp . . .), declared on the basis of the Soviet state's power, for those real political processes of which Lenin was the pre-eminent thinker, and which Mao in turn sought to identify.

Let us note in passing, to mark our discord with the crass equation of Nazism and so-called communism (in effect, the Stalinist state) under the name of 'totalitarianism', that these two political stances remain entirely opposed, even in what concerns the genesis of their entities of reference. For it is precisely *against* the political processes of emancipation linked to the word 'proletarian' – processes they correctly perceive to be unbound, non-assignable, cosmopolitan and anti-statist – that fascisms quite explicitly advocate submission to national and/or racial referential totalities, as well as to their putative representatives. The substantializations of the Stalinist state, on the contrary, are reifications of real political processes; reifications that stem from the impossibility for Leninism to integrate the seizure of the state into its mental apparatus. Whereas the state has always been the alpha and omega of the fascist vision of politics – as a state propped up by the supposed existence of great closed collectives – in the history of Leninism, and later of Maoism, it has never been anything but the obstacle that the brutal finitude of the operations of power opposes to the infinite mobility of politics.

The absolute opposition of these two politics within the century can be given a more philosophical cast. Fascisms seek to oppose the infinite of emancipation with the bloody barrier of a predicable finitude, the denumerable properties of a supposed substance (the Aryan, the Jew, the German . . .). The 'communisms' instead experience the antinomy – pointed out by Marx with his customary genius – between the finitude of the state and the infinite immanent to every truth, including and above all political truth. The mythical referential entities accompany the victory of the fascisms, and inevitably signal the defeat of the 'communisms'.

And yet it's true that, whether they are idealized and turned from the outset into the subjective support of a politics of conquest, or whether they are considered only as pompous names for political stagnation, the century does indeed witness the production of imaginary macroscopic entities and hyperbolic names. These large-scale entities are not the 'we-subject' discussed above. They do not originate in an occurrence or an event; they are inert collectives. Their devotees see them as necessary conditions of any subjectivation, as an objective material that the we-subject either reflects or enacts in practice. I propose to name such entities *the passive body* of subjectivation.

Even in the midst of the challenge posed by state control, why should one not rest content with the real 'we', the 'we' that envelops the 'I' in the effective becoming of an invention of thought? Why has the determination of active singularity so often been obliged to represent itself as the consciousness or experience of objective entities, of mythical hypostases? Why endow action with a passive body? We will have occasion to observe that this formidable objectivation intervenes in the problem of the *naming* of processes, in the theory of names.[36] We may ask ourselves whether, when their allegiance is 'communist', the great macroscopic totalities are not in fact summoned as names (proletarian politics, bourgeois art, the socialist camp, the imperialist camp, state of the workers and peasants . . .) whose only value rests in expediently universalizing a process at the very moment when it lapses into sterility or is frozen into its state form. The name is what allows singularity to assert its worth beyond itself. The century's handling of names is also a prisoner of the Two, of the non-dialectical synthesis. On the one hand, it is important to love active singularities alone (this is fraternity); on the other, these singularities must be historicized, even in those moments when invention is lacking, those moments when, as the French revolutionary Saint-Just put it, 'the revolution is frozen'. The universality of these moments must be made evident through names borne by detectable objectivities.

In the end, the problem is the following: Why does the century require large-scale (objective) collectives in order to give names? Why do political processes of emancipation always take the name of supposedly objective social entities, such as the proletariat, the people or the nation?

I believe it can be shown that we are dealing here with the tribute the century paid to science, and therefore with the residues of nineteenth-century scientism that endure in the midst of twentieth-century voluntarism. Objectivity is indeed a crucial scientific norm. The legitimacy of adequate names for the we-subject was sought within the more or less certain sciences, such as 'historical materialism'. Even Nazism is a racial mythology that presents itself as scientific. To secure its goals of submission and extermination, it thought it could rely on the racialist anthropological jargon that accompanied Europe's imperial expansion ever since the eighteenth century. That this jargon was a tissue of contrived and criminal fictions is plain as day. The 'science' of races is purely imaginary. Note that there also existed an imaginary Marxist science, even if it did not itself determine the revolutionary subjectivities of the century. This Marxism without a real correlate pretended to constitute purely and simply a scientifically legitimate fraternity, and therein lay its strength.

Fourth variation: temporal

The century put forward its own vision of historical time. It had a very ample genealogical vision of political confrontations, thereby following Marx when he wrote that the entire history of mankind was that of class struggle. Academic historians, for their part, worked on long durations, holding the scale of a human life to be a trifling quantity when compared to the flux of significations.[37] Plainly, there was nothing 'humanist' about this history.

It is very striking to see that today we are practically bereft of any thinking of time. For just about everyone, the day after tomorrow is abstract and the day before yesterday incomprehensible. We have entered a period of a-temporality and instantaneity; this shows the extent to which, far from being a shared individual experience, time is a construction, and even, we might argue, a political construction. For example, let us briefly reconsider the 'five-year plans' that structured the industrial development of the Stalinist USSR. If the plan could be celebrated even in works of art, such as Eisenstein's film *The General Line*, it is because, over and above its (doubtful) economic significance, planning designates the resolve to submit growth to the political will of men. The five years of the five-year plan are much more than a numerical unit, they are a temporal material in which the collective will inscribes itself, day after day. This is indeed an allegory, in and by time, of the power of the 'we'. In various ways, the entire century saw itself as a constructivist century, a vision which implies the staging of a voluntary construction of time.

There once existed the immemorial time of the peasantry, an immobile or cyclic time, a time of toil and sacrifice, barely compensated by the pattern of festivities. Today we endure the marriage of frenzy and total rest. On the one hand, propaganda declares that everything changes by the minute, that we have no time, that we must modernize at top speed, that we're going to 'miss the boat' (the boat of the Internet and the new economy, the boat of mobile phones for everyone, the boat of countless stockholders, the boat of stock-options, the boat of pension funds, I could go on . . .). On the other hand, all this hubbub cannot conceal a kind of passive immobility or indifference, the perpetuation of the status quo. This is a type of time upon which the will, whether collective or individual, has no grip: an inaccessible amalgam of agitation and sterility, the paradox of a stagnant feverishness.

Even if, as so often happens in the instant of invention, it was clumsily and dogmatically mishandled, the century's powerful idea of time must continue to inspire us – at the very least against the 'modernizing' temporality that annuls any subjectivation whatsoever. The idea is that if we wish to attain the real of time we must construct it, and that, when all is said and done, this construction depends entirely on the care with which we strive to become the agents of truth procedures. Let us then praise the century for having borne the epic proposal of an integral construction of time.

Fifth variation: formal

What were the century's dominant forms of collective materiality? Let me suggest that this century was the century of the demonstration. What is a 'demo'? It is the name of a collective body that uses the public space (the street, the square) to display its power. The demonstration is the collective subject, the we-subject, endowed with a body. A demonstration is a visible fraternity. The gathering of bodies into a single moving material form is intended to say: 'we' are here, and 'they' (the powerful, the others, those who do not enter into the composition of the 'we') should be afraid and take our existence into consideration.

Throughout the century, the demonstration can only be understood against the subjective horizon of a conviction that 'We could change everything'. It legitimates, in the domain of the visible, the line from the *Internationale*: 'We have been nought, we shall be all!' The demonstration outlines the totality aspired to by a collection of 'noughts', of isolated individuals.

The century was the century of demonstrations, and these demonstrations were enduringly haunted by the insurrectional figure of politics. Insurrection is the final celebration of the body that the 'we' endows itself with; it is the last action of fraternity. Yes, the century's conception of celebration, governed as it was by the paradigm of demonstration and insurrection, always required this celebration to brutally interrupt the ordinary state of affairs. Today celebration – harmless and consensual – is what typically distracts us from every political concern. We observe government experts with furrowed brows reporting that the people want 'strong signs of festivity'. We witness serious newspapers compare the celebrations that accompanied France's footballing victory at the World Cup to the demonstrations that followed the liberation of Paris in 1945. Why not compare them to the taking of the Bastille, or the Long March? These days, 'celebration' is the name for something like a counter-demonstration.

The philosopher should here recall that 'manifestation' is a key Hegelian word; a word that pertains to dialectics, designating the 'coming out of itself' of any given reality.[38] One of Hegel's fundamental theses is that it is of the essence of being to manifest itself. The essence of essence is to appear. On this point the century, so profoundly anti-dialectical in other respects, was very dialectical indeed. For any fraternity – and therefore for a we-subject in the process of being constituted – to demonstrate is to manifest itself. The being of the 'we' is displayed, but also exhausted, in the demonstration. There is great dialectical trust in this monstration. This is because the 'we' is ultimately nothing but the set of its demonstrations. In this sense, the real of the 'we', which is the real as such, is accessible to each and every one in and by the demonstration. To the question: 'What is there that is real?', the century responds: 'Demonstrating.' What does not demonstrate is not.

Sixth variation: critical (again)

One of the great weaknesses of the century's thought, or at least one of its zones of uncertainty, is that it entertained a representational conception of legitimacy. In politics, for example, it widely upheld and practised one of Lenin's later maxims, a maxim presented by its author as 'the ABC of Marxism', but which nonetheless remains dubious: 'The masses are divided into classes, the classes are represented by parties, and the parties are run by leaders.' Parties and leaders draw their legitimacy from a representational operation.

If this conception of legitimacy is tested against the passion for the real it encounters the following obstacle: the real is not represented, it is presented. In all its different inventions – the revolutionary political party, the Manifesto of an artistic school, the integral didactics of a science, and so on – the century never ceased to come up against the lack of correspondence between the real and the represented. The real may be encountered, manifested, or constructed, but it is not represented. That's the stumbling block. If all legitimacy is representational, legitimacy is but a fiction vis-à-vis the real to which it lays claim.

A demonstration or an insurrection, and more broadly a political sequence, or even an artistic creation seized in the violence of its gesture, are in no way representable. Fraternity is not representable. As I've already suggested, the unwarranted appeal to large, inert, macroscopic – and therefore supposedly 'objective' – sets (class-in-itself, race, nation . . .) infects subjectivation by way of its presumed representative legitimacy. But only inertia can be represented. We thereby pass from the real model of event and manifestation to the ideal model of science.

Representation and fake legitimation on the basis of inert totalities are employed to fill in the gaps of what is really presented, which is always discontinuous. Philosophically, the root of the problem is that the real is discontinuous. Lacan puts it figuratively: what there is are 'grains of the real'. In my own vocabulary: there are only multiple procedures of truth, multiple creative sequences, and nothing to arrange a continuity between them. Fraternity itself is a discontinuous passion. In truth, there only exist 'moments' of fraternity. The protocols of representational legitimization attempt to render continuous what is not, to give disparate sequences a single name, such as the 'great proletarian leader', or the 'great founder of artistic modernity' – names that are actually borrowed from fictional objectivities.

Doubtless the epic tale in which the century revelled had its dark underside: it also required false heroes.

Seventh variation: anti-dialectical

I have insisted on the singularity of the theory of the Two, which drives the intellectuality of the century in all its domains.[39] This is an anti-dialectical Two, devoid of synthesis. Now, in every demonstration of fraternity there is an essential Two: that of the 'we' and of the 'not-we'. The century stages the clash between two manners of conceiving the 'not-we'. Either one sees it as a polymorphous formlessness – an unorganized reality – or else one sees it as *another 'we'*, an external and hence antagonistic subject. The conflict between these two conceptions is fundamental, and sets out the dialectics of the anti-dialectical. If, in effect, the 'we' relates externally to the formless, its task is that of formalizing it. Every fraternity then becomes the subjective moment of an 'in-formation' of its formless exterior. In this case, one will declare things like: the apathetic must be rallied to the Party; the left must unite with the centre to isolate the right; the artistic avant-garde must find forms of address which are perceivable by everyone. But then the century sees itself as a formalist century, in the sense that any we-subject is a production of forms. Ultimately, this means that access to the real is secured through form, a conviction obviously shared by the Lenin of *What is to be Done?* (the Party is the form of the political real), by the Russian 'formalists' after the Revolution, by the mathematicians of the Bourbaki school, or, as we've already shown, by Brecht and Pirandello. If, on the contrary, the 'not-we' is unavoidably *always already formalized* as antagonistic subjectivity, the first task of any fraternity is combat, where what is at stake is the destruction of the other. One will then announce that whoever is not with the Party is against it, that the left must terrorize the centre to defeat the right, or that an artistic avant-garde must seek out dissidence and isolation so as not to be 'alienated' within the society of the spectacle.

At the heart of the century, for reasons pertaining to the anti-dialectics of any primordial duality, the properly dialectical contradiction between formalization and destruction plays itself out. It is to this derived contradiction that Mao gave form, in an altogether innovative text,[40] by distinguishing 'antagonistic contradictions' – which are in fact without synthesis, or anti-dialectical – from 'contradictions among the people', which bear on how the antagonistic contradictions themselves are to be dealt with, and ultimately on the choice between formalization and destruction. Mao's essential directive is never to treat the 'contradictions among the people' in an antagonistic manner. In other words, to *resolve the conflict between formalization and destruction by means of formalization.*

This is perhaps one of the most profound lessons, but also one of the most difficult, that the century has bequeathed to us.

10

Cruelties

I will begin abruptly, with two quotations. Here is the first, extracted from a vast poem, certainly one of the century's greatest, dating most probably from 1915. It is presented here in the translation by Edwin Honig and Susan M. Brown:

> A symphony of sensation rises, incompatible and analogous,
> An orchestration in my bloodstream of tumultuous crimes,
> Of spasmodic bloody orgies resounding in the ocean,
> Raging like a hot gale in my soul,
> A hot dust cloud dimming my lucidity,
> Making me see and dream all this through my skin and veins
>   only!
>
> Pirates and piracy, ships and the moment,
> That maritime moment when the prey is seized,
> And the prisoners' terror approaches madness – that moment
> With all its crimes, horror, ships, people, sea, sky, clouds,
> Winds, latitude and longitude, outcries –
> How I wish in its Allness it became my body in its Allness,
>   suffering,
> My body and my blood, my whole being in one livid crimson glob
> Burst in bloom, like an itching wound, in the unreal flesh of
>   my soul!
>
> To be as one with all those crimes, to be part and parcel
> Of all those raids on ships, the massacres, the rapes!
> To be all that happened where the plunder was!
> To be all that lived or died where the bloody tragedies took
>   place!
> To be the grand-sum-total-pirate of piracy at its height,

And the grand-sum-total-victim, but in flesh and bone, of all the
    pirates of the world!

And here is the second, taken from a play, and written fifteen years
later (the translation is by John Willett):

THE FOUR AGITATORS:
What we decided was:
In that case he must vanish, and vanish entirely
For we can neither take him with us nor leave him
Therefore we must shoot him and throw him into the lime pit, since
The lime will burn him up.

THE CONTROL CHORUS:
Was that the only answer?

THE FOUR AGITATORS:
With so little time we could think of no other.
Like an animal helping an animal
We too would gladly have helped him who
Fought for our cause with us.
For five minutes, in the teeth of our pursuers, we
Considered if there was any
Better possibility.
(Pause.)
So what we decided was straightaway
To cut our own foot away from our body. *It is*
A terrible thing to kill.
But not only others would we kill, but ourselves too if need be
Since only force can alter this
Murderous world, as
Every living creature knows.
It is still, we said
Not given to us not to kill. Only on our
Indomitable will to alter the world could we base
This decision.

THE CONTROL CHORUS:
Go on speaking, and be sure
We sympathise with you.
It was so hard to do what was correct
Nor was it you who judged him, it was
Reality.

What do these two texts have in common? Obviously neither their authors nor their style, but not even their subjective stance or figure of commitment. What they have in common is that they both regard the real as inseparable from cruelty, from a sort of fascination with what takes the form of the most abominable crime.

The first text is a short fragment from the *Maritime Ode*, a poem signed by Álvaro de Campos, one of the 'heteronyms' of the Portuguese poet Fernando Pessoa. The second is taken from the sixth scene of *The Decision*, one of Bertolt Brecht's so-called 'didactic' plays.

Though Pessoa is the elder of the pair, historically the two men are not so far apart – except that the Portuguese poet started writing before the war of '14 and, dying prematurely in 1935, did not experience the Second World War. This difference notwithstanding, both writers are at the peak of their creative powers in the twenties and thirties.

The gap between them derives from something other than time; it stems from the relationship between centre and periphery in the Europe of that time. Brecht, whom I situated in the lesson entitled 'A new world. Yes, but when?', combines all the strands of European drama: Germany, the two wars, Nazism, communism, exile, the relationship to the United States, 'real socialism', and so on. Pessoa proudly chooses to identify with Portugal alone, which is to say with the margins of Europe, in a small country first benumbed by impotent republics and then by the dictatorship of Salazar, whose dreary authoritarianism – bringing nothing but the preservation of things and an avaricious, well-policed hoarding – is entirely alien to the flamboyance of fascism. It is here that Pessoa, becoming on his own the greatness that Portugal lacked, writes what is without doubt the most intense and most varied poetry of the century. Yet it is symptomatic that – as far as I'm aware – Pessoa and Brecht completely ignored each other's existence.

Not only are the two poets separated by the sites of History, no link can be established between their personal fates.

Born in South Africa and a virtuoso of the English language, Pessoa, having returned to Lisbon as a very young man, will never again leave that city. His life constitutes a synthesis between the relative invisibility of the commercial clerk and the activism of the avant-garde poet. Like Portugal, in its temporary misfortune, Pessoa knows that he's sheltered from History. Nevertheless, he traverses it obliquely (this is one of the meanings of that great poem entitled *Oblique Rain*). In order to do this, he must keep at bay every unilateral vision of things, and construct, in his solitude, an extremely complex mental world. In short, Pessoa substitutes politico-historical intensity – which in his own country had been snuffed out ever since the end of the great period of discoveries – with the complexity of the constructions of thought. A crucial element in this operation is the 'becoming-many' to which he gave the name 'heteronymy'. Pessoa's poetic oeuvre effectively presents itself under four names and is really the untotalizable set of four oeuvres altogether different in style, breadth, metaphysics, and so on. These heteronyms are Alberto Caeiro, Álvaro de Campos, 'Pessoa in person', and Ricardo Reis.[41] It is as if a man had taken it upon himself to put into writing all the virtualities of Portuguese poetry in the century, to create a poetry worthy of the planetary historical situation from which historically existing Portugal had withdrawn. Pessoa struggles against temporal sclerosis by inventing a poetic complexity without precedent.

Brecht, for his part, is immediately confronted with the complexity of situations and does not need to create their poetic space. His problem is rather that of finding some simple, organic and potent reference points in a situation which is not only complex but knows itself to be such. This is why he'll become a great man of the theatre – theatre being the archetypal art of simplification, of stylized force. Brecht asks himself which new theatrical poetics will wield the direct power to educate the public about the epoch's murky development.

Finally, we could say that the greatest gap between Pessoa and Brecht originates in the fact that while one fights simplification through a poetics of complexity, the other tries to trace the paths of an active poetic simplification in the midst of complexity.

It is thus all the more striking to see them converge in the almost indulgent representation of extreme violence, of the most radical cruelty. It is on this point that they are both of the century. Cruelty, in fact, constitutes an important theme for the literary twentieth century. Of course, this insistence of cruelty in the arts can easily be referred back to the omnipresent cruelty of states. However, as an explanation this is a little limited. What we need to consider is cruelty as both material and source of literary production. Throughout the century, cruelty has been less a moral question than an aesthetic one (yet another debt to Nietzsche). One can think of Artaud and his call for a 'theatre of cruelty', of Bataille's reflections on sacrifice, or, as we've already seen, of the rather serene hardness that characterized writer-adventurers such as Lawrence or Malraux when faced with the worst kinds of violence.

In Pessoa, cruelty is grasped through the metaphor of the pirates. In the background, we are dealing with a colonial cruelty initiated by the Portuguese themselves. For Brecht, under the name of 'the agitators', we are dealing with the Communist Party: both with what the Party requires and with what it is capable of in matters of cruelty and the rational justification thereof. For what the agitators actually decide is to liquidate the dissenting 'young comrade' who wants to break with the Party but knows too much to be left in the hands of the enemy.

In both cases we are dealing with the textual establishment of a place of cruelty. We are faced with that moment when the individual is in some way transcended by something vaster than himself: Piracy as the emblem of the devouring maritime place or the Party as the figure of History. This is a moment in which personal subjectivity explodes, dissolves, or is otherwise reconfigured. Ultimately, cruelty is the moment when the integral dissolution of the 'I' must be decided. As both Álvaro de Campos and Brecht aver, cruelty is necessary so that the 'we' and the idea become one, so that nothing comes to restrict the self-affirmation of the 'we'. The idea can only be embodied in a 'we', but the 'I' only attains its dissolution by assuming – or even desiring – the risk of its own ordeal.

In both cases cruelty is accepted as a figure of the real. For both writers the relation to the real is never given as harmony, but rather as contradiction, abruptness, cut. As Brecht writes, 'only force can alter this murderous world'. For Campos, what must be internalized is the pure multiple 'with all its crimes, horror, ships, people, sea, sky, clouds, winds, latitude and longitude, outcries'. The real always ends up offering itself as an ordeal of the body. The idea that the only real body is the tortured body, the body dismembered by the real, is a terrifying but ancient one. It is the idea seething beneath the image of the pirates, as well as beneath the sinister vision of the body of the 'young comrade' thrown in the limekiln. Isn't the vocation of poetry and theatre to say what is not said, what politics practises but rarely preaches? The wound is what testifies to the body's exposure to the real. Ultimately, the acceptance of cruelty by the militants of a truth follows from the fact that the we-subject is represented as an insensitive – because eternal – body. Sensibility to violence is nothing but the individual component of an immortal 'we'.

The veritable dialectic is therefore placed between cruelty and impassiveness – the impassiveness of truth. The twentieth century maintains that the impassive, universal and transcendent idea is incarnated in a historical body, which in turn comprises bodies that are not impassive, bodies that suffer. Considered as a process, a truth is at once a suffering body (by virtue of its composition) and an impassive body (by virtue of its being as idea). Consequently cruelty is not a problem but a moment, the moment of the paradoxical junction between the suffering body and the impassive body.

As Mandelstam saw, it is metaphorically true that there is something Christly about the century. This is because the century raises the question: What is an incarnation? It poses it in the following form: What is the absolute in history? The emblem of God incarnate is the tortured body of Christ. The century harbours an enduring martyrology, which is the exposition of the tortured body of the Idea.

Philosophically, this is Platonism in reverse. For Plato, the problem is to extricate the Idea from the sensible. Within the century, the question is to grant the Idea its sensible force. A descending anti-dialectic instead of an ascending dialectic.

In the final analysis, everything hinges on the 'I' and the 'we'. What is required is the composition of a mortal and suffering subject, on the one hand, and an impassive and immortal subject, on the other, in such a way that no separation is introduced. The problem then becomes that of knowing what ordeals the absolute of the Idea imposes on an originarily non-impassive body.

The only veritable cruelty is that of the Idea. This is indeed the aspect of cruelty that fascinates our artists. Today we know that when the Idea dies, the hangman dies with it. It remains to be seen whether from the legitimate wish that the hangman die we must infer the following imperative: 'Live without Ideas.'

For the time being, I will not answer this question. Let us return instead to the central point, which concerns how the subject as individuated body is articulated with the subject as anonymous production of the Idea. To tackle this point I will give the word back to Pessoa's *Maritime Ode* and Brecht's *The Decision*, but not without some preliminary clarifications.

The *Maritime Ode* is an immense poem with a solid but extemely complex architecture. It moves from solitude to solitude, so that its last word is not 'we'. The collective cruelty that unfolds in the image of the pirates is a passage – certainly a long, almost interminable passage, but nonetheless a passage, a sort of hallucinated daydream.

Seven moments can be distinguished within the poem.

1   The solitude of the utterance: in Lisbon, an indeterminate 'I', which is nevertheless linked to the poem, gazes, under the sun's rays, at the estuary of the Tagus, the harbour, the dock. A crane circles overhead.

2   The Platonic moment. Solitude comes out of itself by causing the advent of a pure idea of things. As the essence of its vision, it offers the 'great Dock', the essential Dock.

3   This moment is undone by the staging of an absolutely ferocious multiple. This multiple creates a collective call towards the 'we', and solitude is shattered. Here is an extract from this caesura (quote A):

[A]

I want to take off with you, I want to go away with you,
With all of you at once,
To every place you went!

I want to meet the dangers you knew face to face,
To feel across my cheeks the winds that wrinkled yours,
To spit from my lips the salt sea that kissed your lips,
To pitch in with you as you work, to share the storms with you,
To reach like you, at last, extraordinary ports!
[. . .]
To take off with you, divesting myself of me – come now,
    get on with it, get going –
My civilized suit, my genteel behavior,
My innate fear of jails,
My peaceful life,
My sedentary, static, orderly, all-too-familiar life!

4   As an effect of the call that preceded it, there follows
the total explosion of the 'I' into the pirate-multiplicity, a sort
of ecstatic dilation of the personal subject into an absolutely
cruel 'we'. It is from this moment that I take my second extract
(quote B):

[B]

Ah, the pirates! the pirates!
The passion for something illegal and savage,
The passion to do absolutely cruel, abominable things
Like an abstract rut gnawing at our fragile bodies,
Our delicate feminine nerves,
Making great mad fevers burn in our empty gazes!
[. . .]
Let me always gloriously assume the submissive role
In bloody happenings and quartered sensualities!

5   Suddenly, an interruption. As if the momentum of dissolution had reached the limit of imaginative power in matters of
cruelty and submission. In the aftermath, the 'we' comes undone
and something like a melancholic regression towards the 'I' takes
place.
6   Nevertheless, another type of multiplicity still dilates the
creative force of the subject. Unlike that of the pirates, this multiplicity is not dynamic, ecstatic and cruel. It is commercial and

reasonable, busy and diligent. Álvaro de Campos will call it 'bourgeois.' We are in fact dealing with the poem's humanist moment. Quote C is taken from this sixth phase.

[C]

Voyages and voyagers – and so many different types of them!
So many nationalities on earth, so many professions, so many
   people!
So many directions to steer one's life,
And life itself, in the end and at heart, always always the same!
So many strange faces! All faces are strange
And nothing gives one the sense of what's holy so much as
   watching people constantly.
Brotherhood isn't finally a revolutionary idea,
It's something you learn by living your life, when you've got to
   tolerate everything,
And you begin finding amusing what you've got to tolerate,
And you end up nearly weeping with tenderness over the things
   you tolerated!
Ah, and all this is beautiful, all this is human and firmly tied
To the feelings – so human, so sociable, so bourgeois,
So completely simple, so metaphysically sad!
Drifting, diverse, life ends by teaching us to be human.
Poor people! poor people, all of us, everywhere!

7   Unable to incorporate himself into humanism, to bend his word to universal tolerance – understood as both choice and tenderness – the poet retires to a position as close as possible to the initial figure, the position of a solitude that measures, high above the harbour, the circular movement of a crane.

The Decision is a so-called 'didactic' piece written in 1930. Of what is it the teaching or elucidation? Of the Party, the Communist Party conceived as political subjectivity. This subjectivity is made responsible for the tasks of the revolution but, above all, it is the organized paradigm of the articulation between the 'I' and the 'we'. As politically committed as this piece may be, it is clear that in it Brecht speaks of the party as an artist. What interests him is neither conjuncture nor tactics. Brecht wants to manifest on the stage the essence of the party, its generic function in the post-Leninist period.

The title of the piece is very precise. It indicates that the central theme is the party understood as a deciding-machine. What does it mean to say that the Party decides? What are the motives and procedures of a decision taken in the name of the Party? What can the Party demand of its militants in the name of its transcendent capacity for decision? Brecht – and this is an artistic choice on his part, a choice to experience extremity – dramatizes an abominable decision. The piece tells the story of Russian communist agitators sent to China. The stage – the abstract figure of the Communist International – is therefore the entire earth, just as for Pessoa the pirates served to name a cosmic violence. Where the agitators find themselves, the people's situation is terrible and is at risk of deteriorating. But political logic commands them not to act immediately. A young comrade thinks that, despite this logic, they must act immediately in the name of the people's suffering, which he cannot bear to see continue while the political cadres do nothing at all. The other militants try to bring him back to political rationality, against immediate sentiment, but to no avail. Since he resists, thereby jeopardizing the whole group – which acts as we-subject or Party – his comrades decide to execute him and to throw his body in a limekiln.

Brecht does everything in his power to make the spectator sympathize, or even identify, with the young comrade. This is because the young comrade speaks for the ordinary individual subject. In the remote register of pure political reason the legitimate subjectivity of this subject will be contrasted with the strategic logic that belongs to the discourse of the 'we'.

I quote a fragment of the debate between the Party's communist activists, taken from scene 6.

THE YOUNG COMRADE:
Who do you think is the Party?
Does it sit in a big house with a switchboard?
Are all its decisions unknown, all its thoughts wrapped in secrecy?
Who is it?

THE THREE AGITATORS:
We are it.
You and I and them – all of us.
Comrade, the clothes it's dressed in are your clothes, the head
    that it thinks with is yours
Where I'm lodging, there is its house, and where you suffer an
    assault it fights back.
Show us the path we must take, and we
Shall take it with you, but
Don't take the right path without us.
Without us it is
The most wrong of all.
Don't cut yourself off from us!
We can go astray and you can be right, so
Don't cut yourself off from us!
That the short path is better than the long one cannot be denied.
But if someone knows it
And cannot point it out to us, what use is his wisdom?
Be wise with us.
Don't cut yourself off from us!

THE YOUNG COMRADE:
Because I am right I cannot give way. My own two eyes tell me
    that misery cannot wait.

THE CONTROL CHORUS:
One single man may have two eyes
But the party has a thousand.
One single man may see a town
But the Party sees six countries.
One single man can spare a moment
The Party has many moments.
One single man can be annihilated
But the Party can't be annihilated
For its techniques are those of its philosophers
Which are derived from awareness of reality
And are destined soon to transform it
As soon as the masses make them their own.

Formally, the whole scene is built on pronouns (you, I, we). This
point is so striking that it drew the attention of the formidable
linguist and critic Roman Jakobson, who devoted a remarkable

article to the play of pronouns in one of the scenes.[42] Jakobson's article confirms the idea that when we are dealing with creative action the real is only given through the subsumption of an 'I' by a 'we'. Whence Brecht's particularly concise formula: 'We are it.'

But the leitmotiv of the quoted passage is 'don't cut yourself off from us'. The demand of the 'we', whose concrete form is the 'Party', appears as a demand for inseparateness. Brecht does not contend that one must obtain the pure and simple dissolution of the 'I' into the 'we'. Far from it, since 'we can go astray and you can be right'. The ultimately very subtle maxim proposed by Brecht is that the 'I' abide within the 'we' *in an inseparate form*. The maintenance of this inseparateness is precisely what is at stake in the debate. Concretely, this means that the 'young comrade' can and must fight inside the Party for his conviction (that it is necessary to act right away), but that he cannot insist on this stance as a decision separate from the stance of the others. When the young comrade says 'Because I am right I cannot give way', he misunderstands how the real is constructed at the inseparate point of articulation between the 'I' and the 'we'; he misunderstands the Party as form of the capture of this real. Instead, he should say: 'I am right, but my rightness only becomes real by yielding, be it provisionally, to the "we" which alone grants it political existence.' In addition, to infer from an 'I am right', an 'I cannot give way', which takes *the form of separation with the 'we'*, amounts to replacing politics with morality, thus precisely eliminating the real of the situation. The essence of the 'we' is not agreement or fusion; it is the maintenance of the inseparate.

The 'we' in Álvaro de Campos is very different, for it is the ecstatic 'we' of violence. Its construction takes place through the cruel proliferation of a kind of dilation and extenuation of the individual. The 'I' is immersed in the voluptuousness of an absolute submission ('always gloriously assume the submissive role / In bloody happenings and long-drawn-out sensual abandon!'); a masochistic submission that goes well beyond voluntary servitude, since it is ruled by a pleasure principle rather than by mere consent. The dissipation of the 'I' plays off energy against inertia. It is first of all a matter of tearing off the 'civilized suit', of breaking with a 'sedentary, static, orderly, all-too-familiar life', and 'take off with you to every place you [the pirates] went!' This tearing away authorizes one's disappearance as a personal subject, letting oneself be swallowed up by the ferocious 'we' which is animated by 'the passion to do absolutely cruel, abominable things'.

Ultimately, Álvaro de Campos and Brecht testify to the existence of two main figures of the 'I'/'we' relation within the century.

1 A figure of dissolution, which advocates the ecstatic disappearance of the 'I' into a violent and organic 'we'. This is a sort of cosmic naturalization of the 'I' into the 'we' of orgiastic cruelty. The sexual element is often present in this figure, alongside drugs, alcohol and idiocy.[43] Or the poem, music and dance.

2 A figure of the inseparate, which is more dialectical. The 'I' enters into an inseparable connection with the 'we', but it subsists, and is included within the 'we' as an internal problem. The political element is paradigmatic here, remaining very close to the military element, as well as to the novelistic or cinematic, inasmuch as these arts accept their epic origin.

A more detailed examination of the texts should allow us to isolate the respective maxims of ecstatic fusion and inseparate articulation, insofar as they relate to the formalization of the real.

1 Quote A from *Maritime Ode*

The fundamental word in this poetic onslaught is 'with', the signifier of the absorption of the 'I' into a nomadic 'we'. Alongside the obsession with departure and voyage – Campos's 'take off [. . .] to every place you went' – we find again the theme of anabasis, in which the operator of the construction of the new subject is the 'upward and back', the figure of the crossing of oceans or deserts.

Álvaro de Campos lucidly indicates the condition presupposed by this collective nomadism: the break with the familiar and the settled. We encounter here a profound point, which I think is correct: for the individual to become a subject it is necessary that he overcome fear – the 'innate fear of jails' of course, but even more the fear of losing all identity, of being dispossessed of the routines of place and time, of an 'orderly, all-too-familiar life'.

This theme haunts the century, which was often, in its actions as well as its words, a call to courage. What immobilizes the individual, what leads to his powerlessness, is fear. Not so much the fear of repression and pain, but the fear of no longer being the little something that one is, of no longer having the little one has. The first gesture that leads to collective incorporation and creative transcendence is ceasing to be afraid.

We like our life to be orderly so as to avoid insecurity. And the subjective guardian of this orderliness is fear. It is this fear that makes us incapable of wanting the real of the Idea. It follows that one of the fundamental questions is that of knowing how not to be a coward. The very power of thought is at stake. This question is treated in innumerable works between 1920 and 1960, in novels but even more in films. Perhaps the greatest contribution of the United States to the thematic of the century is to have placed at the heart of its cinema the question of the genealogy of courage and of the intimate struggle against cowardice. This is what makes the western – in which this struggle is paramount – a solid, modern genre, and what has enabled it to yield an inordinate number of masterpieces.

This preoccupation with the link between courage and the Idea has no doubt lost much of its vigour today. For the century, to be a coward was basically to remain where one is. Ordinary cowardice has no content save for a conservatism obsessed with security. This is precisely what Álvaro de Campos declares: the obstacle to the ecstatic becoming of the furious 'we' is 'peaceful' or 'sedentary' life. Yet this is exactly the kind of life that is glorified nowadays. Nothing is worth us tearing ourselves away from our ordinary cowardice, and especially not the Idea, or the 'we', which are summarily dismissed as nothing but 'totalitarian phantasms'. So let us mind our own business and have a little fun. As Voltaire, that consummate thinker of humanitarian mediocrity and venomous enemy of Rousseau (the man of courage), once wrote: 'Let us cultivate our garden.'

2 Quote B from *Maritime Ode*

This passage combines two apparently contradictory themes, transgression ('the itch to do something illegal', 'bloody happenings', 'great mad fevers' . . .) and submission ('the submissive role', the 'delicate feminine nerves', the 'empty gazes' . . .). In the poem this will give rise to a long masochist rhapsody, pushed to the point of imagining a body dismembered and dispersed, a fragmented real of 'quartered sensualities'.

One cannot understand this alliance between the most extreme ferocity and absolute submission (yet another anti-dialectical correlation) unless one interrogates the function of passivity, in Álvaro de Campos and beyond. Passivity is in effect nothing but the dissolution of the 'I', the renunciation of any subjective identity. In the end, in order to cease being a coward one must fully consent to becoming. The crucial idea is this: *the reverse of cowardice is not will, but abandonment to what happens.* What tears one away from the ordinary rule, from 'sedentary, static, orderly [. . .] life' is a particular kind of unconditional abandonment to the event. For Campos, this is the abandonment to the nomadic, pirate departure.

I myself underwent a definitive experience of this correlation between transgression and submission. It took place in May 1968 and the years that followed. I felt that the uprooting of my prior existence (that of a minor provincial civil servant, a married father, with no other vision of Salvation besides the one provided by the writing of books), the departure towards a life submitted, ardently submitted, to the obligations of militancy in hitherto unknown places (workers' hostels, factories, markets in the *banlieues*), the clashes with the police, the early morning arrests, the trials – that all of this originated, not from a lucid decision, but from a special

form of passivity, from a total abandonment to what was taking place.

Passivity does not mean resignation. I'm speaking of an almost
ontological passivity, one that changes your being as you are
dragged away and come to depend upon an absolute elsewhere. It
is striking that Campos lays out this passivity – creative as well as
corrosive – under the emblems of femininity. Over time, I have
come to notice that women attune themselves more profoundly
than men to this uprooting abandonment, just as, inversely, they are
terser and more obstinate when it comes to caution and conservatism. The feminine is that which, when it ceases to be the domes-
tic organization of security and fear, goes furthest in the termination
of all cowardice. For this reason, I would like to spare a thought here
for Ulrike Meinhof, a German revolutionary of the Red Army
Faction who committed suicide in her gaol. And also for Nathalie
Ménigon, a French revolutionary of the group Action Directe, currently rotting away in our national prisons. Say what you will, these
women had 'the passion for something illegal and savage'.

3   Quote C from *Maritime Ode*

Campos explains why, in his eyes, this figure of abandonment
must fail. The 'reasoning', if that's an appropriate term, is the following: the one who abandons himself absolutely, who is ecstati-
cally dispersed in the cruelty of universal life, has left behind
ordinary cowardice. In this sense, every greatness is an abandonment, every powerful Idea entails leaving oneself at the mercy of
a fate. But within duration, passivity wears out its creative force.
It can then only turn into acceptance, or tolerance. But tolerance
is the opposite of abandonment. Far from building greatness, tolerance is the basic ingredient of bourgeois humanism. Where the
becoming-other of a subject once stood there now installs itself a
snivelling humanism, in which 'you end up nearly weeping with
tenderness over the things you tolerated'. Where the pirate-
violence of the 'we' once held sway, feelings return, 'so human, so
sociable, so bourgeois'.

This is because, once the energy of beginnings is spent, the unbridled multiple in which the 'I' found the ecstasy of its own dissipation can just as easily become an initiation into the tolerance of differences. It is then that a 'drifting, diverse life ends by teaching us to be human'. This dialectic of discouragement is that of an *other passivity*, of resignation and tolerance, a passivity that makes us exclaim: 'poor people, all of us, everywhere!'

This terminal melancholia is typical of poeticizing thought. Ultimately, Campos thinks that the only greatness lies in departure, in the illegal and polymorphous impetus that shatters ordinary cowardice. But in the devotion to the multiple – the passage from the 'I' to the 'we' – everything is worn away into tolerance and acceptance. So that in the end, through the mediation of a cruel and orgiastic submission, we go from a first cowardice (fear, the pacified, sedentary life) to a second one (religious, bourgeois, and tolerant humanism, which ultimately sees man everywhere and thus concludes that there is nothing but 'life itself, in the end and at heart, always always the same!').

Campos's allusion to fraternity is particularly riveting. It is there I suggested we look for the exemplary subjectivation of the power of the 'we'. When the poet declares that 'brotherhood isn't finally a revolutionary idea', he urges us to distinguish between fraternity proper – which is a separation from the legitimacy of life, an abandonment to the eventual power of the 'we' – and a derived and corrupt fraternity which is made up of nothing but pious humanism and whose formula is that of tolerance for everything, the acceptance of differences and 'human feelings'. These feelings are rightly defined as 'metaphysically sad', since they lead us to renounce any passion for the real.

For the poetic pessimism of Campos it is this second version of fraternity that imposes its law, returning us, unless we tolerate being cowards once again, to complete and utter solitude. This is because the ecstatic and fusional version of the access to the Idea, and hence of the 'I'/'we' relation that is its key in the century, fails to serve as the foundation for any kind of temporality, and is thus dissipated at its very inception. Every insistence is already a mourning.

For Campos, the Idea is an act; it is never the construction of a time.

4   The Brecht fragment

For Brecht, the political problem of the Party, just like the fundamental question of art, is precisely that of not being satisfied with the privileges of the act and the instant, but instead of creating a time, of giving form to a figure of the 'I'/'we' relation that would be endowed with a duration. The Party is the material form of political duration, just as the non-Aristotelian epic is the form of the new theatrical duration. The piece entitled *The Decision* ties these two forms together.

The Leninist conception of the Party derives from an assessment of the workers' insurrections of the nineteenth century, and of the Paris Commune in particular. These insurrections were always crushed. In their own way, they were indeed ecstatic, but invariably ended in bloody repression. No victory is possible if it merely takes the form of an improvisation in the instant. It is thus imperative to submit oneself to a discipline of time. Herein lies the main formal function of the Party. In the wake of the October 1917 revolution, the Communist Parties of the Third International represented the generalization of an experience, that of the Leninist Party. The force of this generalization lay in the idea that, for the first time, the people from below, the proletarians, were going to take control of their own time. They would no longer be in thrall to the spasmodic riot, to the pirate-cruelty described by Campos. A disciplined body would finally be created for them – since without discipline there is no construction of time. But this discipline is nothing other than the acceptance by innumerable 'I's of their connection to a 'we'.

The still revolutionary Communist Party (the one of which Brecht speaks, or dreams, in 1930) is a crystallization of 'I's, a subjective concretion. It has nothing in common with what it will later become: the sinister, impotent Party-State, a half-terrorist, half-demagogical bureaucracy. It is because it is a distillate of thought and pure will that the Party proposes, as Brecht shows, *a singular form of the inseparateness of the 'I' and the 'we'*. The Party designates a particular manner of constructing, through 'I's alone, a 'we' capable of mastering time. The Party, as the agitators say, is 'you and I and them – all of us', 'the head that it thinks with is yours', it is 'we' insofar as it is each and every one.

We can therefore understand why its imperative is 'don't cut yourself off from us'. Unlike the passive ecstasy of the *Maritime Ode*, the political articulation of the 'I' and the 'we' is not a fusion. It is therefore *possible* to separate oneself, but the Party only exists so long as one does not do so. The Party is the inseparate. The Party is each-one-not-without-us. It is the place of the shared, in the sense that no knowledge can be useful unless one first says: 'Share it with us.'

That the Party is the inseparate ultimately means that it is nothing other than a sharing, without it being known beforehand what it is that is shared. The essence of the question is fraternity. 'We' is the shared. If a 'we', like the Party, is made up only of 'I's, there is a constitutive circularity; it means that the inseparate is the law of the 'we', but that only inasmuch as the 'we' establishes its law will there be inseparateness. Discipline is the name for this circularity, the name for the possible effects of the injunction: 'Don't cut yourself off from us!'

In other words, one of the century's imperatives, in all the registers of its thinking and its works, will have been: 'Not without us.'

A very important predicate of the Party – which as we've already noted nourishes the material force of the Idea as embodied in the collective – is that it is indestructible: 'One single man can be annihilated, but the Party can't be annihilated.'

Between 1917 and 1980, the century set out to create the indestructible. Why this ambition? Because indestructibility, or nonfinitude, is the mark of the real. In order to create something indestructible much must first be destroyed. Sculptors are particularly aware of this – they who destroy stone so that through its voids it may confer eternity upon an Idea. The real is the impossible-to-destroy; the real is what resists, always and forever.

One creates a work only if one has the feeling that one is measuring oneself up against this resistance.

Century of epic and resistance, remorseless destroyer, the century will have desired in its works to become the equal of the real whose passion it bore so deeply.

11

Avant-gardes

I will remain faithful to the immanent method established at the very start of this series of lessons and ask the following question: From the standpoint of the works of art which it showed itself capable of producing, what did the century declare with regard to the singularities of art? This is also a way of trying to verify – within one of the principal types of generic procedure – the hypothesis that motivates these lessons, briefly, that the passion for the real is the touchstone for the century's subjectivities. Is there or is there not within the century a will aimed at forcing art to extract from the mines of reality, by means of wilful artifice, a real mineral, hard as diamond? Can we observe, within the century, the deployment of a critique of semblance, a critique of representation, mimesis and the 'natural'? Quite apart from these verifications, which by and large we've already undertaken, we must acknowledge a strong current within the century's thought which declared that it is better to sacrifice art than to give up on the real. We can call artistic avant-gardes of the twentieth century all the different avatars of this current, all of them sporting abstruse monikers, such as Dadaism, acmeism, suprematism, futurism, sensationism, surrealism, situationism . . . We have already glimpsed the century's deliberate iconoclasm in Malevich's *White on White*. The century does not hesitate to sacrifice the image so that the real may finally arise in the artistic gesture. But when it comes to the destruction of the image, we should immediately add that the other tendency is always present: the subtractive tendency, which seeks the minimal image, the simple imaging line, the disappearing image. The antinomy of destruction and subtraction animates the entire process of the deposition of the image and of resemblance. In particular, there is an art of rarefaction, an art of obtaining the subtlest and most durable results, not through an aggressive posture with regard to inherited forms, but through arrangements that place these forms at the edge of the void, in a network of cuts and disappearances. Perhaps the most accomplished example of this path is to be found in the music of Webern.[44]

It is still incumbent upon us to identify, within the art of the century, the sacrificial and iconoclastic forms of the passion for the real, all the while evaluating, on a case-by-case basis, the correlation of destruction and subtraction.

One way of approaching this identification is to examine the meanings of the term 'avant-garde'. More or less the whole of twentieth-century art has laid claim to an avant-garde function. Yet today the term is viewed as obsolete, or even derogatory. This suggests we are in the presence of a major symptom.

Every avant-garde declares a formal break with preceding artistic schemata. It presents itself as the bearer of a power of destruction directed against the formal consensus which, at a given moment, defines what merits the name of art. Now, what is striking is that throughout the century it is always the same thing that is at stake in this break. It's always a matter of going further in the eradication of resemblance, representation, narrative or the natural. We could say that an anti-realist logic pulls the force of art either towards pure subjectivity and the expressive gesture, or towards abstraction and geometrical idealities. Obviously, it is the development of painting which here serves as the major model, but one can also find equivalents in music, in writing (to focus literary creation upon the sole power of language), and even in cinema or the choreographic arts. At its deepest, avant-garde polemic, which adopts the extreme stance of promoting everything previously considered ugly, is directed against the classical axiom that posits the existence of some forms that are more natural, more appropriate, more pleasing than others. An avant-garde aims to break with any notion that there exist formal laws of the Beautiful drawn from the accord between our sensory receptors and intellectual expression. It is a question of having done with the off-spring of Kant's aesthetic, all of which turn the beautiful into a sign of the harmony of our faculties, a harmony synthesized into a reflective judgement. Even if it promotes certain formal devices rather than others, an avant-garde maintains *in fine* that every arrangement of the sensible is capable of producing an art-effect, so long as one knows how to share its rule. There is no natural norm; there are only voluntary coherences, drawing their lot from the fortuity of sensible happenings.

The result is that the declared break does not just affect a certain conjuncture of artistic production, but also those great formal devices that had slowly become hegemonic during the course of Europe's artistic history: tonality in music, the figure in painting, humanism in sculpture, the immediate intelligibility of syntax in poetry, and so on. All of a sudden, the avant-gardes are no longer simply artistic 'schools', they become social phenomena, points of reference for opinion. Fierce polemics are unleashed against them, going well beyond individual works or familiarity with the artists' theoretical writings. This is because an avant-garde affirms – often in the most violent terms – its refusal of the consensus about what does or does not substantiate a judgement of taste, and declares its exception to the ordinary rules for the circulation of artistic 'objects'.

In order to stand their ground in the midst of the storms of opinion they inevitably set off, avant-gardes are always organized. 'Avant-garde' means group, even if this group only comprises a handful of people. An avant-garde is a group that lets its existence and dissidence be known; a group that publishes and acts, and which is motivated by strong personalities, ones that are not too inclined to share power. Sticking to France, consider the exemplary character of surrealism under the direction of André Breton and of its situationist successor under that of Guy Debord.

This organized and often vigorously sectarian dimension already forges a link – at the very least an allegorical one – between artistic avant-gardes and politics (in which communist parties also presented themselves as the vanguards of the popular masses). There is an aggressiveness to the avant-gardes, an element of provocation, a taste for public intervention and scandal. In

retrospect, Théophile Gautier's quasi-military orchestration of
the battle of *Hernani* will have proved an apt anticipation of the
avant-garde practices of the twentieth century. For the avant-
gardes, art is much more than the solitary production of works of
genius. Collective existence and life itself are at stake. Art can
no longer be conceived without an element of violent aesthetic
militancy.

This is because the avant-gardes only think of art in the
present and want to force the recognition of this present. This is
their way of assuming the newly acquired passion for the real.
Invention is intrinsically valuable, novelty as such delectable. Repetition and the old are despicable, so that absolute rupture, which
restricts one to the consequences of the present alone, is salutary.
This is the dominant interpretation, by the avant-gardes, of
Rimbaud's statement: 'One must be absolutely modern.' Art is no
longer essentially a production of eternity, the creation of a work
to be judged by the future. The avant-gardes want there to be a
pure present for art. There is no time to wait. There is no poster-
ity, only an artistic struggle against sclerosis and death; victory
must be achieved, here and now. And since the present is constantly threatened by the past, since it is fragile, it's necessary to
impose the provocative intervention of the group, which alone
ensures the salvation of the instant and the ephemeral against the
established and the instituted.

This question about the time of art is an old one. When Hegel
declares, in his lessons on aesthetics, that art is now a thing of the
past, what he means to say is not that there is no more artistic
activity, but rather that the supreme value of thinking is no longer
the preserve of art, as it had been since the time of the Greeks.
Art is no longer the privileged historical form for the presentation
of the absolute Idea. Obviously, it follows from this that the works
of the past cannot be outdone, since they alone are adequate to
the Spirit's moment of actuality; something that no work in the
present can aspire to, however full of talent or even of genius it
may be.

We can recognize here a properly *classical* conception of art,
and even, within classicism, that conception which opposes the
Ancients to the Moderns. More proof, if needed, of the fact that

Hegel's aesthetics is in no way romantic, and perhaps not even modern. The greatest French artists of the seventeenth century were already convinced that the time for great art had passed, that Greco-Latin antiquity had produced models beyond our reach. Closer inspection reveals that the true basis for classicism lies in essentialism. There is an essence of the Beautiful, which given rules distribute into the different artistic genres. A consummate art is an art that is equal to its own essence, or provides the highest example of what its genre is capable of. But what it is capable of has already been measured and experienced. To present an example is always to re-present it. To say that art must be what it is (that it must effectuate its essence) is at the same time to say that it must become what it has already had the opportunity of becoming. In the end, there can be no distinction for classicism between the past and the future of art.

The avant-gardes, in this respect more romantic than classical, generally maintain that art is the highest destination of a subject; that its full power has yet to make itself felt; and that it is precisely the classical reaction which has constantly hindered art. Thus, contrary to what Hegel said, art is a thing of the present, and essentially so. That the present is the time of art is far more important for the avant-gardes than their own rupture with the past, which is only a consequence and in no way precludes, as one can readily see with surrealism, locating in the past genealogical precursors for the intensities of the present (Sade, some German romantics, Lautréamont).

An avant-garde group is one that decides upon a present – for the present of art has not been decided by the past, as the classicists contend, but rather hampered by it. The artist of the avant-garde is neither heir nor imitator, but rather the one who violently declares the present of art.

The ontological question of twentieth-century art is that of the present. I believe this point is linked to the conviction, oft encountered in the course of these lessons, that the century is a beginning. Classicism can also be defined as the certainty that in art everything began long ago. The avant-garde says: We begin. But the genuine question of the beginning is that of its present. How does one sense, or how does one experience, one's own beginning?

The most widespread response to this question among the avant-gardes is that only the vital *intensity* of artistic creation allows the recognition of a beginning. Twentieth-century art is the attestation of beginning as the intense presence of art, as its pure present, as the immediacy and presentness of its capacity. *The tendency of twentieth-century art is to revolve around the act rather than the work*, because the act, as the intense power of beginning, can only be thought in the present.

The familiar difficulty is that of knowing which doctrine of time or duration envelops the idea of the beginning as norm. It's at this juncture that the thesis of a perpetual commencement rears its head, a thesis that constitutes one of the century's chimeras – and a suicidal chimera at that, one that a number of artists have paid for with their life. But there are other problems, especially the following: If commencing is an imperative, how can it be distinguished from recommencing? How is one to make the life of art into a sort of eternal dawn without thereby restoring repetition?

As we experienced through Álvaro de Campos's frenetic poem, such questions fatally corrode the idea of beginning. The most mediocre or most commercial consequence of this corrosion is the need to periodically invent yet another radical doctrine of beginning, to keep changing the formal paradigm, to replace one avant-garde with another: acmeism with suprematism, sensationism with futurism, and so on. In the seventies and eighties, especially in the United States, this low form of beginning took the guise of an accelerated succession of formal 'mutations', so that the plastic arts began to model themselves on fashion. The high form, which attempts to conserve the present-intensity of the artistic act, consists in conceiving the work of art itself as the almost instantaneous combustion of the force of its own beginning. The guiding idea is that beginning and end should coincide in the intensity of a single act. As Mallarmé already put it, 'the drama takes place all at once, just in time to show its undoing, which unfolds like lightning'. These 'undoings', which are the victory of the pure present, are the hallmark – for example – of certain pieces by Webern; pieces which, in a matter of seconds, graze against the silence that absorbs them; or of certain plastic constructions that are there only to be effaced, or of certain poems eaten away by the white of the page.

Since in such cases the works are uncertain – almost vanished before they are even born, or concentrated in the gesture of the artist rather than its result (as for 'action-painting' in all its various guises) – their gist has to be conserved in the theory, the commentary, the declaration. Through writing, one must preserve the *formula* for this bit-of-the-real extorted by the fleeting passage of forms.

That is why throughout the century the drafting of manifestos and proclamations constitutes an essential activity of the avant-gardes. It's been said that this is proof of their artistic sterility. As you can see, I am diametrically opposed to this retrospective contempt. Contrary to what some maintain, the Manifesto bears witness to a violent tension that seeks to subject to the real all the powers of form and semblance.

What is a Manifesto? The question is of special interest to me in that in 1989 I wrote a *Manifesto for Philosophy*. The modern tradition of the manifesto was established in 1848 by Marx's *Manifesto of the Communist Party*. It effectively appears that a manifesto is something like an announcement, a programme. 'The proletarians have nothing to lose but their chains. They have a world to win,' Marx concludes. This 'world to win' is an option taken on the future. It seems that the programmatic element is alien to the present urgency of the real. It is a matter of finality, of prospective conditions, of a promise. How are we to understand the way in which the imperative of the act and the present inscribed itself into so many proclamations and manifestos? Again, what is this dialectic of present and future, of immediate intervention and annunciation?

It's probably time to say something about André Breton, from whom I will presently draw today's text. Who more than he, within the century, bound the promises of the new art to the political form of the Manifesto? The first and second *Manifesto of Surrealism* are there as clear testimony. But in a more insistent fashion, it is Breton's entire style that is turned towards the future storm, the poetic certitude of a *coming*: 'Beauty will be convulsive or not be at all.' Where then dwells this beauty? This beauty – whose attribute ('convulsive') is plainly that of a violated real, but which is dependent, beyond the present, on the alternative 'to be or not to be', much in the way that Marx could summon human History to face the distressing dilemma 'socialism or barbarism' – where is it to be found? Breton's genius is often concentrated in such formulas. They are formulas which receive their urgency from the image, but in which it is also not certain whether the *thing itself* is already present. In the text I will shortly be reading, we find the following line: 'It's [the rebellion] a spark in search of a powder keg.' The spark is indeed the consummation of the present, but where then is this sought-after 'powder keg'? This problem, which is here localized by writing, is the same as the global one concerning the function of Manifestos. Where can we find the point of balance between the pressure of the real, which is the absolute will of the present, the dissipation of energy in a single act, and what is presupposed by the programme, the announcement and the declaration of intent in terms of waiting, of the foothold sought in an indiscernible future?

My hypothesis is that – at least for those who in the century are prey to the passion of the present – the Manifesto is only ever a rhetorical device serving to protect something other than what it overtly names or announces. Real artistic activity is always eccentric with respect to the programmes that brazenly declare its novelty, just as what is inventive in Heidegger's thought remains foreign to the pathetic announcement, which makes a big impression, of a 'saving return', or of the thoughtful, poetic coming of a God.

The problem, once again, is that of time. The Manifesto is the reconstruction, in an indeterminate future, of that which, being of the order of the act, of a vanishing flash, does not let itself be named in the present. A reconstruction of that to which, taken in the disappearing singularity of its being, no name can be given.

From Wittgenstein to Lacan, this statement traverses the century: 'There is no metalanguage.' This means that language is always tied up with the real in such a way that a secondary linguistic thematization of this bond is impossible. Language *says*, and this 'saying' cannot be re-said in any speech that would itself be appropriate. An informed reading of the Manifestos and proclamations of the avant-gardes must always begin with this axiom: there is no metalanguage appropriate to artistic production. As long as a declaration is concerned with artistic production it cannot capture the present of that production. It is thus in the nature of declarations to invent a future for the present of art.

This rhetorical invention of a future which is on its way to existing in the shape of an act is a useful and even necessary thing, in politics and art as well as in love, where the 'I love you forever' is the patently 'surrealist' Manifesto of an uncertain act. When Lacan says, 'there is no sexual relation', what he also wants to declare is that there is no metalanguage of sex. Now, to say that where there is no metalanguage a projective rhetoric must come to be amounts to a theorem. This projective rhetoric provides a linguistic shelter for what takes place, without however either naming or grasping it. The 'I love you forever' is an altogether expedient rhetorical figure for the protection of the active powers of the sexual bond, even though it bears absolutely no relation to these powers.

To criticize an aesthetic programme for failing to keep any of its promises is to miss the point. Granted, there is nothing 'convulsive' about the undeniable beauties that populate Breton's poetic art. Rather, one should see in it the restoration of a forgotten French tongue, at once carnal, imagistic, and very solidly structured by oratory syntax. But a programme is neither a contract nor a promise. It is a rhetorical device whose relation to what really takes place is only ever one of envelopment and protection.

The avant-gardes activated formal ruptures in the present and at the same time produced – in the form of manifestos and declarations – the rhetorical envelope for that activation. They produced the envelopment of a real present in a fictive future. And they called this double production 'new artistic experience'.

So we should not be surprised by the correlation between vanishing works and staggering programmes. Always precarious and almost indistinct, real action exists in such a way that it has to be pointed out and emphasized by loud proclamations, rather like the circus ringmaster amplifies his calls and orders a drum roll so that a pirouette on the trapeze – novel and daring, but also extremely fleeting – will not be ignored by the public.

Ultimately, the aim of all these constructions is to devote every energy to the present, even if the subjectivation of this present sometimes gets bogged down in the rhetoric of hope. Only the recognition of the fabrication of a present can rally people to the politics of emancipation, or to a contemporary art. Despite its name, even futurism was a fabrication of the present.

What characterizes our present day, which scarcely merits being called, to borrow an expression from Mallarmé, 'a beautiful today', is the absence of any present, in the sense of the real present. The years that followed 1980 remind one of what Mallarmé rightly said about those that came after 1880: 'A present is lacking.' Since counter-revolutionary periods resemble one another far more than revolutionary ones, we should not be surprised that after the 'leftism' of the sixties, we now revisit the reactive ideas that emerged in the wake of the Paris Commune. This is because the interval between an event of emancipation and another leaves us fallaciously in thrall to the idea that nothing begins or will ever begin, even if we find ourselves caught in the midst of an infernal and immobile agitation. We have thus returned to classicism, though we are deprived of its instruments: everything has always already begun, and it is vain to imagine that foundations are built on nothing, that one will create a new art, or a new man.

Indeed, this is what allows one to say that the century is over, since the art of the twentieth century, and its formalization by the avant-gardes, can be defined as the radical attempt to practise a non-classical art.

Some subjectivated foundations for this non-classicism and some of the elements of its programme – together with a number of examples of its protective rhetoric – are contained in the following text by André Breton, whose commentary will conclude this lesson.

It's there, at that poignant moment when the weight of endured suffering seems about to engulf everything, that the very excessiveness of the test causes *a change of sign*, tending to bring the inaccessibly human over to the side of the accessible and to imbue the latter with a grandeur which it couldn't have known without it [. . .]. One must go to the depths of human suffering, discover its strange capacities, in order to salute the similarly limitless gift that makes life worth living. The one definitive disgrace one can bring upon oneself in the face of such suffering, because it would make that conversion of sign impossible, would be to confront it with resignation. From whatever angle you noted the reactions that the worst evil you could conceive of left you open to, I always saw you put the heaviest accent on rebellion. There is, in fact, no more barefaced lie than the one that consists in asserting, even – and above all – when faced with an irretrievable situation, that rebellion is good for nothing. Rebellion is its own justification, completely independent of the chance it has to modify the state of affairs that gives rise to it. It's a spark in the wind, but a spark in search of a powder keg. I revere the dark fire that comes into your eyes whenever you are reminded of the unsurpassable wrong that was done to you and which is inflamed and clouded over again at the memory of the *miserable priests* who tried to approach you on that occasion. I also know that the very same fire raises its bright flames so high for my benefit, twines them into living chimeras before my eyes. And I know that the love which at this point counts on nothing but itself does not recover and that my love for you is reborn from the ashes of the sun. Also, each time a train of thought treacherously brings you back to the point where one day all hope was denied you and, at the precipice where you then stand, threatens, like an arrow seeking a wing, to hurl you again into the abyss, having experienced myself the vanity of all words of consolation and holding all attempts at distraction to be unworthy, I have convinced myself that only a magic formula could be effective here, but what spell could instil in itself and instantaneously give you the whole force of living, of living with all the intensity possible, when I know that it came back to you so slowly? The one I decide to confine myself to, the only one I judge acceptable to call you back to me when it happens that you suddenly lean towards the opposite slope, consists in these words which, when you start to turn your head away, I just want to lightly brush your ear with: *Osiris is a black god.*

This beautiful text, with its sombre and volatile amorous rhetoric, contains a number of maxims worthy of enveloping the real acts of an avant-garde, whatever its name may be. It is taken from *Arcanum 17*, perhaps the least known of Breton's prose pieces; less well known in any case than *Nadja or Mad Love*. It's a relatively late text, one of his mature yet also vaguely disenchanted texts, of the kind dating from the war and immediate post-war period (*Arcanum 17* appeared in 1944). Even if there were nothing in this book apart from the axiom that posits the self-sufficiency of rebellion and the indifference to the pragmatic calculus of results, it would still deserve to be read and reread today.

I wish to make four remarks, in order to structure our reading of the passage.

(1) 'The very excessiveness of the test causes a *change of sign*' The problem posed from the very first lines of the extract is that of the conditions for an affirmative excess. How is one to produce an excess that moves in the direction of the intensity of life, a 'limitless gift', a 'greatness', 'clear flames woven into living chimeras'? By now, we have become acquainted with the nature of this problem. It is a matter of knowing how the fire of *real* life can assure the creative combustion of thought.

On this point, Breton defends a thesis whose appearance is dialectical and whose line of descent is romantic: the only resource resides in pain as a *negative excess*. A creative disposition, be it vital or artistic, must be the conversion of a negative excess into an affirmative excess; of an unfathomable pain into an infinite rebellion. It should carry out what Breton first calls 'a change of sign' and then 'a conversion of sign'. It is indeed a matter of reversal. Not, however, under the constraint of a dialectical progression whose motor would be contradiction, but in the manner that an alchemical operation (the resonance of this theme among the surrealists is well known) transmutes the signs of lead into those of gold.

Notice that Breton does not claim that a creative excess can be directly produced by negating ordinary life. No, there must already be an excess in place, precisely 'the very excessiveness of the test'. There is no alchemy that could change the sign of ordinary states; that could produce a bewitching excess or a creative rebellion on the basis of a neutral sign. One can only pass from an excess that has been suffered and inflicted, or from a terrible, negative sign – a *black* sign (like the god Osiris) – to the hard-won possibility of celebrating what 'makes life worth living'. This passage consists of an operation that is at once voluntary and miraculous, one which inverts the sign of excess, and which Breton calls 'rebellion'.

The crucial lesson in this entire sequence is that knowing how to endure the most terrible suffering is a creative virtue, and that nothing of value would exist were we not *exposed* to excess. Here we find that particular sort of stoicism which encourages desire to extort from life all the intensity it contains. We also encounter here the paradoxical praise of creative passivity that we have come across before, namely in Pessoa's poem. To accept the lesson of the worst is a necessary condition for vital intensity. One must, with rebellious acceptance, 'go to the depths of human suffering, discover its strange capacities' to be able to restore 'the whole force of living, of living with all the intensity possible'. Every affirmation must be conquered, or reconquered, on the basis of a consenting exposure to the negative sign of excess. The risk of a passive exposure to the worst is the deepest resource of an affirmative life. This is because creation can only be a change in the sign of excess, and not the occurrence of excess itself. In this sense, as it pushes the alloy of spirit from the negative towards the positive pole – according to another image cherished by Breton – this is indeed an operation in magnetism. By forcing the passage of 'the inaccessibly human over to the side of the accessible', this operation confronts the subject with its own impossibility, and thus with its rigorously real capacity.

(2) '*Rebellion is its own justification*'   In the experience of the negative, of 'the weight of endured suffering', the fundamental antinomy between resignation and rebellion comes to the fore. In negative excess, the whole problem is that of knowing which of the two orientations the life within us will choose. It is here that volition and magnetic magic become indiscernible. 'Rebellion' means that within the extremity experienced in negative excess abides the certainty that we can change its sign. Resignation, on the contrary, is the acceptance pure and simple of the inevitable

and insurmountable nature of pain. Resignation maintains that the only apt words for pain are words of consolation. But for Breton such words are merely mediocre 'attempts at distraction', since nothing in them points to the surviving possibility of vital intensity.

We then have the very beautiful passage affirming the complete sufficiency of rebellion – which does not need to measure up to its own results – for life. Rebellion is a vital spark (i.e. the pure present) 'completely independent of the chance it has to modify the state of affairs that gives rise to it'. Rebellion is a subjective figure. It is not the engine of change for the situation; it is the wager that the sign of excess can be changed.

It is here that the persona of resignation, which Breton calls *the miserable priest*, makes his entrance. His ruse lies in not simply insisting on the intrinsic badness of rebellion. The 'priest' adopts an insidious voice which is ubiquitous today, in the murmurs and vociferations of politicians, essayists and journalists. Day after day, this voice entreats us to weigh up the worth of rebellion against its results, and to compare it, according to that sole criterion, to resignation. It then establishes, modestly triumphant, that for comparable – or even inferior – objective results, rebellion is extremely costly in terms of lives, suffering and tragedy. In response to this omnipresent 'realist' voice, Breton magnificently declares that what it propounds is nothing but the most 'barefaced lie', since rebellion has no relation at all with the pragmatic calculus of results.

Up until these last few years, one of the most powerful forms of the passion for the real, of action thought in the here and now, of the intrinsic value of revolt (Mao's axiom: 'it is right to rebel'), will have been the proud refusal to appear before the rigged tribunal of results, be they economic, social, 'human' or otherwise. At the heart of the priest's realist plea lies only the reactive desire to oblige subjects to choose the meagre pickings offered to them in exchange for their resignation.

If the century was Nietzschean, it's in part because it regarded the priest as much more than a mere clerk for established religions. A priest is anyone for whom rebellion is no longer an unconditional value; a priest is anyone who measures everything in terms of 'objective' results. Alas, at the century's end the priest is everywhere.

(3) *'My love for you is reborn from the ashes of the sun'*   The century has been a great century for the vision of love as a figure of truth, which is entirely different from romanticism's fatalist and fusional conception of love, as embodied in Wagner's *Tristan and Isolde*. The role played by psychoanalysis in this transformation has been far from insignificant, to say nothing of the successive waves in the struggle for the rights of women. The key issue consists in thinking love not as destiny, but as encounter and thought,[45] as an asymmetrical and egalitarian becoming, as the invention of oneself.

Surrealism was a step in this reconstruction of love as an arena for truth, of love as the procedure that produces a truth of difference.[46] Only a step though, for surrealism still remains in thrall to sexual mythologies that revolve around a fatal and mysterious femininity, the one found walking through the streets of the metropolis, naked under her mantle of fur. This generates a very unilateral masculine vision, whose classical obverse is the hyperbolic praise of Woman. Even in the text quoted above, when Breton reveres 'the dark fire that comes into your eyes', we can discern an idolatry that is more aesthetic than amorous. All the same, surrealism, and Breton especially, did more than merely accompany the movement that saw women climb onto the stage of love just as the masses had climbed upon that of History – so as to become the subject of a truth. When Breton writes that 'the love which at this point counts on nothing but itself does not recover', he says something essential. Love can no longer be mystical fusion, astral conjunction, an Eternal feminine offered up to man, even if it is in order to carry him 'so high'.[47] Love is a dual adventure of the body and the mind; it is the experience and thought of what the Two is, a world refracted and transfigured by contrast. Of this world, there is no recovery.

By linking love to the anti-dialectic of excess, Breton ultimately includes it within the thinking resources of life, within the wager of intensity. After all, as our text testifies, today it is up to a woman rather than a man to be the complete and incontestable heroine of such a wager.

(4) '*Only a magic formula could be effective here*'   I've already said that the power of the act and the real of the pure present do not let themselves be named, that they justify their envelopment 'at a distance' within proclamations and manifestos. However, we must not neglect the attempts by the avant-gardes and their artists directly to match the creative act with a nominal distillate of its power. This is what, following Rimbaud, could be called the 'formula', in the sense in which he wrote: 'I, impatient to find the place and the formula'. Obviously, it should also be understood as the 'magic formula', the one which has the power to open all the secret places ('Open, Sesame!').

Love inspires Breton to find a formula for the devastated woman, made vulnerable by repeated rebellion against absolute unhappiness to being hurled once again 'into the abyss'. It's the only one worthy of her, the only one which is not a consolation, that is, an invitation to resign herself. It is the formula: 'Osiris is a black god.' This formula distils the idea that every metamorphosis, every rebirth, every secondary deification, depends on standing one's ground in the midst of life's most terrible darkenings. The formula conjoins the initial donation of excess in its negative form, the instantaneous forces of rebellious creation, and the elevated language of the Manifestos.

This is because the formula is the supposed point of conjunction between the act in the present and the future that the programme envelops. In politics, everyone knows that the formula is the slogan – when it takes hold of the situation, when it is echoed by marching thousands. Once the formula is discovered, it becomes impossible to distinguish between the material body and the spirit of invention that inhabits it, and like Rimbaud, again, at the end of *A Season in Hell*, one can declare: 'I'll be able to possess truth in a single body and soul.' For Breton, the formula names the change of sign, the rebellious passage from suffering to the affirmative intensity of life. A large part of the century's undertakings – political as well as artistic – devoted themselves to finding the formula, this slightest point of attachment to the real of that which announces its novelty; this explosion in language whereby one word, one word alone, is the same thing as a body.

At the height of its concentration, the art of the century – but also all the other truth procedures, each according to its own resources – aimed to conjoin the present, the real intensity of life, and the name of this present as given in the formula, a formula that is always at the same time the invention of a form. It is then that the pain of the world changes into joy.

To produce an unknown intensity against a backdrop of suffering, through the always improbable intersection of a formula and an instant: this was the century's desire. Which explains why, despite its multifaceted cruelty, it managed – through its artists, scientists, militants and lovers – to be Action itself.

12

The infinite

1 Analogies of dawn

Today, when it seems so remote, how are we to think the intimate link that bound art and politics throughout the century? This link is not uniquely – or even mainly – the one that enslaves art to politics, to official policies and finally to state censorship. Zhdanov's invectives against decadent bourgeois art (by which he meant the whole of contemporary art), or even Mao's informal talks on art and literature at Yenan, are not really what is at stake, and when they are, most often it's only in a secondary and round-about way. The most significant thesis, mainly propounded in the West, and especially by the most innovative and activist currents, is that of art's intrinsic political value and impact. The avant-gardes even went to the extreme of saying that there is more politics to be found in the formal mutations of art than in poli-tics 'strictly speaking'. This conviction was still held by the Tel Quel group in the sixties. Today, some of Jacques Rancière's writ-ings provide a sophisticated echo of it.[48] What was it, in the century's creative operations, that made such an affirmation possible?

I'll begin with a prefatory and wholly descriptive remark in order to link this lesson to the previous one. There is no doubt that among the important benchmarks of the century we should number the appearance of groups that explicitly saw themselves as poetico-political. Such groups assert that they embody the identity between a school of artistic creation and an organization which practises and maintains the intellectual conditions of a political break. We will take the 'poetic' in the term 'poetico-political' in a broad sense, to refer to something like a subjective aesthetic of emancipation. The surrealists, the situationists and, at the end of the line, the group around the review *Tel Quel*, exemplified – respectively in the twenties and thirties, the fifties, and the sixties and seventies – this vocation to make art and politics indiscernible.

Given that all politics comes down to collective actions debated and decided upon in meetings, poetico-political initiatives can no longer simply comprise separate artistic works; they too must result from meetings and collective decisions. In the world of artists as in that of small political groups – not to mention psychoanalytic schools – this facet of things cannot be separated from a great secessionist fury, incessant invectives against this or that figure and protocols of exclusion.

It would be a very interesting project to investigate the institutional question of exclusion as a fundamental practice of all even slightly inventive groups within the century – be they vast state powers, like many of the communist parties, or very small aesthetic factions, like the situationists. It seems that the ultimately solemn conviction that one is in the process of touching on the real leads to a form of extreme subjective feverishness, one of whose manifestations is the incessant designation of heretics and suspects. This chronic preoccupation with purging was not just the exclusive province of Stalinists, far from it. Figures as diverse as Freud, André Breton, Trotsky, Guy Debord and Lacan all instigated merciless proceedings against deviation, banished or stigmatized numerous heretics and disbanded their sects.

Exclusion is surely linked to the difficulty of determining the criteria for legitimate action when the touchstone of action is real subversion. Everything then pushes towards the negative identification which I've already discussed: the essence of the One is in the Two and unity can only be secured through the ordeal of division. Whence the solemn staging of splits and exclusions. One of the great maxims of the French Communist Party in its high Stalinist period – in truth, the only one in which this mediocre party at least *meant* something – was that you did not leave the party, you were excluded from it. You cannot simply have done with the real once you have touched on it. It is the real that judges you unworthy of it. This is another way of saying what we already heard from Brecht: 'Don't cut yourself off from us.'

Truth be told, interrogating ourselves with regard to the frequency of exclusions and splits among poetico-political groups comes down to putting the accent on the word 'politics'. When all is said and done, what does this term name within the century, which lets one transpose the traditional violence of power struggles onto the imperatives of art? The word 'politics' has a history and we must postulate that the century has reinvented its meaning. When art is assigned a political vocation, what does 'political' signify? Ever since the twenties, the word dilates to the point of vaguely designating every radical break, every escape from consensus. 'Politics' is the common name for a collectively recognizable break. In this sense, it's easy to surmise why there are innumerable 'political' groups, artistic as well as psychoanalytic, theatrical as well as civic, poetic as well as musical; why it can be argued, as indeed happened after May '68, that 'everything is political' – sexuality in particular. The word 'politics' names the desire of beginning, the desire that some fragment of the real will finally be exhibited without either fear or law, through the sole effect of human invention – artistic or erotic invention, for example, or the inventions of the sciences. The art/politics connection is incomprehensible if the word 'politics' is not accorded this expanded, subjective meaning.

Notwithstanding the transformations it may have undergone, in the last instance the word 'politics' always refers back to professional politics, the kind that involves power and the state. This is particularly the case when the words 'rebellion', 'revolution' and 'avant-garde' are shared by political art and the art of politics (it was Lenin who once remarked that insurrection was an art). The danger then consists in transforming art's political vocation, its commitment to the real beginning, into an opportunistic enslavement to either party or state. We are faced with two overlapping processes: on the one hand, a process internal to art, which has to do with rupture – with the passion for the real understood as the dawn of Being, invented through the activation of forms; on the other, an external process, which concerns the position of art and artists vis-à-vis effective and organized politics, and revolutionary politics in particular. Revolutionary politics also speaks of rupture and dawn, but it does so in the name of a collective infinite which, more often than not, is portrayed as transcending all particular ruptures. We can no longer avoid the question of the degree of autonomy possessed by artistic revolutions – and a fortiori by artistic avant-gardes – with regard to political revolution, and specifically with regard to the party that leads this revolution or is at least the guarantor of its possibility. For those who reasonably accept the inclusion of artistic revolutions within political ones there are moments when the absolute freedom claimed by art must turn into absolute submission to the directives of the party. This dialectical enigma is just one among the many disjunctive syntheses through which the century's passion for the real manifested itself. It is not tantamount to a formal contradiction. Between Louis Aragon the surrealist, selling his pornographic daydream *Irene's Cunt* on the sly – the Aragon who will later address these lines to the feminine icon:

> Your eyes so deep that perching over them to look
> I saw all the suns come to drown themselves within
> Your eyes so deep I can no longer recall

and the same Louis Aragon who, speaking about the socialist Léon Blum, declares 'fire on the wise bear of social democracy!'; who watches over literary orthodoxy in conformity with Zhdanov's directives; or who writes a strange poem about the return to France of Maurice Thorez, Secretary-General of the French Communist Party, after a long stay in a Soviet hospital, a poem as obsequious as it is lyrical – 'And the wattman stops his machine, he returns, he returns . . .'; between these 'two' Aragons there is no need to postulate some form of schizophrenia, despite what he himself later tried to make others believe. There is instead the real paradox of moments when creation and obedience become indiscernible, and this other paradox, perhaps just a variant of the first, which is that of the subsumption of the spirit of revolt and invention by the imperative to dissolve the 'I' into a 'we' – a 'we' that is sometimes uncertain about the collective freedom which it was meant to organize. There is also the far more widespread confusion between the acrid flavour of revolt and the rather greasier taste that accompanies the exercise of power over others.

The idea advanced through the mediation of these paradoxes or confusions is that in the end one cannot – on pain of blindness to the singularity of particular sequences – call every promise of a dawn of thinking a 'politics'. The revenge of the real upon an *excessively unified* grasp of its fragmentation has signified that neither the art of the avant-garde nor the practice of revolutionary politics benefited from their announced fusion. Today we know that they constitute two distinct truth procedures, two heterogeneous confrontations between the thinking invention of forms and the indistinctness of the real. Yet we know this only because we've re-thought the fate of the avant-gardes, and hailed, for all time, their splendid and violent ambition.

By the same token, even in the period of the poetico-political groups, the veritable essence of this 'fusion' was to function as a vector for a much older question, one pertaining to the truths of art as such: the question of artistic objectivity, of what the arts *produce*.

2   Romantic infinite, contemporary infinite

Contemporary artists have all been led, at one time or another, to interrogate the very notion of the 'work'. We have already mentioned the reason why: the primacy of the act, viewed as the only thing capable of measuring up to the real present. The finitude and immobility of the canvas, for example, its inactive exposition and commercial objectivity, were subjected to criticism from an early date. Today the canvas is often replaced by ephemeral 'installations'. Just as in politics the idea of producing an ideal community has been forsaken (so that we find Blanchot and Jean-Luc Nancy reflecting upon an 'inoperative' community and Giorgio Agamben writing about a 'coming' community), it's been argued that what matters in art is the act or gesture, not the product. Incidentally, this converges with the critique of the fetishism of results that I have myself promoted. In its most radical form, the orientation towards an inoperative art maintains that art itself, conceived as a separate activity, must disappear, that it must realize itself as life. This hyper-Hegelianism proposes to overcome art by means of an aestheticization of the everyday. It also represented one of the fundamental orientations within situationism – with the proviso, of course, that this becoming-art of life be immanent, intensely subjectivated and never offered up as a spectacle. Guy Debord's films (especially his arresting *In girum imus nocte et consumimur igni*), attempt, at one and the same time, to be acts (destructive ones even) and the manifestos of these acts. They seek to pronounce the end of cinema as a production of spectacles and to realize this end in films that are to be non-films. (The truth is that they are – and this is no mean feat – nothing more than beautiful, nostalgic meditations. But this is another story.)

In my view, this interminable and tortured debate about the uselessness of works and the staging of acts, in art as elsewhere, is emblematic of a task that the century set itself but could never carry to its conclusion. This is the task of finding the means for a decisive break with romanticism.

What torments the century? It is its striving to have done with the romanticism of the Ideal: to abide in the abruptness of the effectively-real, but to do so with subjective means (a dark enthusiasm, an exalted nihilism, the cult of war . . .) that remain irreparably romantic.

This insight helps us to understand the century's uncertainties, as well as its ferocity. Everyone says: 'It's time to stop dreaming, to stop singing the praises of the Ideal. Action! Up with the real! The end justifies the means!' – but the precise relationship, within this strained subjectivity, between the finitude of desires and the infinity of situations is still tainted by romantic exaggeration. The persistence of the romantic element explains the rage perceptible in the century's anti-romanticism: the relentless struggle of action against itself and of all against all; a struggle that was to last until the advent – through fatigue and saturation – of today's putative, painful peace.

But in the final analysis, what is romanticism? It is two things, subtly entwined throughout many works and proclamations.

(a) Art is the descent of the infinity of the Ideal into the finitude of the work. The artist, elevated by genius, is the sacrificial medium of this descent. This is a transposition of the Christian schema of the incarnation: the genius lends Spirit the forms it has mastered so that the people may recognize its own spiritual infinitude in the finitude of the work. Since in the end it's the work that bears witness to the incarnation of the infinite, romanticism cannot avoid making the work sacred.

(b)   The artist lifts subjectivity to the heights of the sublime by testifying that it possesses the power to mediate between reality and the Ideal. Just as the work is sacred, so is the artist sublime. What we are here calling 'romanticism' is an aesthetic religion, what Jean Borreil called the advent of the artist-king.[49]

To have done with romanticism in art thus involves deconsecrating the work (to the point of repudiating it in favour of Duchamp's readymade, or of temporary installations) and divesting the artist (to the point of advocating the dispersion of the artistic act within everyday life). In this respect, the twentieth century is no doubt the first to set itself the objective of an atheist art, of a truly materialist art; this is what makes Brecht, perhaps the artist most brutally aware of what is at stake here, into one of the century's key players. But why is it that artists, philosophers and essayists so often linger within the domain of what they're fighting against? Why do they still make such use of romantic pathos? Why does the prose of Breton or Debord – to say nothing of Malraux's in his writings on art, or Heidegger's when he entrusts the poets with the shelter of being, or that of René Char, this talented poet who sometimes takes himself for Heraclitus – why then are all these forms of rhetoric ultimately so close to that of Hugo, even in their curious staging of the sublime *posture* of an artist-thinker meditating upon History?

It is because the infinite is at stake and because, in terms of its link to the real, this question is far from having achieved within the century a clarification capable of authorizing a serene departure from romanticism. Even today, the fundamental lessons of Cantor – that isolated, shuddering prophet of a wholly secularized conception of the infinite – are a long way from penetrating the dominant discourse of artistic modernity.

How can art assume the compulsory finitude of its means while incorporating the infinity of Being into its thinking? Romanticism proposes that art is precisely the coming of this infinity into the finite body of the work. But it can only do so at the price of a kind of generalized Christianity. If we are to break with this latent religiosity, we need to discover another articulation of the finite and the infinite. This is what the century proved incapable of doing, collectively and programmatically – oscillating as it did between the perpetuation of a romantic subjectivity that would harbour the infinite within itself, at least as a programme for emancipation, and the integral sacrifice of the infinite, which is actually the elimination of art as a form of thought. The torment of contemporary art in the face of the infinite situates it between a programmatic forcing that announces the return of romantic pathos, on the one hand, and a nihilistic iconoclasm, on the other.

No genuine artist, however, can be reduced to collective impasses, even when he or she publicly partakes in their utterances. The artist's work outlines an intermediary path between romanticism and nihilism, reinventing each and every time – even if rarely in an explicit manner – an original idea of the real-infinite. This idea comes down to acting as if the infinite were nothing but the finite, once the latter is conceived not in its objective finitude, but in the act from whence it arises. There is no separate or ideal infinite. The infinite is not captured *in* form; it *transits through form*. If it is an event – if it is *what happens* – finite form can be equivalent to an infinite opening.

In its effective process, rather than in the declarations of the avant-gardes, twentieth-century art is marked by an enduring formal unease, a complete inability to uphold a doctrine of local arrangements, or even of macro-structures. Why? Because form constitutes the transit of being – form's immanent overcoming of its finitude – and not simply an abstract virtuality for a descent of the Ideal, under whose thrust it would merely need to 'shift' the established devices (*dispositifs*). Indeed, there can no longer be any established devices for the production of art. There is only *the multiplicity of formalizations*.

Commentators, who for the most part can be counted among the partisans of the current Restoration – which is clearly also an artistic reaction, the alpha and omega of which is the sinister, antiquarian mania for 'baroque' interpretations of every kind of music – often maintain that 'contemporary art' (a bizarre expression, if we consider that sometimes we are talking about works, like those of Schoenberg, Duchamp, or Malevich, that are almost a century old) was 'dogmatic', or even 'terroristic'. They can go ahead and call the passion for the real 'Terror', I won't object; but when they denounce what they deem to be an obstinate preoccupation with formal *a priori* they're guilty of spectacular idiocy. Quite the reverse, the century is marked by an unprecedented variability in its imperatives of construction and ornamentation, being enticed not by the slow historical movement of the equilibrium of forms, but by the urgency of this or that experimental formalization.

The art stigmatized by the agents of the Restoration strives to bring about the ruin of incarnation – the Christian figure of the work's finitude – and, at the same time, to retain it as the support for an opening of form in which the infinite would come about *as disincarnation*. Of course, the most radical vision consists in replacing the objectivity of the work with the precariousness of events, formal arrangements made to be uninstalled, or even with 'happenings' that are coextensive with their own duration. There is also a recourse to improvisation in all its forms, because improvisation un-limits form, prohibiting its anticipation or even the identification of stable points of reference within it. After all, that is why jazz – that astonishing laboratory for improvisation – is truly an art of the century.

Installations, events, happenings, improvisations: everything conspires to orient artistic research towards a sort of generalized theatricality, inasmuch as theatre has always assumed its own status as a precarious art, a craft tied to innumerable public contingencies.[50] That, once its form has been partially but rigorously decided, the infinite could emerge from scenic happenstance – this is the century's ideal, the directive through which it arduously sought to extricate itself from romanticism. It is the ideal of a *materialist formalization*. According to this ideal, the infinite proceeds *directly* from the finite.

On this point, the philosopher should note that the century is engaged in a constant debate with Hegel around the theme of the 'end of art'. This time, however, the debate takes place in a kind of unconscious proximity, rather than according to an obsessive, albeit antagonistic, reference.

To take stock of this proximity it is necessary to read, in the section of *The Science of Logic* entitled 'Quantity', the passage entitled 'Quantitative Infinity'. The synthetic definition proposed by Hegel (I will borrow his vocabulary here) is that (the quantum's) infinity comes to be when the act of self-overcoming is once again taken up into itself. Hegel adds that in this moment the infinite exceeds the sphere of the quantitative and becomes qualitative, becomes 'a pure quality of the finite itself'. In other words, just as in contemporary art's presentation of its real concept, the infinite is effectively a *qualitative determination of the finite*. But under what conditions? It is here that the Hegelian analysis is of use.

Hegel starts by acknowledging that the finite, taken in its concrete reality, is always, as a concrete category, a becoming or movement. What assigns this movement to finitude is its repetitive character. The finite is what comes out of itself only in order to remain within itself. This is what Hegel calls the 'surpassing' (*das Hinausgehen*). The finite is what surpasses itself *within itself*. In other words, it is what, coming out of itself in order to produce the Other, remains within the element of the Same. Instead of an alteration of self there is only an iteration.

I find the idea that the essence of the finite is not the boundary or the limit – which are only vague spatial intuitions – but rather repetition, very profound. It is indeed the 'compulsion to repeat' which Freud, and later Lacan, will ascribe to the finitude of human desire, a desire whose object always comes back to the same place.

Hegel goes on to posit that surpassing, in its guise as a repetitive series – as the deferment of the exit from oneself within the Same – is the 'bad infinite' (*das Schlechte-Unendliche*); the one, for example, which makes it so that a number is followed by another number, and so on 'ad infinitum'. The bad infinite represents the repetitive sterility of surpassing. In this respect it is nothing but the finite itself viewed from the standpoint of its negative determination (repetition).

It is at this juncture that Hegel's analysis takes an interesting turn. Up to now, we've considered surpassing, which is the concrete being of the finite, only *in its result*: repetitive sterility, iteration, and the insistence of the Same. As Hegel notes, however, thereby anticipating today's artists, we can attempt to grasp and to think surpassing no longer in its result, which is nothing but a 'bad infinite', but *in its act*. Here one must distinguish, and try to prise apart, the act and the result, the creative essence of surpassing and the failure of creation. Or, as we would put it today, the gesture and the work. The fact that an act is sterile does not mean that we are exempt from thinking it *as such*. Hegel then discovers that there is something *really infinite* in the 'bad infinite', namely the act of self-surpassing, provided one manages to separate it from repetition. In Hegel's vocabulary, this detachment from repetition, and thus from the result, is called the 'returnedness into itself'. Against the tyranny of the objective result, the 'returnedness into itself' of the act of surpassing makes it possible to think the 'subjective' ground of the finite, that is to say, the real infinite immanent to the movement of the finite. The infinite as pure creation is thereby attained by taking hold of that which makes the obdurate activity of surpassing count 'in itself', and not by virtue of subsequent repetitions. It is this immanent creative power, this indestructible capacity to overstep boundaries, which is the infinite as *quality* of the finite.

We should remark that twentieth-century art also interrogates itself about the new forms of repetition. In a text that has become too famous, Walter Benjamin indicates (on the basis of photography, cinema, printing techniques, and so on) that the century introduces the artistic series, the power of technical reproducibility. What is at issue in the artistic emphasis upon the serial object (Duchamp's bicycle wheel, or the forms of collage already present in cubism) is the circumscription and staging of the repetitive act outside of the brute value of repetition. These artistic gestures exhibit the Hegelian 'returnedness'. Many of the century's artistic projects attempt to make perceivable, in an instance of repetition, the power of the act of repetition itself. This is precisely what Hegel calls the qualitative infinite, which is *the visibility of the power of the finite*.

Ideally, the twentieth-century artwork is nothing other than the visibility of its own act. This is the sense in which it overcomes the romantic pathos of the descent of the infinite into the finite body of the work. That is because the artwork has nothing infinite to show, save for its own *active* finitude. If the 'work' of art is ruled by this norm, it's easy to understand why it is not exactly a work, and even less a sacred object. If an 'artist' does nothing but confer visibility upon the pure act immanent to any repetition, it is clear that he or she is not exactly an artist, a sublime medium between the Ideal and the sensible. The anti-romantic programme of deconsecrating the work and de-sublimating the artist is thereby achieved.

The fundamental problem that now arises is that of the trace, or of the visibility of the visible. If our only infinite resource is to be found in pure active quality, what is the trace of this quality which would allow it visibly to separate itself from repetition? Are there traces of the act? How can we isolate the act from its result without resorting to the ineluctably sacred form of the work?

Let us illustrate this problem by means of an analogy: can a choreography be rigorously annotated? In the wake of Russian ballets and Isadora Duncan, dance is a crucial art precisely because it is only act. The paradigm of a vanishing art, dance does not produce works in the ordinary sense of the term. But what is its trace, where does it circumscribe the thinking of its own singularity? Is there only ever a trace of its repetition, and never of its act? Art would then amount to the unrepeatable within a repetition. It would have no other destiny than that of giving a form to this unrepeatable. Have we solved the problem then? I'm not so sure. For if the unrepeatable admits of a form, is it not because its result is itself a repetition? Would this not mean that art treats the unrepeatable only as though it were the formal instance of repetition? Here we would need to contrast two senses of the word 'form'. The first, traditional (or Aristotelian) sense is on the side of the formation of a material, of the organic appearance of a work, of its manifestation as a totality. The second sense, which belongs to the century, sees form as *what the artistic act authorizes by way of new thinking*. Form is therefore an Idea as given in its material index, a singularity that can only be activated in the real grip of an act. Form is the *eidos* – this time in a Platonic sense – of an artistic act; it must be understood *from the side of formalization*. Formalization is basically the great unifying power behind all the century's undertakings – from mathematics (formal logics) to politics (the Party as *a priori* form of any collective action), by way of art, be it prose (Joyce and the odyssey of forms), painting (Picasso, the inventor of a suitable formalization in the face of every occurrence of the visible) or music (the polyvalent formal construction of Alban Berg's *Wozzeck*). But in 'formalization', the word 'form' is not opposed to 'matter' or 'content', but is instead coupled to the real of the act.

All these extremely difficult questions stirred the century. My hypothesis is that it is because of a post-romantic conception of the infinite – qualitative as well as vanishing – that the art of the century inscribed itself paradigmatically between dance and cinema. Cinema offers a technical reproducibility that is both all-encompassing and indifferent to its public. It realizes itself as an 'iteration work', as a permanently available impurity. Dance is the opposite: a pure instant, forever effaced. Between dance and cinema lies the question of what a non-religious art could be. An art in which the infinite is drawn from nothing besides the effects of the act – real effects of what at first is only exhibited as a repetitive vacuity. An art of formalization rather than of the work. An art far removed from the business of humans.

3   Univocity

Infinite in its act, art is not the least bit destined to the satisfaction of human animals in their tepid everyday life. Instead, it aims at forcing a thinking to declare, in its area of concern, *the state of exception*. Whilst accounting for the act, the qualitative infinite is what exceeds every result, every objective repetition, all the 'normal' subjective states. Art is not the expression of ordinary humanity, of that which within the human obstinately strives to survive, or, as Spinoza would put it, to 'persevere in being'. Art bears witness to the inhuman within the human. Its aim is nothing short of compelling humanity to some excess with regard to itself.

This is why artistic declarations and manifestos are so ominous, so leaden. In this respect, the art of the century, just like its politics or its scientific formalisms, is starkly anti-humanist.

And that is indeed what it is reproached with today. We hear calls for a humanist art, an art abhorring what man is capable of doing to his fellow man, an art of human rights. It is certainly true that from Malevich's *White on White* to Beckett's *Waiting for Godot*, from Webern's silences to Guyotat's lyrical cruelties, the fundamental art of the century doesn't care a jot about man. Quite simply because it considers that man in his ordinary state does not amount to much, and that there is no need to make such a fuss about him – all of which is quite true. *The art of the century is an art of the overhuman.* I agree that, at first glance, it is a sombre art. I don't say sad, distraught, or neurotic. No: sombre. An art in which joy itself is sombre. Breton is right, Osiris is a black god. Even when it is frenetic and Dionysian, this art is sombre because it is not devoted to anything within us – human animals busy with their own survival – that would be immediate and relaxing. Even when it advocates the cult of a solar and affirmative god, the modalities of this stance remain sombre. Nerval's 'black sun' is the image that best prefigured the art of the century, and perhaps the century in its entirety. It is not a tranquil light that bathes this nascent world. It is a sun made for the Phoenix, and we can never forget the ashes from which it arose. Let us listen to Breton, once again: art – like love, politics, and science at its most ambitious – is reborn from 'the ashes of the sun'. Yes, the century is an ashen sun.

The overhuman demands the abolition of all particularity. But, as the animals that we are, our only simple pleasure is to be sought in particularity. Hence the fact that what men will remember the century by has nothing to do with their satisfaction. What the century desires – in the construction of socialism as in minimal art, in formal axiomatic as in the conflagrations of mad love – is a universality without remainder, without adherence to any particularity whatsoever. Like Bauhaus in architecture: a building that nothing renders particular, for it is reduced to a translucent, universally recognizable functionality; the kind of functionality that has forgotten every index of stylistic particularity. It is easy to see that the apposite slogan is that of formalization, at the borders of the real, and that it is precisely this which immediately produces the austere impression of an indifference towards the judgement of men.

The overhuman is that which, having dispensed with particularities, withdraws from all interpretation. If the work must be interpreted, if it can be interpreted, it is because too much particularity still survives within it, because it has failed to reach the pure transparency of the act, because it has not bared its real. Such a work is not yet univocal. Humanity is equivocal, overhumanity univocal. But every univocity is the result of a formalization whose localizable real is constituted by the act.

The century will have been the century of univocity. This is what I hope will outlast the current Restoration, which is all the more mendacious and equivocal in that it claims to be both humanistic and convivial. Deleuze forcefully affirmed the univocity of being, and our time will indeed have desired – through works inhabited by a universality without remainder – to be the inhuman rival of being.[51] In every domain, it will have unfalteringly explored the paths of formalization.

I maintain that the thought of being qua being is nothing other than mathematics. So it is not surprising, in my view, that the matrix of the century's grandiose projects was the attempt, undertaken by the century's mathematicians between Hilbert and Grothendieck, 'to break in two', as Nietzsche would say, the history of mathematics, in order to establish a comprehensive formalization, a general theory of the universes of pure thought. To produce in this manner the steadfast certainty that every correctly formulated problem can be solved. To reduce mathematics to its *act*: the univocal power of formalism, the naked force of the letter and its codes. Bourbaki's great treatise is France's contribution to this immense intellectual project. It is necessary to lead everything back to a unified axiomatic; to compel formalism to demonstrate its own coherence; to produce – once and for all – the 'mathematical thing', never abandoning it to its piteous and contingent history. Everyone must be offered an anonymous and complete mathematical universality. The formalization of the mathematical act is the enunciation of the mathematical real and not an *a posteriori* form stuck onto an unfathomable material.

Bourbaki's monumental *Treatise* is the mathematical equivalent of Mallarmé's poetic project of the *Book*. With the difference that the *Treatise*, albeit unfinished, exists, and – as Mallarmé wished – 'in many tomes', unlike the *Book*. Yet more evidence that, as we've argued from the start, the twentieth century actually carried out what the nineteenth merely projected.

Just as it's become commonplace to point to Mallarmé's supposed 'failure', today, at a time when even within mathematics 'concrete modesty' is the norm and especially when mathematicians all too often aspire to become financial analysts, people like to say that the Bourbaki project failed. This is only true if we reduce it to one of its aspects, the most dated, the least innovative: the desire for logical closure (or, as logicians say, 'completeness'). Granted, Gödel showed it is impossible for a mathematical formalism armed with the resources of elementary arithmetic (which is indeed the minimum . . .) to contain a demonstration of its own consistency. But the Bourbaki project's passion for the real is only peripherally attached to the property of completeness, which instead goes all the way back to the systematic ambitions of classical metaphysics. What matters is that the formal presentation of mathematics envelops a founding radicality which characterizes the nature of its act. In my view this point remains a necessary requirement of thought, for mathematicians as well as philosophers.

Some have interpreted Gödel's technical result to mean that every formalizing stance leaves a remainder. Consequently, the century's dream of univocal access to the real must be abandoned. Not being formalized, the untreated, intractable residue will have to be interpreted. We must retread the ragged and equivocal paths of hermeneutics.

It's striking that this is not the lesson that Gödel himself – after Cantor, the greatest genius in the examination of the essence of mathematics – draws from his own demonstrations.[52] He sees in them a lesson of infinity, as well as the ransom of ignorance that must be paid every time knowledge is extorted from the real: to partake in a truth is also to measure that other truths exist, truths we do not yet partake in. This is indeed what separates formalization, as both thought and project, from a merely pragmatic employment of forms. Without ever being discouraged, one must invent other axioms, other logics, other ways of formalizing. The essence of thinking always resides in the power of forms.

Today, there can be no doubt that it is advisable for us to remain Gödelian, at least if we wish to safeguard within us the inhumanity of truths against the animal 'humanity' of particularisms, needs, profits and blind archaicisms.

What are our axioms? And what consequences must follow, implacably drawn from these axioms? Indifferent to the opinion of the agents of the Restoration, we are obliged to answer these questions. And no one will divert us from this task.

The century having come to an end, we have to make its wager ours, the wager on the univocity of the real against the equivocity of semblance. To declare anew, and perhaps this time (who knows?) win, the war within thought which belonged to the century, but which already opposed Plato to Aristotle: the war of formalization against interpretation.

This is a war that possesses numerous less esoteric names: The Idea against reality. Freedom against nature. The event against the state of affairs. Truth against opinions. The intensity of life against the insignificance of survival. Equality against equity. Rebellion against tolerance. Eternity against History. Science against technics. Art against culture. Politics against management. Love against the family.

Yes, we have all these wars to win – as the Chuvash poet says – 'among the jolting breaths of the unsaid'.

13

The joint disappearances of Man and God

These days – that is in the fourth year of the twenty-first century – we hear of nothing save for human rights and the return of the religious. Some nostalgics of the brutal oppositions that captivated and laid waste to the twentieth century even propose that our universe is organized around the deadly clash between a West upholding human rights (or freedoms, or democracy, or the emancipation of women . . .) and religious 'fundamentalists', generally Islamic and bearded, partisans of a barbarous return to traditions originating in the Middle Ages (cloistered women, obligatory beliefs, corporal punishments . . .).

In France, this game is even joined by certain intellectuals truly anxious to promote – in a conflictual field now dominated by the war of Man (or the Law) against (a terrorist) God – a surrogate master signifier. Renegades of the leftism of the seventies, it is nevertheless they who remain inconsolable that 'Revolution' has ceased to be the name of every authentic event; that political antagonisms no longer provide us with the key to the History of the world; that the absoluteness of Party, Masses and Classes is spent. So here we have these poor intellectuals, deprived of any real resort, and symmetrically placed to the bearded false prophets and their petroleum God, busy turning the extermination of the Jews by the Nazis into the single and sacred Event of the twentieth century; identifying anti-Semitism as the destinal content of the history of Europe; turning the word 'Jew' into the victimizing designation of a surrogate absolute; and the word 'Arab', barely hidden behind the word 'Islamist', into the designation of the barbarian.

From these axioms it follows that the state of Israel with its colonial policy is an outpost of democratic civilization, and that the American army is the ultimate guarantor of any acceptable world.

My stance, with regard to this pathetic 'grand narrative' of the final combat between humanist democracy and barbarian religion is stunningly simple: the God of monotheisms has been dead for a long time, no doubt for at least two hundred years, and the man of humanism has not survived the twentieth century.[53] Neither the infinite complications of state politics in the Middle East nor the spongy mindsets of our own 'democrats' have the least chance of resuscitating them.

The clash of civilizations, the conflict between democracies and terrorism, the fight to the death between human rights and the rights of religious fanaticism, the promotion of racial, historical, colonial or victimizing signifiers, such as 'Arab', 'Jew', 'Western', 'Slav' – all this is nothing other than an ideological shadow play behind which the only real drama is taking place: the painful, dispersed, confused and slow replacement of the defunct communisms with another rational path towards the political emancipation of the large human masses currently consigned to chaos.

Make no mistake, I am no longer concerned with the 'French' or the 'European'. Elsewhere, I have proposed the pure and simple dissolution of these national categories.[54]

On this basis it is interesting to reread a page of the twentieth century to which I personally bore witness: the last spasms of the old concept of man, in its correlation to the definitive retreat of the divine.

Let us first take a step back.

We know that, along with some others, Dostoevsky posed the dramatic question: What happens to man if God is dead? Can there really exist a 'Godless' man?

To gauge the force of this question we must recall the previous disposition of the link between 'man' and 'God', such as its concept was engineered by modern metaphysics. Beginning with the moment when the thematic of man as subject (based on the post-Cartesian motif of self-consciousness) stands out in its own right, what is the philosophical development of the relation between the question of man and the question of God?

Let's proceed at the speed of a historical steam engine.

For Descartes, God is required as the guarantee of truth. Whence the fact that the certainty of science finds in Him its justification. One will rightly say, in Lacan's vocabulary, that the God of Descartes is the God of the subject of science: what knots man and God together is nothing other than truth such as, in the guise of certainty, it proposes itself to a subject.

The second moment is Kant. Here we encounter a major displacement: the tying of man to God is no longer an operator of the subject of science, a subject that Kant renames the 'transcendental subject'. The true relation between man and God belongs to practical reason. As Rousseau desired, it is a tie instituted by moral conscience. Paraphrasing Kant himself, we can speak of a religion within the limits of practical reason alone. Man has no purely theoretical access to the supersensible. The Good, and not the True, opens man to God.

This is very close to today's American God, who is sufficiently vague to possess no other employable attributes than the ones used to promote the conquering humanism of 'human rights' and 'democracy'. A God whose whole national function is to bless the humanist soldiers busy bombing and invading barbarous lands. Besides which there is only his private function: to bless good heads of the family.

With Hegel, we have a new displacement. What he calls God is the absolute becoming of spirit, or the absolute Idea, 'the absolute as subject', or the concrete Universal. More precisely, the absolute becoming of subjective spirit, which is our own becoming, completes the unfolding of God. We could say that Hegel proposes an immanent knotting: God is the process of a supposedly complete man.

This eschatological vision is particularly foreign to the chaotic beginning of our twenty-first century. Every figure of the absolute is now viewed with suspicion – in the name of finitude, which is the ontological essence of 'democracy' – especially the one that would immanently absolutize this or that becoming of a human vanguard.

It is nevertheless only in this sense ('God' being reduced to nothing but an old name for the truths into which we are capable of incorporating ourselves) that I remain – like anything of worth in the twentieth century – Hegelian.

Finally, there is positivism, which radicalizes the immanence of God to man as outlined by Hegel. In effect, for Auguste Comte, God is humanity itself – the living and the dead mixed together – a humanity that he renames the 'great Being'. Positivism proposes a religion of humanity, which is the result of the process of the scientific immanentization of the True.

All along, through the True, the Good and the History of immanence, we observe the trajectory of what is for us the most important point: a nominal undecidability circulates between 'man' and 'God'. Are we dealing with a divinization of man, a kind of Christianity in reverse? Or, closer to the theme of the incarnation, a humanization of the divine? Both rather, thrown into a state of reversibility. A divine analogy is maintained, but in a figure which has become inseparable from man. We could say that the essence of classical metaphysical humanism is the construction of a predicate which is undecidable between the human and the divine.

The single stake of Nietzsche's desperate intervention is to undo this predicate, to decide at the very point of the undecidable. God must die, and Man must be overcome.

It might appear that Nietzsche is standing up against religion, in particular against Christianity. But he pontificates about God and priests only to the extent that they constitute a figure of human (im)potency. The famous statement 'God is dead' is obviously a statement about man, at a moment when, after Descartes, Kant, Hegel and Comte, God is undecidably bound up with man. 'God is dead' means that man is dead too. Man, the last man, the dead man, is what must be overcome for the sake of the overman.

What is the overman? Simply man without God. Man as he is thinkable outside of any relation to the divine. The overman decides the undecidability, thus fracturing the humanist predicate.

The problem is that the overman is not yet here. He must simply *come*. And since the overman is nothing but man strictly speaking, man untied from God, it must be said that, prophesying the whole of the twentieth century, Nietzsche makes man into a programme. 'I am my own forerunner,' Zarathustra declares. The overman is the unknotting to come of the History of man.

The twentieth century thus begins – we have repeated this in more than a few ways – under the theme of man as programme, and no longer as given.

Let us note that a certain twenty-first century, under the sign of human rights as the rights of the natural living being, of finitude, of resignation to what there is, tries to return to man as a given. I've said this already: it does so at the very moment when science (finally!) authorizes the transformation of man all the way into his infrastructure as animal species. Meaning that this 'return' has already failed. And that our question remains, now more than ever: What can the programme of a man without God actually promise us?

We experienced, in the glorious sixties of the century of which I speak, that concerning this question there are two conflicting hypotheses.

Here the textual elements could be, regarding the first hypothesis, Sartre's *Search for a Method*, published in 1959 in *Les Temps modernes*, before becoming the introduction to the *Critique of Dialectical Reason*. And, regarding the second hypothesis, the famous passage from Foucault's *The Order of Things* (1966) devoted to the death of man.

The first great hypothesis is that Godless man must take the place of the dead God. We are not dealing with a process of immanent divinization. We are dealing with the occupation of an empty place.

Make no mistake, the effective occupation of this place is, of course, impossible. At the end of *Being and Nothingness*, Sartre basically says that man's passion inverts the passion of the Christ: man loses himself to save God. Except that, he adds, the idea of God is contradictory, so that man loses himself in vain. Whence the famous formula with which the book concludes: 'Man is a useless passion.'

Later Sartre will come to understand that this nihilist romanticism remains merely ornamental. If the project of man is to make himself arise at the place of the absolute, the essence of man is this project itself, so that its 'realization' is not the measure of its unfolding. There are historical practices homogeneous to this project, others which are not. So there is a possible humanist reading of what we should or should not do, even if the supposedly complete figure of the man-god is ontologically inconsistent.

I think that this theme of the impossible, albeit necessary (or real), occupation of the place left empty by the gods can be referred to as a radical humanism. Man is his own absolute, or more precisely, he is the endless becoming of the absolute that he is. We could almost say that Sartre raises to the absolute, or transforms into metaphysics, the programmatic dimension of revolutionary politics, especially in its communist version. Man is what man must invent. This is the content of what offers itself less as a personal morality than as a hypothesis of emancipation. The only duty of man is to make himself arise as a unique absolute.

Of course, this hypothesis communicates with a whole swathe of Marxism. It reconnects to the primordial insights of the Marx of the *1844 Manuscripts*: generic humanity carries within itself (under the name of 'proletariat') the wherewithal to make its own essence arise, beyond the alienations that deploy it within concrete History. That is why Sartre will assert both that the content of positive knowledge is the alienation of man, and that the real stake of this knowledge is the movement whereby one 'exists' – alienation qua programme of disalienation. One will say simultaneously that 'Marxist Knowledge concerns alienated man' (because servitude is the actual historical milieu in which freedom exists, thus making the free man into a mere programme) and that the stake (which is no longer of the order of Knowledge) is that 'the questioner understand how the questioned – which is to say himself – lives out his alienation, how he surmounts it and alienates himself in this very surmounting'.

Man as programme is this: the existential comprehension of the surmounting of the alienation of man, in view of an emancipation whose stages always constitute *new* forms of alienation. Or, the dialecticization of the (objective) knowledge of servitude through the (subjective) comprehension of its condition, which is freedom: 'practical freedom can be grasped only as the permanent and concrete condition of servitude, that is, through this servitude and by it, as that which makes it possible, as its ground'.

The word 'ground' recapitulates the metaphysics of radical humanism: man is the being who is his own programme and who, by virtue of the same movement, grounds the possibility of a programmatic knowledge of himself. As Sartre puts it: 'The ground of anthropology is man himself, not as the object of practical Knowledge, but as a practical organism producing Knowledge as a moment of his own *praxis*.'

To occupy the place of the dead God is to become the only *ground* of what one is.

The second great hypothesis – whose principal content is Nietzschean – is that the absenting of God is one of the names for the absenting of man. The joyous catastrophe affecting the divine figure (the gods, Nietzsche repeats, died of laughter) is at the same time the gay science of a human, all too human catastrophe: the dissipation or decomposition of the figure of man. The end of humanism. As Foucault writes: 'It is no longer possible to think in our day other than in the void left by man's disappearance.' And, just like Nietzsche, Foucault no longer aims to counter those 'who still wish to talk about man, about his reign or his liberation' with anything other than 'a philosophical laugh – which means, to a certain extent, a silent one'.

The hypothesis covered by this laugh, or by this silence, is in truth that of the historical advent of a radical anti-humanism.

We could thus say: a certain philosophical twentieth century lets itself be identified, at its midpoint, around the fifties and sixties, by the confrontation between radical humanism and radical anti-humanism.

As is the wont of the dialectical thinking of contradictions, there is a unity of the two conflicting orientations. That is because both of them treat this question: What becomes of man without God? And they are both programmatic. Sartre wishes to ground a new anthropology in the immediacy of *praxis*. Foucault declares that the disappearance of the figure of man is 'the unfolding of a space in which it is once more possible to think'. Radical humanism and radical anti-humanism agree on the theme of Godless man as opening, possibility, programme of thought. That is why the two orientations will intersect in a number of situations, in particular in all the revolutionary episodes.

In a certain sense the politics of the century, or revolutionary politics more generally, creates situations that are subjectively undecidable between radical humanism and radical anti-humanism. As Merleau-Ponty saw perfectly – but only to draw from the undecidable indecisive conclusions – the general heading could very well take a conjunctive allure: 'humanism *and* terror'. While the twenty-first century opens with a disjunctive morality: 'humanism *or* terror'. (Humanist) war against terrorism.

This conjunctive dimension, this 'and', which can already be registered in the thinking of Robespierre or Saint-Just (Terror and Virtue) – a conjunction that authorizes us, forty years later, to write, without a hint of paradox, 'Sartre *and* Foucault' – does not hinder, but rather demands, in order that we may be worthy of what happens, to formalize the conflict of radical orientations. This is a conflict that empirically also constitutes the shift, in the century, between the fifties, on the one hand, and the sixties and seventies, on the other. That is, before the eighties brought back to the surface, like a dead fish, a disjunction which is deprived not only of any radicality but also of any universalizable hope.

What is philosophy for radical humanism? Sartre says it loud and clear: it is an anthropology. There is an anthropological becoming of philosophy. This becoming is obviously dependent on the creation of man by man. Philosophy is ultimately a provisional anthropology which awaits the historical or sequential effectuation of the programme constituted by the absoluteness of man.

In the framework of radical anti-humanism one disdains from the outset the word 'philosophy'. Why? Because, Foucault tells us, 'Anthropology constitutes perhaps the fundamental arrangement that has governed and controlled the path of philosophical thought from Kant until our own day.' But for a Nietzschean, to say 'anthropology' is also to say 'theology', or even 'religion'. All of a sudden, philosophy, formed for a long time as anthropology, becomes suspect. One will thus – following Heidegger – prefer the word 'thought' to 'philosophy'. At bottom, 'thought', in the radical anti-humanist vision (de facto anticipated by Heidegger in the twenties), designates what replaces philosophy when one abandons anthropology, with which philosophy has been compromised for far too long. As Foucault, who nevertheless retains the programmatic style, says, we need 'to think without immediately thinking that it is man who is thinking'. To think 'in the void left by man's disappearance', and so *begin* to think.

Thus, at the border between the fifties and the sixties, and under the single slogan of the death of God, there are two definitions of the tasks of philosophy:

(a) A general anthropology accompanying a concrete process of emancipation (Sartre);

(b) A thinking which lets an inhuman beginning arrive (Foucault).

Sartre is someone who comes too late. He proposes to reactivate radical humanism, which was already the basis of Stalin's voluntarist terrorism – Stalin, who, let us repeat, had written of 'Man, the most precious capital'. Moreover, in a very Hegelian (or 'young Marxist') style, Sartre imagines his humanist anthropology, not only as a comprehensive knowledge accompanying revolutionary *praxis*, but also as the concrete becoming of thought, as the historical incorporation of philosophical intellect: 'The reintegration of man, as concrete existence, at the core of anthropology, as its constant support, necessarily appears as a stage in the "becoming-world" of philosophy.'

In the end everything happens as if Sartre proposes to the USSR and the Communist Party a spiritual supplement at the very moment when, as paradigmatic figures of emancipation, this state and that party are reduced to political corpses.

Sartre thus delineates the pathetic and formidable figure of a fellow traveller without a path on which to travel.

If, at the end of the sixties, the anti-humanist programme prevails (and, in my view, persists as our starting point) it is because it is the bearer of the coupled ideas of the void and the beginning. These ideas will reveal their usefulness for the revolts of 1968 and then at the start of the seventies. It was common then to think that something was near, that something would happen. And that 'something' deserved devotion, precisely because it was not the umpteenth edition of humanism, precisely because it was a figure of inhuman beginning.

It is clear that this question of humanism ends up designating a division with regard to History. Radical humanism maintains the Hegelian thematic of the historiality of the True. What the programmatic word 'man' designates is a certain historical *work* of man. The second volume of the *Critique of Dialectical Reason* was after all supposed to be devoted to History, from ancient Egypt to Stalin. 'Man' is the essentially normative notion that allows an understanding of the monumental work of the history of emancipation.

Under the sign of anti-humanism, Foucault proposes a vision of History in discontinuous sequences, historical singularities, which he calls 'epistemes'. 'Man' must then be understood merely as one of the words used by modern philosophical discourse. All of a sudden, History as the continuity of sense, or the becoming of Man, is a category as obsolete as that of the discourse that supports it (philosophy qua anthropology). What we must be absolutely and single-mindedly attentive to is the question of knowing whether something is beginning, and in which discursive networks this beginning is situated.

Is history a monument or a succession of beginnings? In the century, 'man' is the bearer of this alternative.

The programme of the Godless man has therefore had two stances at its disposal. Either man is the historical creator of his own absolute essence or he is the man of inhuman beginning, who installs his thought in what happens and abides in the discontinuity of this arrival.

Today we witness the simultaneous abandonment of these two propositions. We are no longer offered anything more than the restoration of classical humanism, but without the vitality of the God (whether present or absent) that sustained its exercise.

Classical humanism without God, without project, without the becoming of the Absolute is a representation of man which reduces him to his animal body. I maintain that if we exit the century through the simultaneous termination of the two programmes of thought constituted by radical humanism and radical anti-humanism, we will necessarily endure a figure which makes man simply into a species.

Sartre already said that if man does not have communism, integral equality, as his project, then he is an animal species of no more interest than ants or pigs.

That's where we are. After Sartre and Foucault, a bad Darwin. With an 'ethical' touch of course, since if we're dealing with a species what should we be worried about, save for its survival? Ecology and bioethics will provide for our 'correct' development as pigs or ants.

Let's not forget, however, that a species is, above all, *what can be domesticated*.

If I wished to scandalize, I would say that my conviction is that this domestication, which subtends the project-less humanism that is inflicted upon us, is already at work in the promotion, as spectacle and norm, of the victimized body.

Why is it in effect that today it is never really a question of man except in the form of the tortured, the massacred, the famished, the genocided? Is it because man is no more than the animal datum of a body, whose most spectacular attestation, the only saleable one (and we are in a kind of supermarket), as we've known ever since the time of circus games, is suffering?

We could say that what contemporary 'democracies' wish to impose upon the planet is an animal humanism. In it man only exists as worthy of pity. Man is a *pitiable animal*.

This dominant ideology that characterizes this beginning of the twenty-first century wants absolutely to destroy the point held in common by Sartre and Foucault. Namely, that man, if he is not the infinite programme of his own absoluteness, deserves only to disappear. Sartre and Foucault think the following: either man is the future of man (Sartre) or he is his past (Foucault). He could not be his own present without being reduced to the lineaments of the animal he contains, or which represents his infrastructure. Today's reactionaries, for instance those who wrote the pamphlet *Why We Are Not Nietzscheans*,[55] on the contrary declare: man is the only present of man.

One will agree however that, were this to be the case, and in view of what our present is like, man would not be worth a fig.

In the retroaction of animal humanism, the common traits of radical humanism and radical anti-humanism are easier to see.

These common traits are three in number:

(1) Sartre and Foucault outline, on the basis of man or of his void, an open figure. In both cases, what is at stake is a total project. For Sartre, anthropology broadens philosophy to span the dimensions of the world. For Foucault, to abide in the absence of man is to surmount 'the obstacle standing obstinately in the way of an imminent new form of thought'. For both Foucault and Sartre, the key question is the opening of an unprecedented possibility, a possibility of thinking for the one, of the humanization of Being for the other. 'Man', whether as becoming or vacuity, is nothing other than one of the names for this possibility, for this opening.

(2) Sartre and Foucault both manifest a fierce hostility to substantialist categories. Sartre rails against any substantial separation of practical freedom from its alienations. It is impossible to 'suppose that the freedom of the project can be found in its full reality *beneath* the alienations of our society'. Inseparable from what keeps him at a distance from his own absoluteness, man is a trajectory of disalienation, or a project, but never a separable identity. Foucault, for his part, cruelly mocks those 'who still ask themselves questions about what man is in his essence'.

The man of animal humanism, on the contrary, is a substantialist or natural category, which we attain through empathy in the spectacle of suffering. Even such a lively talent as Guy Lardreau[56] has felt it necessary to assist in this oppressive metaphysics of pity. But pity, when it is not the subjective instance of propaganda for 'humanitarian' interventions, is nothing but the confirmation of the naturalism, the deep animality, to which man is reduced by contemporary humanism.

Our age, at least in what concerns the 'Western' petty-bourgeois, is the age of ecology, of the environment, of the opposition to hunting – whether it is the hunting of foxes, whales or man. We must live in our 'global village', let nature do its work, affirm natural rights everywhere. For things have a nature that must be respected. It is important to discover and consolidate natural balances. The market economy, for example, is natural, we must find its balance, between some unfortunately inevitable millionaires and the unfortunately innumerable poor, just as we should respect the balance between hedgehogs and snails.

We live within an Aristotelian arrangement: there is nature, and beside it right, which tries as much as possible to correct, if needs be, the excesses of nature. What is dreaded, what must be foreclosed, is what is neither natural nor amendable by right alone. In short, what is *monstrous*. And in fact Aristotle encountered, in the guise of the monster, delicate philosophical problems.

Foucault and Sartre harboured, with regard to this neo-Aristotelian naturalism, a genuine hatred. In actual fact, both the one and the other, as they should, start out from the monster, from the exception, from what has no acceptable nature. That is the only basis from which they envisage generic humanity, as what stands beyond every right.

(3) Sartre and Foucault each propose a central concept, which underlies their definition either of man or of thought as beginning, project, opening. For Sartre existence (or *praxis*) is an operator of this type. For Foucault it is thinking, or thought. For the one, existence is what must be understood within alienation itself, and it remains irreducible to knowledges. For the other, thinking is something other than the simple execution of the discursive formations of an 'episteme'. Let us agree (as Platonists) to call these operators Ideas. We can then say that the fundamental imperative of animal humanism is 'Live without Ideas'.

Through the great voices of Sartre and Foucault, the century asked: The coming man, the man who must come, in the guise of an existence or of a thought, is he a superhuman or an inhuman figure? Is the figure of man to be dialecticized, surmounted? Where else will we install ourselves? In an 'elsewhere' that Deleuze declared to be 'interstellar'.

At the century's end, animal humanism wants to abolish the discussion itself. Its main argument, whose obstinacy we have already encountered several times, is that the political will of the overhuman (or of the new type of man, or of radical emancipation) has engendered nothing but inhumanity.

But that's because it was necessary to *start* from the inhuman: from the truths to which it may happen that we partake. And only from there can we envisage the overhuman.

About these inhuman truths, Foucault was right to say (as was Althusser with his 'theoretical anti-humanism' or Lacan and his radical dehumanization of the True) that they oblige us to 'formalize without anthropologizing'.

Let call our philosophical task, on the shores of the new century, and against the animal humanism that besieges us, that of a *formalized in-humanism*.

'European nihilism' and beyond: commentary by Alberto Toscano

Through an inevitably partial and regrettably restricted selection of subjects, this complement to Badiou's lessons has the following aim: to explore the presence throughout the century of a thinking of subjectivity transversal to the subtractive and destructive orientations excavated and delineated in the pages above. This thinking too is a thinking of the inhuman, but of an inhuman that manifests itself in an inertia to formalization, always threatening to neutralize the trajectories of singular subjects in its own opaque advance.

What happens when the militant subjects of the century seek to confront a faceless subject of the century – to which they bestow names like War, or Capital? How do subjects measure their own transformative capacities over and against processes and tendencies that often appear impervious to the proliferation of formal experiments and seemingly inexorable decisions? It is at the labile border between multiple subjective inventions and the overwhelming, anonymous and material force of an inhuman Subject, that is, at the very edge of catatonic impotence and debilitating despair, that the subjects *of* the century tried to be more than mere subjects *to* the century.

1   The C Factor

I'd like to begin with a twofold inversion of the methodological principle that inaugurates Badiou's lessons. Two questions then: What became of *philosophy* in the century? And: What of philosophy now, at the cusp, in this grey zone barely beyond the century, in the long wave of what these pages condemn as the Restoration – a time wherein, we may hazard to assert, certain larvae of novelty are beginning to be perceived? In sum: What consequences might the practice of philosophy draw from its travails in the century?

For many of the century's philosophers, especially the ones either alien or inimical to the anti-humanist *belle époque* of the concept, the watchword was not affirmation, or construction, or foundation, but *crisis*. Needless to say, this was inextricably a crisis registered and a crisis engendered (or, to put it with Deleuze, counter-effectuated). In any case, an initial inspection would warrant the impression that in what concerns bold, methodological postulates and unbridled, systematic invention, the nineteenth century of Schelling, Feuerbach, Marx, Comte, Nietzsche or Peirce had nothing to envy the twentieth.

If we consider the period until the onset of the Second World War, many of the efforts of recognizably philosophical figures, however bold and provocative, were really aimed at *integration*, at the organic recomposition of a putatively divergent or fragmented world of thought and practice. The fact that this integration, in its most lucid variants, was often obliged to fashion for itself a language of radicality, does not dispel its (ultimately frustrated) desire to master the disparate elements and phenomena surrounding it – the fragmentation of the intelligible world into a kind of unprocessed debris at the mercy of inscrutable forces. Indeed, we may be forgiven for the suspicion that much of the century's philosophy was tempted to *neutralize* environing novelties, if only to maintain its own sovereignty.

To put it differently, for all of its burgeoning terminological inventiveness, sectarianism, and much decried hermeticism, a large share of the century's philosophy – and phenomenology *in primis* – sought to present itself as a kind of supra-cultural *organon* that would provide an ultimately *unifying* repartition of all strata of human activity. And whether the nemesis was the molecular iterability of 'journalism', the voluble 'masses', or the impieties of 'science', there is something ineluctably conservative, be it *radically* so, about many strains of the century's philosophical production. Alas, surrounded by the active, albeit often inconsistent, performance of (European) nihilism, much of philosophy could still only muster the phantom of a *diagnosis*, availing itself of the subjective figure of the physician (or of the pre-Galilean physicist) to enact a kind of scalar reduction of the century, to provide it with a new, unitary principle of *measure*. Philosophy, the measure for an immeasurable age?

Arguably, and despite its lasting lag vis-à-vis the inventiveness of its time, this metric anxiety, this attempt to reinvent its own eminence, led philosophy into an unstable mixture between two images of crisis: a crisis *of culture* (philosophical culture included) and a crisis *for the sake of immanence* (in the sense of a crisis that introduced the need for philosophy to abdicate its transcendent sovereignty). Furthermore, these two images of crisis found themselves combined in an unstable and often nebulous admixture in the widely shared theme of a *critique of representation*. We could almost say that it was by registering the ambient failure of traditional principles of *ordering* (somewhat hastily collected under this rubric of representation), and in trying to fashion new instruments of measurement and integration, that philosophy found itself obliged to aggravate its own crisis, and to do so by breathing a strange new life into that most (late) scholastic of terms, *ontology*.

Bearing this constellation of terms in mind, we could venture that the radical conservatism, as well as the vaunted revolutionism, that accompanied much twentieth-century philosophy, can be seen to derive from the way in which it both suspended and prolonged its own crisis within the horizon of representation, understanding that horizon as primarily, if implicitly, cultural (or socio-political). Whence the frequent attempt to collapse philosophy's own self-criticism into a struggle with and within culture, and above all to force a transitivity between the political category of representation (with its apparatus of contractual and electoral mediations) and the philosophical category of representation (with all of its Kantian connotations). This equivocation has functioned as a key operator in the subordination of philosophy – passed off as mastery and control – to what Lacan irreverently dubbed the C *Factor*, culture.

The supremely equivocal notion of representation is also what has often rendered philosophy incapable of responding to extra-philosophical innovation as anything but a fanaticism, which Kant had defined, in the *Critique of Judgment*, as 'the delusion of wanting to SEE something beyond all bounds of sensibility, of dreaming according to principles (raving with reason)'. Fearing a fanatical and inscrutable Subject of the century, a nihilistic subject of cultural disintegration, many of philosophy's self-appointed guardians have been quick to quash the restless subjects of the century, wherever they menaced its sovereignty and security. Whether opening up to some variety of alterity, restraining us within the bounds of the possible, or hallucinating the immediately political or aesthetic consequences of philosophy, the themes of crisis and representation perpetuate the impotent mastery of philosophy over a field, culture, whose very existence the century has thrown into question. Is it not perhaps by abandoning the reciprocal *closure* of philosophy and culture *via* the theme of representation, that philosophy may renovate itself and really internalize and unfold the theme of crisis, discovering, as it were, new ways of raving with reason?

2   The strategic brain of man directing

Let us look for our new fanaticism ('to SEE the infinite . . .') in cinema, and specifically in that period of Soviet cinema that sought to mutate the eye from theatrical spectator to revolutionary agent, whose emblem and concentrate is to be found in the work of Dziga Vertov and his associates. The documents I'm concerned with (stenographic records of meeting, appeals, manifestos, poems, and of course, the films themselves), date from 1922 and 1923. They register the ontological stakes of Vertov's revolutionary cinema, as well as of its troubled articulations with the polit-

ical injunctions of his time (1923 is the very year of the first draft
of Mandelstam's 'The Age', discussed in Badiou's second lesson).
In many regards they are exemplary of the mimetic politics of the
century's vanguards.

Issuing from Vertov's own 'cell', the 'Council of Three' (in
which he was flanked by Mikhail Kaufman, his cinematographer
and brother, and Elizaveta Svilova, his editor and wife), they identify a *subject* (the *kinoks* or 'cinema-eye men'), an *enemy* (cinematography as theatre of memory and the representation of man:
'"Cinematography" must die so that the art of cinema may live.
WE *call for its death to be hastened*'), a name of *being* (movement),
and the basic *element* of aesthetic construction and articulation
(the interval).

Throughout these texts we can identify three crucial demands,
related respectively to the question of genre, the struggle with the
aesthetic of humanism and the relation to politics: (1) the cinema
must die so that the art of cinema may live; (2) the eye must be
emancipated from man; (3) we still need a cinematic October.
Point 1 is strikingly encapsulated in a poem contained within an
appeal from 1922. Confrontationally adopting the second person,
addressed amongst others to 'You – exhausted by memories', it
seeks to dramatize the death of a cinema of representations (or
even of Eisenstein's 'attractions', still too 'thematic' for the *kinoks*)
as the necessary prelude to the emergence of a cinema that would
develop the autonomous life of sensation in the montage of movement. The sheer violence of the image is striking, a violence done
directly to the cinema *as organism*:

> A friendly warning:
> Don't hide your heads like ostriches.
> Raise your eyes.
> Look around you –
> There!
> It's obvious to me
> as to any child.
> The innards,
> the guts of strong sensations
> are tumbling out

of cinema's belly,
ripped open on the reef of revolution.
See them dragging along,
leaving a bloody trail on the earth
that quivers with horror and disgust.
It's all over.

Sensation (or movement), revealed by the incision of the Vertovian image of cinema, bears a striking affinity with Adorno's demand apropos of the New Music in his 1967 rapprochement with the Darmstadt school, 'Vers une musique informelle': 'it would be necessary to eliminate unsentimentally every vestige of the organic that does not originate in its principle of artifice, its thoroughgoing organisation'. Neither are we in the thrall of a vitalism/mechanism dichotomy. Vertov does not oppose the *mechanism* of montage to the *organic body* of cinema. He dissolves this opposition in order to demonstrate how the new cinema transfigures the physiological and theatrical eye of the habituated spectator into a kino-eye, a sort of transhuman conduit for a life of sensation that can only be experienced in its vital truth to the degree that it is machinically constructed and composed.

This brings us to point 2. The 'emancipation of the camera' from the habituated eye is the very condition for this 'inhuman' experience of the life of sensation. Together with many of his contemporaries, Vertov will thus come, in this cinema which could be termed a 'communism of sensations' or a 'communism of movements', to equate the promise of revolution with a liberation from the human depicted as a *habitus* of representation. In Vertov's cinema the revolution is in principle the harbinger of an unfettered, inhuman sensation.

In the transvaluation of the eye into the 'kino-eye' we see the century's promise – at the intersection of political and aesthetic militancy – that the emancipation of human subjects will entail the emancipation of the inhuman from the representational *habitus* of humanity. Yes, this is a break from reality into the real but into a real that will never be sundered from its *construction*: 'The mechanical eye, the camera, rejecting the human eye as crib sheet, gropes its way through the chaos of visual events, letting itself be drawn or repelled by movement, probing, as it goes, the path of its own movement. It experiments, distending time, dissecting movement, or, in contrary fashion, absorbing time within itself, swallowing years, thus schematizing processes of long duration inaccessible to the normal eye.' Vertov's cinema is thus marked by a systematic *anachronism*, a capacity to 'denature' time and envelop it, along with movement as an element, material, or rather, as a *medium* of construction.

This project will be wrecked by the hardening of the revolution, by a socialist state that could endure only insofar as it was itself endlessly and expediently *represented*, played out in idolatrous icons, in garish clichés of mastery. In the notes and journals that track the disintegration of the *kinoks* and Vertov's increasing desperation at his marginality (from 1934: 'We went about covered from head to foot with naphthalene, our irritated skins unable to breathe, smeared with stinking caustic liquids, fighting off attacks of lice. Our nerves were always on edge, and we controlled them by willpower. We did not want to give up. We had decided to fight to the finish') the incessant demand – point 3 above – is for an October in and for cinema.

What does this demand entail? *That the art of the revolution must never represent the revolution.* A generalized parallelism must be invented between political and artistic militancy, the services rendered by the latter taking the form of an *enactment* of the revolution, a *transposition* of revolutionary injunctions into its own domain, specified to its own categories (not the people, but movement; not the party member, but the *kinok*; not labour, but the interval . . .).

In proposing his inhuman cinema of movement – or his cinema of inhuman movement – Vertov unravelled the very image (political *and* aesthetic) of the organic as the impossible intersection of necessity and act, of life and decision, of the deepest passivity and the purest act. In its place, and predicated on the founding postulate of his cinematic ontology (Being is Movement), he instituted the dialectic of, on the one hand, a material of sensation that is both time and movement, and, on the other, the interval as principle of artifice. The kino-eye is a fracture in the fabric of the habits of representation giving onto the life of sensation, but this life is in turn constructed through and through, contracted and dilated, connected and disconnected by 'the strategic brain of man directing'.

Is this wholly anti-naturalist practice of articulation (as Vertov pointedly remarks, the cinema is not actually made of movements, but of intervals), founded on the conviction that the real can be 'experienced' but *only* through the discipline of artifice, not a testament to the possibility not just of an *enthusiasm* (the name of Vertov's first sound film . . .), but even of a *fanaticism without terror*, beyond the sombre antinomy of necessity and decision?

3 The language of war

What Badiou dubs the 'century of war' was also drawn to a far less 'constructible' inhumanity than the one of Vertov's machinic aesthesis. In the (battle)field of literature, perhaps no two voices are as diametrically opposed, no two characters as dissonant, as those of Karl Kraus and Ernst Jünger. Yet I would briefly like to explore the possibility that in the very contrast of their opposing works we may be able to orient ourselves within war in the twentieth century and the twentieth century as war (to borrow the title of an essay by Jan Patočka); that we may begin to delineate those coordinates of conflict, political and otherwise, which emerged from the European cataclysm of 1914, in order to understand the manner in which the subjects of the century may have come to mimic war – conceived as a generalized figure of opposition and destruction – and to assume it as both the object and the element of experience (in this instance, of writing).

How, in the artifice of language, is war to be experienced and articulated? How is it to be identified and subjectivated? But in order for these questions to be posed, and to draw their formal consequences, we first need to ask: Is *novelty*, the novelty of the century and the century as novelty, the mark of this war?

The choice of literary form is our first clue. Reflecting the ambiguous nature of the war of 1914, both Jünger and Kraus opt for forms which are *not* those of the experimental avant-garde. Their works inhabit an aesthetic limbo between the century which will emerge as a consequence of the Great War and the literary habits of the late-nineteenth century. A wilful incongruity between the means and the content of expression is at work, an incongruity which is perhaps the only way that such an experience could have been recorded.

In Kraus, this incongruity takes the shape of a kind of hallucinatory archaism, what he calls a theatre of Mars: a sprawling satire, or monstrous tragedy, which takes place in five acts containing over 200 scenes and whose actual production would have required well over ten hours. It is telling that Kraus refused offers to produce *The Last Days of Mankind* (1914–22) during his own lifetime, preferring to present it by instalments within his publication *Die Fackel* and 'performing' it himself in his famous public readings.

Given the premises of Kraus's enterprise, the dramatic form is both required and impossible. Required, because both Kraus's object (the manifestation of war in the voices of *doxa*, in the palpable *disintegration* of language) and his method (a combination of dialogue and collage, with two-thirds of *The Last Days* being made up of citations) wish to make the war 'speak for itself'. Impossible, because Kraus postulates that there is no literary form adequate to the linguistic catastrophe that both accompanies and exacerbates the war. Indeed, as he puts it in the text which served as the germ to *The Last Days, In These Great Times* (1914), these are times 'in which things are happening that could not be imagined and in which what can no longer be *imagined* must *happen*, for if one could imagine it, it would not happen'.

The only thing to be done then is to *record* the catastrophe in the myriad voices of an unprecedented horror, a European hecatomb, with the ridiculous simulacra of 'culture' – slogans and words whose eerie banality and ludicrous verve Kraus deftly 'arranges' with the cruellest and most acute auditory capacity. Against any techno-romantic attempt to find the war's novelty in the affective phenomenology of combat, Kraus offers up his ghastly vignettes, culled from his Viennese environs, ranging from attempts to turn Goethe's poetry into elegies for submarines to organized tourist trips to the sites of Europe's carnage.

At the core of Kraus's desperate project is the heuristic principle that the war can only be properly assessed on its 'surface', specifically within the collapse of language, a collapse punctuated by bitter laughter. As he puts it in the 'Premise' to *The Last Days*: 'I've depicted what others have limited themselves to doing.' For Kraus, to participate in war is precisely not to comprehend it; to be prey to the war's becoming is inevitably to fall for the martial kitsch with which it persuades thousands into a futile, ludicrous sacrifice. *This war cannot produce a subject.*

Instead, in a manner that for Kraus remains obscure, *war is itself a kind of subject*, a relentless movement that turns mankind into 'human material', language into propaganda, and whose drive is to be found in an opaque amalgam of finance and technics. The only position, the only marginal subjectivity left is that of the 'conscientious objector', of the critic whose sole task is to echo this 'chorus of an impious ritual'; to force the war and the century to listen to themselves, negatively attesting in dramatic satire for an impossible redemption, in the grey zone past the 'point of no return' signalled by the war and suffered by language. The century's novelty marks, indeed, 'the last days of mankind', days when war will have become indiscernible from peace.

Again, it is in formal or stylistic terms that we can grasp how alien Jünger's experience of war is to that of Kraus. That the war is both recounted (in *Storm of Steel*, published in 1920) and recalled (in *The Adventurous Heart*, the 1929 version, published only in 1979) in a journal is testament to what we can call the *thesis of the soldier*, juxtaposing it with Kraus's *thesis of the critic*. If the thesis of the critic is that war can only be experienced in exteriority, through the effect of satire, then the thesis of the soldier is that war can only be authentically experienced in interiority, in the revelation of impersonal force through the ecstasies of combat.

While for Kraus war-the-ventriloquist testifies through the puppet of journalism, in Jünger it is only for the soldier (in this respect the cousin of the *flâneur*) that war, undergone in the sundering of the comforts and habits of individuality, is revealed to be the element of a properly inhuman intensity. Whence the composure pervading Jünger's stylistic exercises in military asceticism, in the spoliation of self. While both his reception and much of his rhetoric was fiercely nationalistic in character, it is clear that for Jünger war was never truly within the domain of politics.

In his writing, which filters expressionism (witness the accounts of nature) and surrealism (witness the obsession with all things oneiric) through the sieve of the soldier's *ethos*, war is the occasion for a refined literary phenomenology of disindividuation. Constant musings on alternately ravaged and transfigured landscapes surrounding the trenches eventually lead Jünger to the Heraclitean conclusion that perhaps war is a 'condition of things' (a temptation that also runs through Terrence Malick's recent war film *The Thin Red Line*, in which nature is 'at war with herself' . . .).

Once the search for intensity has evacuated antagonism of all political content, there emerges, as Jünger proposes in the conciliatory preface to the English edition (a preface for the enemy, as it were), a sort of community of soldiers, an uncanny, inhuman empathy which reveals itself in combat, 'when the chaotic vacancy of the battlefield has its murderous and decisive interludes'. This is 'life' making its irruption in combat, as an intensity-in-movement devoid of any intrinsic organic armature, a vitalism that only appears at the very limits of organism, whether this be physiological, political, or aesthetic in nature.

And just as shame and sarcasm accompany as affects Kraus's project of 'auditory' critique and negative redemption, so for Jünger it is the affects of dignity and resolve, these badges of the warrior, that mark the presence of a project of inhuman (de)subjectivation. What characterizes these affects is precisely their lack of affiliation to any actual end as such, their being evaluated only in terms of their intensity, of their uncompromising immersion in the real at the cost of any pedestrian 'realism' whatsoever.

As Jünger writes in *The Adventurous Heart*: 'At the incomparable school of war, life offered itself to its highest flux, its most extreme possibilities.' Fanatical, like so many of the century's figures, even in his diagnosis of *total mobilization* Jünger will never cease to affirm the claims of infinite intensity and infinite movement over the vicissitudes and specificities of historical conjunctures. How does this passion for the dynamic infinite affect the very concept of the century?

This is what Jünger says: 'Faced with the infinite tension which, for a pious heart, makes the temporal pale, the tension between two centuries does not amount to much, and even less that between two generations, or even two individuals. And yet the individual, in the midst of these conflicts, whatever the importance of their meaning, takes part in all these tensions – it is only in them and thanks to them that he can attain a clear idea of what he likes to call his century.' The century thus finds its singularity marked out by an obliteration of time at the hands of the overwhelming movement of life.

Where then lies the affinity between the martial aesthete, Jünger, and the acerbic pacifist, Kraus? In the fact that, whether experienced in exteriority, in the ruin of language at the hands of *doxa*, or in interiority, in the ecstasy of combat, the war is the element of an inhuman movement that nullifies the self-evident legitimacy, intelligibility and standing of any institutional universe or experiential life-world.

In terms of thresholds, whether this signals a cosmic-aesthetic invariant (Jünger), or a demonic historico-cultural drift (Kraus), the 'magical zero-point' of the first and the point of no return of the second both crystallize a diagnosis that we could summarize in the following terms: war is the domain of an impersonal transformation of human affairs, ambiguously coextensive with capital and technics, yet never entirely reducible to them. This martial mobilization turns everything into its indifferent material, destroying any topology wherein a subject could install itself, save as an aesthetic automaton (Jünger) or a powerless scribe (Kraus).

The war is thus characterized as a global event or symptom of the obliteration of boundaries. Crucially, as these divergent trajectories both elucidate, this entails that the realms of politics and action have no autonomy whatsoever, since the global character of both has definitively sapped their capacity for independent subsistence. No wonder then that for both Kraus and Jünger, the warring parties are of secondary importance, tributary to the autonomous becoming of war.

This characterization of the century of war as a century which sees the end of demarcation has weighed heavily upon the fate of political thought following the war of 1914. If taking war as a paradigm entails this deviation into an amorphous, inhuman movement, doubling as a sort of global destiny, can we judge that the century's politics has been incapable of extricating itself from this condition, unable to think conflict without its dissolution into a violence whose essence is not political, but rather obscurely ontological – an impure admixture of technics, finance, physiology and aesthetics, masquerading as cosmic destiny? To resist the mobile opacity of this global violence would seem to demand an immanent delineation of the realms of political action.

What would it be to think the link between politics and violence (to think *conflict*, to think the *adversary*) in such a way as to avert the dissolution of politics by a generic violence, but also to consider the contemporary figures of violence, without evacuating them from politics? Having seen the violence of war captured in the expression of intensity (Jünger) and in its negative presentation through *doxa* (Kraus), could we envisage a (political) language that would, instead of matching or miming its destructive force, *articulate* violence, establish its contours? Is this not the condition for a politics that would finally escape the paradigm of war, a paradigm that condemns it to death *as politics*?

4   Enemies

The century's thinking of political conflict finds one of its more forceful and more symptomatic heralds in the work of Carl Schmitt, ever the object of instructive revivals. I say 'symptomatic' insofar as we encounter here one of the rare instances of a rigorous (juridico-political) 'internal' formulation of National Socialism, articulating the epochal and institutional singularity of its doctrine – or the way, to recall Badiou, in which Nazism could be said to constitute a political thought.

This is all the more significant to the extent that the Nazi theses of Schmitt's 1933 tract *State, Movement, People* cannot be simply ascribed to his much-descried 'opportunism', amounting instead to terminal resolutions of those contradictions inhering in his formulation of the autonomy of the political. That these theses arose from an attempt to counter the dissolution of the political in the plurality of interests, a tendency coextensive with the doctrine of liberal parliamentarianism, qualifies Schmitt's thought not only as an exemplary case of the century's practical and speculative limitations but also as a necessary point of transit for any thorough reckoning with the standing of the problem and the place of politics in a twenty-first century that is arguably yet to come.

Schmitt's concept of the political is indeed an offspring of the century, and indirectly, of the trenches that gave rise to the literary gestures of Kraus and Jünger. We could even say that Schmitt's project lies in the transformation of the intensity of combat into the condition for a critique of the cacophony of *doxa* and the phantasmagoria of petty interests. If the question governing Schmitt's thought can be stated as *What is a political entity?*, then it is a question firmly rooted in the paradigm of war, but precisely in a war whose *political* character requires reassertion.

This much is starkly stated in *The Concept of the Political* (1932): 'The friend, enemy, and combat concepts receive their real meaning precisely because they refer to the real possibility of physical killing. War follows from enmity. War is the existential negation of the enemy. It is the most extreme consequence of enmity. It does not have to be common, normal, something ideal, or desirable. But it must nevertheless remain a real possibility for as long as the concept of the enemy remains valid.' The dissolution of the political in the impurity or intensity of violence is countered by Schmitt with the thesis that only in the assumption of war as possibility does politics attain autonomy. But can the political withstand this variation on the paradigm of war, without once again being overcome by the opacity of violence? Any answer must turn to the structure, the *topology* of the Schmittian position.

Given that the categories of the political must themselves remain autonomous, it appears that the only 'substance' of the political entity, the *friend*, is its standing as the instance of a 'dualization': the friend declares itself in the same act whereby it declares its enemy; it decides itself and its other. Politics is born of the Two, the Two of the possibility of *killing*. Again and again, Schmitt will affirm that this 'dualization' is unique and autonomous – while any opposition can be *politicized* by the possibility of killing, the substance of the political can never be drawn from anywhere other than the decision, from the 'insubstantial' possibility of killing.

This stance is informed by Schmitt's abiding disdain for any abstract normativity, his insistence on the fact that the political (and its juridical effects) can only be thought *in situ*. Now, the Hobbesian consequence is that while there is indeed a political entity, the *friend*, more specifically, the *state* of the friend, there is no political *domain*. If politics is conflict, dualization, then it depends on the decision regarding the Two, but this very decision precludes any independent experience of the political. Paradoxically, once the political, in the form of the *state of friends* and/or of the *state sovereign*, determines itself in dualization, it disappears as a domain.

The political here is not merely the drawing of the line that distinguishes friend and enemy, norm and exception, it is in a sense this line itself, and *nothing but this line*. The political itself, like the sovereign, becomes what Schmitt called a 'borderline concept'. In a sort of transcendental topology of the political (later carried over into the realm of geopolitics, see the post-war *Der Nomos der Erde*), the political decision is the one that decides upon the domain (i.e. the state, in Schmitt's authoritarian framework) but precisely insofar as the domain itself must be made safe from the extremity of conflict. This liminal autonomy of the political turns into the death of politics. The political is the dark side of the state, a state predisposed to disposing of men.

But defining the political at the limits of the state is not enough. Even if the basic entity, the object of Schmitt's juridico-political inquiry, remains the state, the *political* entity only arises in the situated response to the question: *Who decides?* For a thinker for whom intensity was not a category of the new, *danger* becomes the only criterion of true decision. The political decision, and therefore the political entity, thus appears to possess two sides, two moments. Firstly, is there danger? Must the norm be suspended to cope with this danger? This beckons the figure of the sovereign. Secondly, who is dangerous? Who reveals the possible need to kill? Thus appears the enemy (and the friend).

Note that both these questions *presuppose* the existence of the political entity. The political decision as such presupposes itself, it is the real, extreme, possibility of its 'normal' substance. And, indeed, without this substance the coincidence of friend and sovereign in the bosom of the state – which, according to Schmitt, constitutes the problem of democracy – would not obtain. Schmitt's adherence to the Nazi Party, crowned by the publication in the same year of *State, Movement, People*, also represents the recognition of a solution, in a concrete situation, to a set of theoretical difficulties.

The first amendment to Schmitt's pre-Nazi position, as evidenced by the title, is the tripartite distinction that distinguishes the political subject (the NSDAP and the SA), its administrative-institutional apparatus (the State), and the non-political body politic (the population). While all three constitute the State in the extended sense, what we have here is a first sketch of the very subject of politics. *Who decides? The Party, for the people, through the State*. The reciprocal determination of these three components radically enhances the scope of the political.

The new, in the form of a global suspension of the norm in favour of permanent norm-making, irrupts into Schmitt's thinking. Once the exception becomes a state, the decision is no longer exceptional. But the problem remains, how is the political decision a decision *of* the political entity *for* the political entity? Or, how is Nazism to be a 'sovereign democracy'? Schmitt's solution is, with the Party as subjective element of political action, to equate the sovereign with the *Führer*, and the friend with the race.

Whence the heading of the crucial fourth section of Schmitt's essay, *The Principle of Leadership [Führerprinzip] and the Identity of the Race: Fundamental Concepts of National-Socialist Right*. If the political is, in the last instance (and in the Nazi case, in every instance), a matter of the decision on enmity, and such a decision must be made *in situation*, not according to abstract principles or transcendent norms, then the right based on this decision must be based on the transitivity, or, more strongly, the immanence of sovereign and friend. This is indeed exactly what is stated in the 1933 essay with regard to the *Führerprinzip*: it is a concept of an immediate contemporaneousness and of a real presence. *For this reason*

it includes, as a positive requirement, an unconditional racial identity (*Artgleichkeit*) between the *Führer* and the partisans. The con-
tinual and infallible contact between the *Führer* and the partisans,
as well as their reciprocal fidelity, are based on racial identity.

The affirmation of the political, with enmity and exception as
its specific traits, thus culminates with the National-Socialist thesis
of the identity of *Führer* and race. It is at this apex of course that
the political must, once again, become indiscernible from its
opposite, that the autonomy of the political transmutes into the
unchecked, exterminatory sovereignty of the bio-political. To
counter the concrete interests cloaked in the abstractions of liberalism with the real possibility of the political decision, Schmitt
must – while inadvertently confessing the strictly political, deci-
sionistic character of the Nazi state – naturalize the political, so
as to draw from the concrete situation the substance of right.

Whether in conservative or totalitarian garb, Schmitt's affirmation of the political in terms of the rights of exception collapses
into a depoliticization, into an obliteration of antagonism as complete as it is radical. Is this the price to be paid for thinking the
political in situation? Are the primacy of the political and the affirmation of conflict doomed to such a catastrophic destiny? The
fact that Schmitt's theories, and his belated fidelity to National
Socialism, were founded on a critique of the liberal ideology that
today reigns hegemonic makes facing his legacy all the more
urgent. Three sets of problems demand attention:

The first is what we could call *the problem of neutralization*. If
an immanent determination of the political, and its separation
from the non-political, is achieved at the price of a generalized
depoliticization – while the neutralization of the political is a
transparent cloak for a brutality that disavows the very terms of
political conflict – what protocol for the distinction of political
from non-political domains could forestall both identitarian hegemony and destruction, on the one hand, and the non-political
legitimation of political force, on the other?

Second is *the problem of the State, or of the substance of the political*. What sort of political adversary can we envisage that would
not be identified with an essentially non-political category (race,
nation, creed . . .)? Can we foresee a politics that would avert the

disaster of finding substance in the situation without falling into a merely liberal formalism? How is this to be done when the entrepreneurial state exists as the very foreclosure of the Two, or when, as neo-liberal Empire, it equates the enemies of order with the enemies of humanity *tout court*?

Third, and finally, is *the problem of conflict and novelty*. What is the difference between a theory of antagonism which endeavours to exterminate, for whom decision takes the form of selection rather than election, and one founded on novelty? Is the new itself, as what is offered generically to its future partisans, what prevents enmity from turning into destruction? Can adversaries ever be encountered in a relation of symmetry? In other words, under what conditions can conflict be endured, articulated?

5   The ends of the global

This host of questions is especially germane when we turn to the examination of a category, anticipated by Schmitt – albeit in obscurantist and hopelessly corrupted terms – that has come to dominate both the Restoration and many of the attempts at terminating its neutralizing grip. This is the category of the *global*.

The cessation of the Cold War was greeted by the partisans of 'market democracy' as the incorporation of the communist bloc – the paradigmatic 'closed society' – into the planetary dynamic of capitalism. The rejoicing at a finally integrated world had of course been anticipated, in an entirely opposite affective register, by the many thinkers, throughout the century, of the malevolent integration of a planet seemingly stripped of hope or purpose.

In terms of the Cold War itself, we could meditate, all due differences aside, on the theories of a fundamental, though often surreptitious, convergence between all political camps under the aegis of state capitalism (starting with the theses of Friedrich Pollock in the thirties and moving on to the heated disputations in the Trotskyist galaxy). A similar intuition, regarding the underlying isomorphy not of Nazism and the New Deal (as in Pollock), but of the USA and the USSR, could be located in the various theories of bureaucratic power that criss-crossed the New Left.

On the eve of the alleged 'death of communism', it was given voice in Guattari's annotations on Integrated World Capitalism or Debord's prophecy of the tendential merger of the Western diffuse spectacle and the state-socialist concentrated spectacle into an integrated spectacle – graced, it seems, with the most insidious aspects of its progenitors.

In a more metaphysical vein, the closure of any horizon for the subjective political will was implicit in the parallel (and therefore incommensurable) paths of, on the one hand, the Frankfurt School dialectic of Enlightenment, and, on the other, the questioning of technology that Heidegger deployed once any hope of a 'third way' between the twin nemeses of Americanism and communism had been quashed.

We could say that at a profound level the century seems to herald an extreme cancellation of any humanist horizon for action. At times, it is hard to discern how a new subject could be hatched from a humanity so petrified by compulsion. No surprise then that scraps of messianicity or negative instances of a Pauline *katechon* (another term beloved of Schmitt) surface in these thoughts of a corrupt totality. What's more, taking a cue from Fredric Jameson's searing explorations of the postmodern, and from his rereading of it in the half-light of Adorno's negative dialectic, we can argue that the garish kaleidoscope of postmodernity, with all its gadgets and hybrids, renaissances and regurgitations, is nothing but a poorly concealed defence formation against the paralysing lessons of all those thinkers who saw in the century a stifling process of the exhaustion of possibilities, worthy of the gravest existential and political claustrophobia.

Already in 1905, in the first edition of *The Protestant Ethic and the Spirit of Capitalism*, one of the most acute inheritors of Nietzsche's analysis of European nihilism wrote the following lines, which prefigure a whole contemporary discourse that links political to ecological closure (not to mention the return of energetic preoccupations to the forefront of what David Harvey, in *The New Imperialism*, has identified as the current drive to 'accumulation by dispossession'): 'The mighty cosmos of the modern economic order (which is bound to the technical and economic conditions of mechanical and machine production) . . . today . . . determines, with overwhelming coercion, the style of life *not only* of those directly involved in business but of every individual who is born into that mechanism, and may well continue to do so until the day that the last ton of fossil fuel is consumed.'

In these strangely prescient lines from Max Weber we have once again the temptation – present in much of the pessimistic strain of thought that hones in on a planetary European capitalism as a kind of benighted totality – to think of crisis and catastrophe as the only point of flight from the alienating Moloch of modernity. What we also have is a harking back to an aspect of Marx's thinking that has recently been foregrounded by the likes of Moishe Postone. This is the idea that, to use an expression from *Capital*, the 'automatic subject' of contemporary society is not man, or labour, or humanity, but capital itself (qua value). In this schema of domination, men become mere bearers (*Träger*), or personifications of capital. The expropriation of subjects by the Subject of capital appears complete.

Without entering into the possible aporias of such a reading, we can nevertheless recognize it as the culmination of one of the century's darker intuitions, and as the imposition of a question: What if the subjects of the century are incessantly undone, circumvented, manipulated by a Subject which is both made up of nothing but their very actions and simultaneously an abstraction over which they seem to exercise no ultimate control?

Incidentally, it might be fruitful to reflect here on the different subjective options that might arise out of such a recognition. For instance, the emergence of the kind of reformist subjects who, reasonably resigned to the force of the impersonal, nevertheless seek to harness and tame it, with no shortage of inventiveness or boldness – just think of the career of John Maynard Keynes. Or the active nihilists of capital, those neo-liberal subjects who sing the lurid praises of acceleration in quasi-futurist tonalities.

Perhaps one of the unfinished lessons of the century lies precisely in the elaboration of new ways for subjects to evade the fate of being mere supports of a global, automatic, and abstract Subject, and to do so – unlike many of the subjects of the century – without necessarily needing to occupy the supposed place of that Subject, without needing to match it in ferocity and creative destruction.

The other side of 'globalization' and 'postmodernism' (these twinned words of the Restoration) does not simply lie in the mechanisms of planetary integration and the baleful visions of totality that forecasted and accompanied them, but in the very antagonisms that 'integration' brought to the fore. Not least of these is one of the inexhaustible legacies of the century, that of anti-colonialism.

Despite the facile and almost invariably racist retrospective glance that sees inevitable failure in the reclamation of freedom and the sundering (soon sutured by more circuitous and often more brutal means) of the colonial bond – the assault on what W. E. B. Du Bois called 'the problem of the Twentieth Century ... the problem of the colour line' – one of the lessons of the century might lie in the possibility of a break, a salutary inter-ruption in the (political, technological, metaphysical) dialectic of Europe. One of the more accomplished poetic attempts to give speech and sound to this emancipation from the European mould can be found in the West Indian poet Edward (Kamau) Brath-waite's superlative 'new world trilogy' of dispossession and recla-mation, *The Arrivants* (1967–9) – for instance in the following two stanzas from 'Negus':

It is not
it is not
it is not enough
to be pause, to be hole
to be void, to be silent
to be semicolon, to be semicolony;

fling me the stone
that will confound the void
find me the rage
and I will raze the colony
fill me with words
and I will blind your God.

Despite its flaws, and what we might call its 'organicist' penchant for a humanity made 'whole', I think that we may gain from returning, in the waning light of the century, to one of the strongest pronouncements of this rage, one of the most forthright attempts to think what it would be like truly to 'raze the colony': the declaration of another humanism in the famous conclusion to Fanon's 1961 *The Wretched of the Earth*. This is not in order to postulate a fantasmatic outside in this age of real subsumption, but rather to reflect on what it might mean to think the century in terms of a suspension of a dense and seemingly univocal dialectic, a specifically 'European' fate that haunted so many of its subjects. Rather than emphasizing the formation of another bloc, the improbable cohesion of the Third World, or even the salutary reminder of the intimate ties between civilization and limitless barbarity, what remains most vital in this text is a gesture towards the possibility of putting what we might still call 'European nihilism' at a distance, that is to say, neither forgetting nor prolonging its basic coordinates.

Fanon enjoins: 'Come then, comrades, the European game has finally ended; we must find something different. We today can do everything, so long as we do not imitate Europe, so long as we are not obsessed by the desire to catch up with Europe.' Reading these lines now, along with the injunction not to labour to create 'a third Europe' (after Europe and the USA), we can regard them, I would propose, as befitting not just that irreducible plurality of political situations that once went under the heading of 'Third World', but as perfectly apt for 'Europe' itself, inasmuch as it desperately needs to evade what Fanon calls 'the stasis of Europe', 'this motionless movement where gradually dialectic is changing into the logic of equilibrium'. In the same way that Fanon required the Third World to forge the means for its separation from the terminal European dialectic, moving beyond the twentieth century today – for political subjects inscribed in multiple and asymmetrical territorial or political realities – might also require a distance from a certain European legacy, which in too many ways has become the 'obscene caricature' that Fanon enjoined his readers to escape.

In that respect, another century – if another century is possible – could do worse than to recall the closing salvo of Fanon's book: 'For Europe, for ourselves and for humanity, comrades, we must turn over a new leaf, we must work out new concepts, and try to set afoot a new man.' But it should do so by meditating on the possible split internal to the very notion of a new man. For in numerous respects the century's 'activism' towards the new man remained hostage to the active nihilism that Nietzsche delineated and countless others recast, a nihilism whereby the often exhilarating, but ultimately crushing, burden of subjects lay in assuming, nay, *accelerating* a movement not of their own making, a movement whose supposed Subject (History, Capital, Being . . .) turned novelty into a kind of inexpiable sacrifice and the human into a 'medium', at once glorious and wretched, repulsive and fetishized. To heed Fanon's call today is also to invent new ways to deactivate the mythological machines which, under the signifier 'Europe', still hold in place the impasses and antinomies that the century visited upon its subjects, that 'tradition of dead generations' which – whilst harbouring the material for 'new concepts' – also, to put it with Marx, 'weighs like a nightmare on the brains of the living'. As these lessons suggest, it is only through exacting experiments in formalization, unsparing in their dislocations of our cognitive and cultural coordinates, that such nightmares may be dissipated, if not for the sake of new men then at least for that of new thoughts, and of the subjects that will be traversed by them.

Notes

*The asterisks in the text refer to the notes in the translator's 'Remarks on the translation' (see pp. 217–23). All the sources for the translations used in the text can be found in the 'Select bibliography' (see pp. 224–5).

1   *The Blacks*, like almost all of Genet's texts after the first novels (that is, all the texts following the publication of Sartre's massive *Saint Genet, Actor and Martyr*), is a crucial document on the century, insofar as it articulates the relationship between white Westerners and what we could call their black historical unconscious. Similarly, *The Screens* attempts to make theatre out of the terrifying colonial war in Algeria. It does not do this in terms of anecdotes, but on the basis of what unfolded within the war in terms of subjects. It is the sole attempt of its kind, with the exception of Guyotat's splendid and solitary *Tomb for 500,000 Soldiers*, which turns the war into a sort of materialist poem, akin to that of Lucretius.

Genet's literary attempt culminates in what I consider his masterpiece, *Prisoner of Love*. This time we're dealing with a work of prose rather than a theatrical piece. *Prisoner of Love* elevates to eternity a crucial moment in the Palestinians' war against Israel, and also, with the Black Panthers, a moment in that secret and perpetual civil war which we call the United States.

2   I do not think that Bossuet – and particularly his *Sermon sur la mort* (Sermon on Death), from which I quote – is much read these days. Nevertheless, he's one of the strongest voices in French history. We must pay tribute to Philippe Sollers, who has obstinately argued for Bossuet's importance for many years. For anyone interested – as we expect the reader of these pages to be – in the balance sheet of centuries, it is important to read Bossuet as the most consequent

defender of a providential, and therefore rationalist, vision of human history, albeit one that exceeds the resources of our intellect.

3　That the enumeration of the dead constitutes a balance sheet for the century is what the 'new philosophers' have been arguing for more than twenty years; they who've endeavoured to subject all thinking of politics to the most regressive 'moral' injunction. The recent publication of *The Black Book of Communism* must be regarded as an altogether ill-timed, historicist appropriation of this regression. Nothing of what is broached in that publication, under the catch-all name of 'communism', regarding political experiences that differed vastly in both their inspirations and their stages – and which, moreover, spanned seventy years of history – is in the least bit intelligible if we stick to this balancing of accounts. The enormous massacres and pointless loss of life that did in fact accompany some of these political experiments remain absolutely subtracted from all thinking if we adopt the methods of *The Black Book*, which after all claims to be devoted to them. Yet what is not subjected to thinking insists, endures. Contrary to what is often said, it is thought that forbids repetition, not memory.

4　In the wake of the discourse on the 'totalitarian' character of the politics of emancipation, or of non-liberal politics, some thought it advisable to seek out its roots in the French Revolution, particularly in its central, Jacobin episode. As a result, ever since the late seventies we've been subjected to inanities about Robespierre-as-Stalin, or even, by way of counterproof, about the liberating genius of the Vendéans in the face of the provincial 'genocide' plotted by the republicans. This is the sense in which, for some extremists of the Restoration, the twentieth century – if its essence is to be found in the totalitarian abomination – begins with the Committee of Public Safety.

5　For the information transmitted to the Allies concerning the process of extermination and the gas chambers, see in particular the crucial work by Rudolf Vrba, *I Escaped from Auschwitz* (Robson, 2006) (originally published as *I Cannot Forgive*).

　　This reading should be complemented by Cécile Winter's article, entitled 'Why the Word Jew is Unpronounceable', now published in my *Circonstances 3*, and to be included in Steven Corcoran's translated collection of my articles, *Polemics* (Verso, 2006). Among other things, Winter's article comments upon the way in which the editing of Claude Lanzmann's *Shoah* cuts through Vrba's testimony.

The fundamental book on the stages of the genocidal project remains Raul Hilberg's *The Destruction of the European Jews*, 3 vols (Holmer and Meier, 1985).

For a comprehensive picture of the problems posed to thought by the balance sheet of Nazi politics, as well as by the revisionism which bases itself on the denial of the gas chambers, the reader should consult the collective volume edited by Natacha Michel: *Paroles à la bouche du present. Le négationnisme: histoire ou politique?* (Words in the Mouth of the Present. Negationism: History or Politics?) (Al Dante, 1997).

6   Among the rare testimonies on the savagery of colonization by the French artists of the century we must obviously cite Gide's *Travels in the Congo*. But also a trifling little thing, one of Ravel's *Chansons Madécasses*, whose refrain is: 'Dwellers of the shore, don't trust the whites'. Ravel was a man who turned down the legion of honour because the French government supported every possible and imaginable manoeuvre against the Bolshevik revolution in Russia.

7   In the initial phase of the Cultural Revolution, some party leaders, Lin Biao among them, rallied behind the slogan 'Change what is deepest in man'. It quickly became apparent that this transformation of the depths of the human invariably required a dictatorship of steel and inordinately violent score-settling, simply in order to produce some very aleatory results. What's more, this forced delivery of the new man was denounced, in a later sequence of the Cultural Revolution, as a 'leftist' excess. Lin Biao himself, carried to the heights of power in 1969, lost his life in the midst of this counter-current in September 1971; it's likely he was liquidated in a corridor during a meeting of party leaders. This episode remains classified in China as a State secret.

8   For Mandelstam's poems of the twenties, the reader should refer to the *Selected Poems* edited and translated by Clarence Brown and W. S. Merwin, as well as to the translations and commentaries in Steven Broyde's study, *Osip Mandelstam and his Age: A Commentary on the Themes of War and Revolution in the Poetry (1913–1923)* (Harvard Slavic Monographs, Harvard University Press, 1975).

9   Here is the poem on Stalin, in Brown and Merwin's translation:

Our lives no longer feel ground under them.
At ten paces you can't hear our words.

But whenever there's a snatch of talk
it turns to the Kremlin mountaineer,

the ten thick worms his fingers,
his words like measures of weight,

the huge laughing cockroaches on his top lip,
the glitter of his boot-rims.

Ringed with a scum of chicken-necked bosses
he toys with the tributes of half-men.

One whistles, another meows, a third snivels.
He pokes out his finger and he alone goes boom.

He forges decrees in a line like horseshoes,
One for the groin, one for the forehead, temple, eye.

He rolls the executions on his tongue like berries.
He wishes he could hug them like big friends from home.

It is not uninteresting to compare this Russian poem from the thirties to a French poem from 1949, signed Paul Eluard, some fragments of which I reproduce here:

And today Stalin dissolves our sadness
Trust is the fruit of his brain of love
The cluster reasonable in its full perfection

Thanks to him we'll never know autumn
Stalin's horizon is forever reborn
We live without doubt and even in the deepest shadows
We produce life and regulate the future
For us there is no day without a morrow
No dawn without noon no coolness without heat

[. . .]

For life and men have chosen Stalin
To embody on earth their boundless hope

To think the subjectivity of the century in connection with the Stalinist sub-species of the genus 'communism' is, in sum, to think the gap between these two texts – without immediately rushing to say that Mandelstam was in the right and Eluard in the wrong. Although in a way this is obvious, it produces no effects for thought. It's more interesting to directly consider the *truth* of this statement by Eluard the ex-surrealist, to wit, that the name 'Stalin' effectively designated, for millions of proletarians and intellectuals, the power of living 'without knowing autumn', and above all, the power of producing life without having to doubt.

10   The memoirs of Mandelstam's wife, Nadezhda (*Hope Against Hope,* translated by Max Hayward, Harvill Press, 1999) represent a captivating document about the life of the intelligentsia under Soviet power, and about the stages that led from the activism of the twenties to the fears, silences and 'disappearances' of the thirties. We learn there for example that Yezhov, the principal organizer of the 1937 terror, in which tens of thousands of people were shot by firing squads and hundreds of thousands deported, was actually a refined intellectual, well known in poets' and writers' circles. It seems that, generally speaking, the passion for being confronted with the 'hard core' of action led numerous members of the intelligentsia into the ranks of the police or the secret services. This is also what took place in England, where the 'communism' of the Cambridge intellectuals chiefly manifested itself in their aptitude for espionage and infiltration. These trajectories may be considered as perverse variants of the passion for the real.

11   It is important to read, or reread, the preface to the *Phenomenology of Spirit.* It is beyond doubt that this is one of the texts of the nineteenth century that has the greatest resonance for the twentieth. We could even say that this text, untimely when it was first written, became entirely pertinent around 1930.

12   I have commented upon this formula in great detail in the pamphlet from the Perroquet conferences entitled, appropriately enough, *Casser en deux l'histoire du monde?* (Breaking the History of the World in Two?). A variant of that essay can be found in *Pli: The Warwick Journal of Philosophy,* 11, under the title 'Who is Nietzsche?'

13   Heidegger's texts on poetry are legion. The more equivocal among them are probably also the most significant for what we're seeking here: the century's extreme points. See *Elucidations of Hölderlin's Poetry,* translated by Keith Hoeller (Humanity Books, 2000).

14   From the *Silhouette of a Serpent* to *The Young Fate,* the serpent is indeed one of Valéry's animals; just as it is, along with the eagle, one of Zarathustra's. When it comes to the century, Valéry is not a thinker who can leave us cold, far from it. The serpent as emblem designates the bite of knowledge, the awakening to the lucid consciousness of oneself. Note that, in his own way, Valéry also poses the great question that we're pursuing here: How are we to guar-

antee our access to the real? In his most accomplished poem, *The Graveyard by the Sea*, he concludes, very much in the vitalist style of the century, that the real is always a separation from reflection, a plunge into the immediate and into the instant, an epiphany of the body:

> No, no! Up! And away into the next era!
> Break, body, break this pensive mould,
> Lungs, drink in the beginnings of the wind!
> A coolness, exhalation of the sea,
> Gives me my soul back! . . . Ah, salt potency,
> Into the wave with us, and out alive!

15 It is the heroine of Claudel's play *The City* (translated by John Strong Newberry, Yale, 1920) who, in the third act, declares: 'I'm the promise that cannot be kept.' It is interesting to immerse oneself in Claudel and to compare him to Brecht, who admired him a great deal. Cloaked in a dense, almost medieval Catholicism, Claudel too arrives at the conviction that what touches the real is never either knowledgeable wisdom or ordinary morality. What is required instead is a definitive and deracinating encounter, together with an absolute stubbornness in pursuing the consequences of this encounter to their very end. Claudel also believes that the individual is merely the fragile sign of forces and conflicts that, precisely because they exceed him, grant him access to the greatness of an intimate transcendence. He too considers humanism (in his eyes a Protestant abomination) and liberalism (likewise) to be paltry doctrines worthy of condemnation.

16 This book is entitled *Le Nombre et les nombres* (Number and Numbers) (Seuil, 1990). An English translation is forthcoming from Polity.

17 Among the French publications that try to elude consensual liberalism and safeguard some of the intellectual forces of the century, we should mention *Le Monde Diplomatique*, from which the majority of these figures are culled. The limitation of this monthly is that, coruscating as it may be with regard to social situations and the enormities of economic injustice, it remains rather deferential when it comes to properly political questions, and rarely dares to venture into what is ultimately essential: the critique of parliamentarianism and of the 'democratic' theme that serves as its screen; a critique that implies the articulation of an entirely different conception of

politics and of democracy. To cut to the chase, this is the conception proposed by the Organisation Politique, of which I am proud to be a militant.

18 On this point one should consult the excellent short essay by Dominique Janicaud, 'The Theological Turn of French Phenomenology', translated by Bernard G. Prusak, in *Phenomenology and the 'Theological Turn': The French Debate* (Fordham, 2000).

19 Jean-François Lyotard gave expression to a kind of melancholic farewell to the century (to 'modernity') when he declared the end of 'grand narratives'. For him, this meant above all the end of Marxist politics, the end of the 'proletarian narrative'. He did this with elegance and profundity, scouring the refinements of contemporary art for something capable of relaying – in the discontinuous and the infinitesimal – the lost Totality and the impossible Greatness. One should read *The Differend: Phrases in Dispute*, translated by Georges Van Den Abbeele (University of Minnesota, 1988).

20 The concept of 'disjunctive synthesis' lies at the heart of Deleuze's conception of the 'vitality' of Being, which is the same thing as its productive univocity. It designates the power of the One that manifests itself even in the most divergent series. I tried to reconstruct this position (and rationally to demarcate myself from it) in my *Deleuze: The Clamor of Being*, translated by Louise Burchill (University of Minnesota, 1999).

21 On this point, see the study on Lenin and time in Sylvain Lazarus's great work *Anthropologie du nom* (Anthropology of the Name) (Seuil, 1996).

22 Trotsky's *History of the Russian Revolution* is an excellent book, there are no two ways about it. It achieves a lucid balance between the epic sense of the 'irruption of the masses' (the formula is taken from the book) and marxisant political analysis.

23 The work of Erich Maria Remarque articulates different dramas within the century, from his great classic on the war of 1914 (*All Quiet on the Western Front*, translated by A. W. Wheen, Little and Brown, 1929) to the figures of wandering, action, and disconsolate love from the inter-war period (*Three Comrades*, also translated by Wheen, Ballantine, 1998).

24 The brevity and poverty of the history of the United States, beyond the current hegemonic Empire, is such that those few episodes within it whose political weight is indisputable have been subjected to pitiless examinations and powerful artistic formalizations. This is the case with the Civil War, of course, and more generally with the

question of the South. It's also the case with the persecution, chiefly aimed at artists and intellectuals, at the end of the forties and the beginning of the fifties, unleashed under the pretext of anti-communism. The committee against so-called 'un-American' activities was presided over by Senator McCarthy, which is why this period bears the name of 'McCarthyism'. It was a particularly intense time, since everyone was required to snitch on everyone else. Those who informed in order to avoid suspicion and keep their jobs were numerous and sometimes famous. The most debated case is without doubt that of the great filmmaker Elia Kazan. Innumerable artists, actors, scriptwriters and directors appeared before the committee. Ever since, American art, and particularly cinema, is replete with allusions to this period.

25 Althusser, who took interest in Lacan's enterprise very early on, connected the Marxist concept of ideology directly to the imaginary effect of unconscious formations in psychoanalysis. In the end he made the 'subject'-instance, what he called 'interpellation as subject' (*interpellation en sujet*), into the motor that explained the efficacy of both ideologies and their material apparatuses. See Althusser's article 'Ideology and Ideological State Apparatuses'.

A personal testimony: In 1960, I was a student at the École Normale Supérieure and had just discovered, with extreme enthusiasm, Lacan's published texts, when Althusser, at the time in charge of philosophy at the École, asked me to prepare a synthetic presentation for my fellow students on what was then a completely ignored author. I did this in two talks which to this very day serve me as internal guides.

26 Bearing in mind the moralizing tendency displayed by contemporary French historians, and even, as François Furet's book on communism shows, the coquettishness with which they assume the role of mere liberal propagandists, it is no doubt to English and American scholars that one should look for intellectually convincing studies of the Stalinist period in the USSR. Even so, a fruitful starting-point for considering what the 'little father of the people' may have represented as a *figure* is to be found in the documents collated and discussed by Lilly Marcou under the title *Les Stalines vus par les hôtes du Kremlin* (The Stalins as Seen by the Hosts of the Kremlin) (Julliard, 1979).

Concerning the Siberian Gulag in particular, nothing compares to Varlam Shalamov's novellas, collected in English under the title *Kolyma Tales* and translated by John Glad (Penguin, 1995). These novellas are undoubtedly one of the century's masterpieces. They are vastly superior to Solzhenitsyn's ponderous constructions, which – as it has since become apparent to everyone but his fervent admirers among the French apostates of Maoism – tend to reinforce a Slavophile and somewhat anti-Semitic mindset.

27   A small and excellent book on this question is Pierre Broué's *Les Procès de Moscou* (The Moscow Trials) (Julliard, 1964), published in the outstanding (and now defunct) French series Archives, which also included the book by Lilly Marcou mentioned in the previous footnote. Reading all the books published in this series is the best possible way of learning about some important fragments of universal history.

28   One must reread the extremely dense passage in the *Phenomenology of Spirit* devoted to the Terror. By way of a simple invitation, I offer here the following extract, in A. V. Miller's translation:

> When the universal will maintains that what the government has actually done is a crime committed against it, the government, for its part, has nothing specific and outwardly apparent by which the guilt of the will opposed to it could be demonstrated; for what stands opposed to it as the *actual* universal will is only an unreal pure will, *intention. Being suspected*, therefore, takes place, or has the significance and effect, of *being guilty*; and the external reaction against this reality that lies in the simple inwardness of intention, consists in the cold, matter-of-fact annihilation of this existent self, from which nothing else can be taken away but its mere being.

29   For all the questions relating to the French Revolution, as seen from an anti-dialectical perspective, see Sylvain Lazarus's study 'La Catégorie de révolution dans la Révolution française' (The Category of Revolution in the French Revolution), in *Anthropologie du nom*.

30   Since when it comes to the Cultural Revolution everything is now either forgotten or covered over by slanderous journalism, one is obliged to refer to sources contemporaneous with the event that were both impartial and measured. A book that allows one to form a synthetic idea of the initial phase (the only phase to contain any universal lessons) of what the Chinese then called the Great Proletarian Cultural Revolution (GPCR) is Jean Esmein's *The Chinese Cultural Revolution*, translated by W. J. F. Jenner (Anchor Books, 1973).

31   Simon Leys – in other respects a man of talent – is the main pro-
      ponent of anti-Maoist sinology. His essay *The Chairman's New
      Clothes: Mao and the Cultural Revolution* (translated by Carol App-
      leyard and Patrick Goode), originally published in 1971 at the
      height of the Cultural Revolution's intellectual popularity, func-
      tioned at the time as a sort of iconoclastic bomb. That Simon Leys
      is honoured as the courageous vanguard of the renegade, counter-
      revolutionary spirit certainly does justice to the courage of opinion
      that he showed; one which his followers, all of them repentant
      Maoists, have never displayed – neither at the time, when 'every-
      one' was a Maoist, themselves included, nor today, when this same
      'everyone' only comprises penitents, which they're so eager to be.
      But we're still not convinced that his books are praiseworthy. It is
      up to the reader to judge.

32   Concerning the meeting between Heidegger and Celan, and more
      generally the place to be accorded Celan in today's philosophical
      interrogations, one should consult Philippe Lacoue-Labarthe's indis-
      pensable book, *Poetry as Experience*, translated by Andrea Tarnowski
      (Stanford University Press, 1999).

33   Though it upsets this closure, we are obliged to mention here the
      case of Gennady Aygi, Chuvash poet of Russian (and Chuvash)
      tongue. Regarding Aygi – whose only peer in the use of form, albeit
      coming from a completely different experience, is Celan – we can
      say that he comes under the heading of that which, within the
      century, takes stock in thought of the powers of language. Antoine
      Vitez, always ahead of everyone else when it came to knowledge of
      the world's great poets, liked to call him 'the Mallarmé of the Volga'.
      By way of an introduction, one should read *Aïgui*, by Léon Robel,
      in the famous series Poètes d'Aujourd'hui (Poets of Today) (Seghers,
      1993).

34   Natacha Michel's doctrine is summed up in a small and essential
      book, entitled *L'Écrivain pensif* (The Pensive Writer) (Verdier, 1998).

35   Two articles by Jacques-Alain Miller remain canonical in terms of
      what happens to the concept of the subject when the latter is deter-
      mined by a logic of which it is not the centre but rather the lateral
      effect. The first is called 'La suture' (Suture), the second 'Matrice'
      (Matrix).

36   On names and their avatars in the century's thought, see J. C.
      Milner's indispensable essay, the title of which already indicates its
      pertinence for our question: *Les Noms indistincts* (Indistinct Names)
      (Seuil, 1983).

37 The *Annales* school, whose initial inspiration came from Marc Bloch, promulgated a theory of the 'long time-span' (*temps long*) whose manifesto is Fernand Braudel's great book *The Mediterranean and the Mediterranean World in the Age of Philip II*, translated by Siân Reynolds (University of California, 1995). That some see Furet's enterprise as a continuation of this school is at least as surprising as the fact that some regard Habermas's work – all of which operates under the sign of legalism – as a continuation of the Frankfurt School, and therefore of Adorno's negative dialectics.

38 One can find a potent exegesis of this Hegelian theme in Michel Henry's noteworthy treatise *The Essence of Manifestation*, translated by Girard Etzkorn (Kluwer, 1973).

39 There is a debate in which I've been involved, with Christian Jambet in particular, centring around whether the century's anti-dialectics is indeed a theory of the Two, or whether it is not rather a theory of the One – but a paradoxical One, of the kind thematized by certain neo-Platonists and later by the Iranian thinkers of Shi'ite Islam. On this point, the reader should consult Jambet's book *La Grande Résurrection d'Alamût* (The Great Resurrection of Alamut) (Verdier, 1990).

40 Mao's two great essays on dialectics are 'On Contradiction' and 'On the Correct Handling of Contradictions among the People'. The first of these texts (written in 1937) elicited the admiration of Brecht, who cites it in his journal entries from the early fifties. Althusser put it to subtle use in the mid-sixties in his crucial article 'Contradiction and Over-determination'. I myself commented on both these texts in my essay from the mid-seventies, *Théorie de la contradiction* (Theory of Contradiction) (F. Maspéro, 1975). The complete and utter disappearance of these texts from all bookstores, without exception, is a sign of the times, when we would instead be happy to see them included in some university syllabus or other.

41 Regarding the theoretical function of heteronyms in Pessoa's poetry, and in particular the intellectual stance that such a 'technique' authorizes with respect to the relations between poetry and metaphysics, one should refer to the only genuine 'specialist' in these questions, Judith Balso. While awaiting the publication of her synthetic work *Pessõa, le passeur métaphysique* (Pessoa: The Metaphysical Smuggler), one should read her article 'L'hétéronymie: une ontologie poétique sans métaphysique' (Heteronymy: A Political Ontology without Metaphysics), in the volume *Pessoa. Unité, diversité, obliquité* (Pessoa: Unity, Diversity, Obliqueness) (Christian

Bourgois, 2000), which collects the papers from the Cerisy collo-
quium on Pessoa.

42   Roman Jakobson's article is entitled 'The Grammatical Structure of
      Bertolt Brecht's Poem "Wir sind sie"'. In effect, the choral passage
      of *The Decision* about the identity of the Party also circulated as a
      separate poem.

      Let's add the following: some thirty years ago, under the hege-
      monic banner of linguistic formalism, the works of Jakobson and
      Benveniste were widely known. It is high time they were read again,
      since over and above that which opened up a vast field of influence
      for them – what is quite mistakenly termed 'structuralism' – these
      works are, within the century, crucial works of thought. The same
      holds for the (anthropological) works of Mauss and Dumézil, for
      Koyré's (in the thinking of the sciences), or for the (historical) works
      of Marc Bloch or Moses Finley – to mention just a few among the
      mighty dead.

43   Sexuality as a vector of the dissolution of the 'private' and well-
      policed Ego into the forces of the cosmos is a major theme in
      D. H. Lawrence's novels. One may, if one so wishes, reread *Lady
      Chatterley's Lover*, but better still – since it captures the logic of
      fusion in legendary, metaphysical emblems – is *The Plumed Serpent
      (Quetzalcoatl)*.

      The most accomplished example of the role of alcohol in the
      subversion of the usual limits of the 'I' is without doubt to be found
      in Malcolm Lowry's *Under the Volcano*.

      As for idiocy understood as an 'elementary' dilation of the Ego,
      it is exalted by the character of Benji in Faulkner's *The Sound and
      the Fury*.

44   Anton Webern's musical oeuvre shines, diamond-like, at the heart
      of the century. It is the century's most admirable distillate, in that
      extremely far the implementation of the subtractive approach to
      the real it pushes. Elementary, though infinitely complex, sus-
      pended, albeit rich in surprises, almost inaudible, though prodi-
      giously varied in its sonic effects, it offers to silence ornaments
      as sublime as they are impalpable. Nevertheless, it shows that by
      separating oneself too much from destruction one doubtlessly
      distances oneself from any kind of politics, in favour of a sort of
      mysticism without descendants. The paradox of Webern is that of
      having served, from the fifties onward, as the universal referent for
      a programme – the serialist one – whose intention the structures
      of his work effectively seemed to legitimate, but from which its

sensorial effect, the kind of mysterious prayer that animates it, is altogether removed.

Webern was accidentally killed by an American soldier during the liberation of Vienna. Archimedes, another (mathematical) genius without any immediate heirs, was killed, no less accidentally, and a couple of millennia earlier, by a Roman soldier during the conquest of Syracuse.

45   Among contemporary philosophers, there is no doubt that Jean-Luc Nancy is one of those who has meditated most adequately on love in its link to flesh rather than sex. But this is just one among the many different themes that Nancy interrogates – with the acuity but also the equanimity which is his stylistic signature – with a view to elucidating where we find ourselves at the century's end. So let us, without further ado, read the collection *A Finite Thinking*, edited by Simon Sparks (Stanford University Press, 2003).

46   A significant facet of Jacques Derrida's oeuvre turns not only around the destinal sense to be given to difference (his crucial contributions from the sixties on this point are widely known – read or reread *Writing and Difference*, translated by Alan Bass, University of Chicago Press, 1980) but, in an ever more insistent fashion – raising the suspicion of some 'religious' virtuality winding through the labyrinth of his thinking – around the dis-connection between difference and alterity (the Other), a question for which Emmanuel Levinas is necessarily an interlocutor and sexuation forms an inexhaustible matrix.

47   Appraising a certain eighteenth century (including Napoleon within it), the century that saw the sexual invention of Woman, the ageing Goethe thus concludes *Faust II* (in Stuart Atkins's translation):

> All that is transitory
> Is only a symbol;
> What seems unachievable
> Here is seen done;
> What's indescribable
> Here becomes fact;
> Woman, eternally
> Shows us the way.

48   In this line of thought (which in Rancière doubles and nuances the archaeological-workerist line, while still remaining steeped in the nineteenth century), one should first of all mention the very remark-

able edition of the seminar he directed and which, like the book that collects its presentations, bore the significant title *La Politique des poètes* (The Politics of the Poets) (Albin Michel, 1992). But also – this time turned mainly towards the problem of prose – the short book *La Parole muette* (The Mute Word) (Hachette, 1998).

49 Before his all too early death, Jean Borreil had proved his originality by surveying the great archetypes that issued – at the juncture between social effects and literary creations – from what one could call the discourse of the arts. His synthetic work is entitled *L'Artiste-roi* (The Artist-King).

50 The exploration of everything the century owes to theatre, and of the innumerable and sometimes infinitely subtle links that connect this art to the different intellectual formations of the century, is carried out in exemplary fashion in François Regnault's books and articles. Begin with *Le Spectateur* (The Spectator) (Beba/Nanterre Amandiers/Théâtre National de Chaillot, 1986). Then, in order to verify that Regnault's axioms enable the creation of a new thinking of the history of the theatre, read *La Doctrine inouïe. Dix leçons sur le théâtre classique français* (The Unheard of Doctrine: Ten Lessons on Classical French Theatre) (Hatier, 1996).

51 I use the word 'being' deliberately, since I place myself without hesitation within the 'Western' ontological tradition. One should be aware that this decision is itself trans-valued in the proposals of François Laruelle. For Laruelle, access to the real is barred by the philosophical decision to erect being as the central concept. What guarantees this access, under the (rather unexpected) name of 'science', is what Laruelle names the 'vision-in-One'. Such an approach, which suspends the philosophical decision, takes the name of non-philosophy. For the details, which as always are what counts, see *Philosophie et non-philosophie* (Philosophy and Non-Philosophy) (Pierre Mardaga, 1989).

52 Surely it is not a bad thing to end this fleeting examination of the century with a reading of Gödel's fundamental article: 'What is Cantor's Continuum Hypothesis?' I'll say it again: the fact that 'structuralist' meditations may have saturated these authors does not mean that today one can conceive of doing philosophy without having read the canonical texts of Cantor, Frege and Gödel. And also those great philosophical texts conditioned by mathematics, which are the essays of Cavaillès, Lautman and Desanti.

53 With regard to God, I refer the reader to the first chapter of my *Court Traité d'ontologie transitoire*, now translated by Norman

Madarasz as *Briefings on Existence: A Short Treatise on Transitory Ontology* (SUNY, 2006). The chapter is entitled 'God is Dead'. The German translators of the *Court Traité* used this as the title for the whole book, *Gott ist tot*. With regard to the death of Man, I propose instead my *Ethics: An Essay on the Understanding of Evil*, translated and introduced by Peter Hallward (Verso, 2000). In that book I dissect the tenets of human rights. In brief, my maxim – adapted from an anarchist slogan – could be: 'Neither god nor man.'

54   In *Circonstances 2*, in an essay now included in *Polemics*, translated by Steven Corcoran (Verso, 2006), I propose the fusion of Germany and France, with the aim of engendering a new power that would cancel out its initial components, and would subordinate to itself the slow and chaotic construction of Europe. The piece is entitled 'The Power of the Open: On the Necessity of Fusing Germany and France'.

55   The collective book published some time ago under this title brought together a number of young (or less young) intellectual midgets wishing to publicly strangulate the great figures of the sixth decade of the twentieth century – something that had already been attempted, in the pensum entitled *La Pensée 68* (translated into English by Mary H. S. Cattani as *French Philosophy of the Sixties: An Essay on Anti-Humanism*, University of Massachusetts Press, 1990) by the future bonze Renaut and the future minister Ferry.

56   In *La Véracité* (Veridicality) (Verdier, 1993), Lardreau desperately tries to found a sensitive (or materialist) moral theory on the feeling elicited by the suffering of the other. He is still, at this stage, a '*nouveau philosophe*', in other words an ideologue of humanitarian interventions. However, we can say that he is not *truly* one.

Remarks on the translation

* *p. 11* Though the French translation of this poem (which Badiou himself undertook with Cécile Winter, on the basis of extant French versions) is entitled *Le Siècle*, none of the English translations of which I am aware have chosen to translate the title as 'The Century'. Both Broyde (whose translation I have reproduced), and Merwin and Brown, give the title as *The Age*, while Greene (whose translation featured a foreword by Nadezhda Mandelstam), and Raffel and Burago, opt for *My Time*.

Everything hinges on the rendering of two terms in the first stanza of the poem, *vek* and *stotelij*. Remaining with Broyde, we have the following: 'My age [*vek*], my beast, who will be able / To look into your pupils / And with his own blood glue together / The vertebrae of two centuries [*stotelij*]?' In a certain sense, this reverses Badiou's French version, in which the subject of the poem is precisely *the century* (*vek*), that beast whose survival depends on the gluing together of two *epochs* (*stotelij*).

To abide with the methodological decision governing these lessons, does this issue of translation intimate a problem for philosophical meditation? It's not entirely clear, at first, that the terms *vek* and *stotelij* are subject to a univocal determination, whether lexically or thematically (which is another way of saying that a real decision inevitably accompanies their translation). In other poems from the same period, as Broyde notes, we get lines such as 'In the veins of our century [*stotelija*] flows the heavy blood of extraordinarily distant, monumental cultures', or 'The prehistoric years [*gody*] when life thirsts for unity, when the backbone of the age [*vek*] is becoming straight', or again 'Children are playing knucklebones with the vertebrae of dead animals. / The fragile chronology of our era [*ery*] is coming to an end.' While these poems suggest a panorama of epochal ambivalence and infirmity (also by contrast with 'the prehistoric years') similar to the one of the poem under consideration, they still do not seem to lead us towards a self-evident distinction between 'age' and 'century' obtaining across Mandelstam's production.

With respect to the poem *Vek*, this distinction can even lead to a contrasting hypothesis, voiced once again by Broyde, when he says that 'the age [like the child and the lamb] is young too (two centuries old)', that the dying or broken age 'was' the union of two centuries (with a further ambivalence whether this is the nineteenth century *and* the nascent twentieth, or the eighteenth and nineteenth, *as opposed to* the twentieth). Likewise, considering other poems of the twenties, an unequivocal figure of the *vek* itself (however we wish to translate this term into English) is not readily available; arguably, an effect of oscillation or undecidability is built into it by Mandelstam, and no more so than in the superb *January 1, 1924*, where Mandelstam writes (in Broyde's translation): 'The age-sovereign [*veka-vlastelina*] has two sleepy apple-eyes / And a beautiful clay mouth, / But to his aging son's hand, which is growing numb, / He, dying, will press himself.' Here too, the twentieth century, the 'aging son', bears no glad tidings of redemption. I am grateful to Professor Donald Fanger for his valuable suggestions regarding Mandelstam's vocabulary and its rendering into English.

* *p. 12* Translation slightly modified. Perhaps the most widely available English translation of *The Age*, by Clarence Brown and W. S. Merwin, presents us with another intrigue, in this instance of a more interpretive-historical than purely terminological order. In their *Selected Poems*, the translators select a version of *Vek* with a different second stanza from the one discussed in Badiou's lesson. Mandelstam's replacement is dated 3 February 1936. Nowadays this version is canonical in the English-speaking world. Here is the amended version in its entirety:

> My animal, my age, who will ever be able
> to look into your eyes?
> Who will ever glue back together the vertebrae
> of two centuries with his blood?
> Blood the maker gushes
> from the throat of the things of earth.
> Already the hanger-on is trembling
> on the sills of days to come.
>
> Blood the maker gushes
> from the throat of the things of earth
> and flings onto a beach like burning fish
> a hot sand of sea-bones,
> and down from the bird-high net,
> out of the wet blocks of sky

it pours, pours, heedlessly
over your death-wound.

Only a metal the flute has melted
will link up the strings of days
until a time is torn out of jail
and the world starts new.
The age is rocking the wave
with human grief
to a golden beat, and an adder
is breathing in time with it in the grass.

The buds will go on swelling,
the rush of green will explode,
but your spine has been shattered,
my splendid derelict, my age.
Cruel and feeble, you'll look back
with the smile of a half-wit:
an animal that could run once,
staring at its own tracks.

Are there any hypotheses we could postulate or consequences we could draw from this singular decision (by no means a common practice for Mandelstam) to alter the poem a whole thirteen years after its composition? (Or to *date* this alteration: some commentators speculate that the change was made far earlier or was part of the original, which is itself dated 9 October 1922.)

This amendment to *The Age* takes place in the midst of Mandelstam's exile to Voronezh, in Russia's Black Earth Region, with his wife Nadezhda – a period of material penury and isolation that also saw the writing of some of his most crystalline, essential verses. The date of the amendment thus falls between the dates covering the first (April–July 1935) and second (December 1936–February 1937) of the so-called *Voronezh Notebooks*. As for the specific dates, we have no clues (if that is what we should be looking for . . .) as to what could have prompted this considerable revision.

Though the original second stanza had ended in sacrifice, it remained woven out of a subtle and not entirely disparate constellation of terms; terms, however precarious, of junction and continuity (*backbone, cartilage*), which culminated in the fleeting hint of a synthesis in the third and fourth lines: 'And a wave plays with the invisible backbone.' This wave, that 'the age [. . .] rocks [. . .]/with human anguish,' which in the 1923 version had been tentatively followed by the binding flute, is here transformed into a deluge akin to the painting of the *Sea of Blood* that the Baroque sculptor Gianbattista Bernini had installed before his death bed. 'Blood the maker' no longer gushes simply 'from the throat of the things of earth', but also from 'wet blocks of sky'; any residual hope for the sacrifice to be reversed, for the cartilage to reconstitute itself around the broken backbone, is terminated; the beast is afflicted with a death-wound, made all the worse by the fact that the blood pours onto it and not out of it, with no revitalization in sight.

Its 'cartilage' replaced by 'a hot sand of sea-bones', pure bloody frag-ments without juncture, the age is irrevocably doomed, the fragile promise of a nascent structure starkly revoked, as the wave washing over the backbone is transformed into a heedless pouring over the death-wound. It is therefore all the more interesting to consider the return of this 'cartilage', as it migrates into one of the first poems written by Man-delstam in the *Second Voronezh Notebook*, that is, one of the first after the 1936 version of *Vek*: 'They, not you nor I / have total control over all the endings of words. / . . . / They are nameless. / If you penetrate their cartilage, / you will be the heir of their princedoms.' (See *The Moscow and Voronezh Notebooks*, translated by Richard and Elizabeth McKane, Bloodaxe Books, 2003.) The cartilage, the binding power, is now entirely on the side of the nameless princes who oversee 'the endings of words' . . .

Thanks to John Malmstad for information regarding the dating of *Vek*.

* p. 32 Trading some speculative resonances for ease and efficacy of expression, I have translated *la passion du réel* throughout as 'the passion for the real'. This should not be taken to insinuate that such a passion is a purely intentional affair, since, as it clearly transpires from Badiou's lessons, it is a passion that inhabits subjects as what is in themselves more than themselves. As Aaron Schuster has kindly brought to my attention, and as he has developed in an unpublished text, *la passion du réel* is a term introduced by Lacan in his Seminar IX (1961–2), on identification, in its discussion of neurosis and the *Hausfrau*.

* p. 85 Roger Little, in his *Saint John Perse*, has noted the considerable importance of Eliot's translation of *Anabase* both for Eliot's own poetic development (as evinced by *Ash Wednesday, Journey of the Magi, Cori-olan*) and for that of numerous poets of his generation and the one fol-lowing (Vincent Cronin goes so far as to envisage this act of translation as 'a crucial decision in English literature'). A striking example of its styl-istic influence is given in Auden's 'The Orators' (1932), modelled upon (Eliot's translation of) Canto X of *Anabase*:

Designs for the flow sheet of a mill. Sound of our hammers in the solemn beat of a quarry, and the packing of labelled specimens in japanned boxes. Theories inter-relating the system of feudal tenure with metabolic gradients, and arguments from the other side of the lake on the formation of hanging valleys, interrupted by the daughter of the house with a broken doll.

But the fortunes of Perse's poem must also be considered in light of Eliot's approach to the translation. It is in the diction and scansion, as well as in the lexical choice of his rendering that we can measure the great intellectual and aesthetic distance that separates the two poets. Whereas Perse evacuates the landscape of the poem of the signs of a recognizable civilization, and purges the language from the style of a particular epoch – thus holding true to the nomadism of his object – Eliot is compelled to insert numerous archaisms and to *saturate* the poem, such that, where Perse adopted a sparse, elliptical approach, conveying a certain serenity and indifference in the exercise of power, Eliot's version forces the recognition of a more lofty past, punctuated with the bombast of declamation and with the use of deliberately remote vocabulary. (Consider for example the line given here as 'Beautiful are bright weapons in the morning and behind us the sea is fair', which in Little's more 'literal' version is rendered as 'Weapons are lovely in the morning *and the sea*'.)

In this regard, while not going so far as to affix a time to the poem's errancy, Eliot's very approach to poetic language contravenes Perse's directives, as stated in a letter discussing the connotations of the title:

The word is neutralised in my thinking, attaining the self-effacement of an ordinary term. It must no longer suggest any association to classical ideas. Nothing to do with Xenophon. The word is employed abstractly, incorporated into everyday French with all the necessary discretion, in the simple etymological sense of 'Expedition towards the interior', with a meaning both geographic and spiritual. The word also bears the further etymological meaning of 'climbing on horseback', 'climbing on the saddle'.

It is such a historical *neutralization* of language that ultimately separates the two poets, even – or especially – as one transposes the other into his own tongue. This separation was explicitly noted by Perse himself. Writing to Shlomo Elbaz, the author of a comparative thesis on the two poets, he remarked sharply:

Despite the personal friendship that we have been able to share, everything fundamentally opposed us, in our conceptions of the poetic principle and of literary creation as well as in the human behaviour in the face
of life itself or in the face of the metaphysical threshold.

Perhaps the most important of these oppositions concerns the significance for the poem of *culture*. Eliot's departure from America was driven
by the rejection of the pragmatic commercial pluralism of his origins as
well as by the dogged attempt to attain, through the poetic medium, the
partial (re)composition of an organic universe of social, moral and aesthetic values (though, ideologically speaking, never reaching the fascis-
tic delirium of his fellow expatriate Pound). Tellingly, this enterprise,
marred by its nostalgia, could not but employ two mutually exclusive
strategies: (1) the creation of works constructed out of the brilliant but
eclectic selection and interweaving of references and fragments from disparate, though allegedly 'purer', epochs of literary creation, and intended
as great frescos of the disintegration of the present age; (2) an ascesis of
both speaker and language, aimed at rejoining, through a kind of self-
effacement, an essentially imaginary culture (in this instance, a sort of
heroic Anglicanism). Language was therefore subjected to a disciplinary
regimen largely dictated by a bitter unease with the present and an
attempt to revive fragments of the past, an attempt itself undermined
by the fact that these *could not but be fragments*, not to mention by the
inevitable acknowledgement that the pluralism of the publicist and the
usurer will never be quashed by the eclecticism of the archivist and
curator.

Quite the reverse – explaining both his own feeling of distance from
Eliot as well as the surface tranquillity of his own work – Perse's writing
was intended as a *cure from* and not as a *search for* culture. As he reflected:
'My hostility towards culture is a matter . . . of homeopathy: I believe
that culture itself must be taken to the extreme point where it impugns
itself and, perjured, cancels itself out.' Where a superficial consideration
of his style, so paced and composed, might view Perse as a literary conservative, comparing poorly with some of the formal innovations of Eliot
or Pound, statements such as this reveal him to be a far more radical
inhabitant of a century of the real, a time for which the authority of
culture and the infinite archives of tradition were something that could
be dispensed with in the balance – and the 'solitude', as Perse would put
it – of action.

It is worth noting, in this respect, that *Anabasis* may bear greater
affinities with some of the more iconoclastic figures in American

literature, and specifically with the later writings of William Burroughs – that other 'annihilator' of culture, who, with his collaborator Brion Gysin, had once cut up *Anabasis*, together with the Song of Songs of Solomon, Shakespeare's *Sonnets*, and Huxley's *Doors of Perception* to produce a *Poem of Poems* for radio performance. Some of Burroughs's later fiction, especially *Cities of the Red Night*, can be seen to testify to this subterranean Persean lineage.

It is perhaps in a certain annihilation or scrambling of culture – in Burroughs's 'electronic revolution' for instance – that the greatness of twentieth-century American writing may be discerned. D. H. Lawrence anticipated this in his Foreword to the 1923 *Studies in Classic American Literature*, writing: 'The furthest frenzies of French modernism or futurism have not yet reached the pitch of extreme consciousness that Poe, Melville, Hawthorne, Whitman reached. The European moderns are all trying to be extreme. The great Americans I mention just were it.'

This kind of annotation leaves some questions pending: Doesn't this lineage of active American nihilism – despite the imperial expansion of Luce's 'American Century', and the neo-con vision of its sequel – point to the possibility of a weird continuity between the nineteenth and the twentieth century in what concerns the USA and its artistic subjects? Is there a *sui generis* subjectivity that marks the American (literary) experience in particular – as outlined in Deleuze's diagrams of cosmic imperceptibility? Is this an extreme subjectivity of construction and flight, rather than one of either destruction or subtraction? Today especially, much could be gained from delving into the subjective resources that have long seethed in the interstices of the Empire of Capital.

* *p. 99*   The *Internationale* is quoted here and below, in Charles Hope Kerr's version, as it appeared in the thirty-fourth edition of the International Workers of the World's *Little Red Songbook*. The rather fusty British version, by Martin Glasse, obscures or eliminates many of the most distinctive lines in the original.

* *p. 100*   *Le Moi*, which is customarily translated in Sartre as 'the Me', is rendered in translations of Lacan as 'Ego' (e.g. *idéal du moi* becomes 'ego-ideal'), thus obscuring some of the resonances that Badiou is highlighting in this section.

Select bibliography

Aragon, Louis, *Irene's Cunt*, tr. Alexis Lykiard, Creation, 1996.

Auden, W. H., 'The Orators', in *The English Auden: Poems, Essays and Dramatic Writings 1927–39*, ed. Edward Mendelson, Faber and Faber, 1977.

Aygi, Gennady, *Selected Poems 1954–1994*, tr. Peter France, Northwestern University Press, 1997.

Bonnefoy, Yves, *In the Shadow's Light*, tr. John Naughton, University of Chicago Press, 1991.

Bossuet, Jacques Bénigne, *Sermon sur la mort et autres sermons*, ed. Jacques Truchet, Flammarion, 1996.

Brathwaite, Edward (Kamau), *The Arrivants, A New World Trilogy: Rights of Passage/Islands/Masks*, Oxford University Press, 1988.

Brecht, Bertolt, *Écrits sur la politique et la société (1919–1950)*, tr. from the German by Paul Dehem and Philippe Ivernel, L'Arche, 1971.

Brecht, Bertolt, *The Decision*, tr. John Willett, in *Collected Plays: Three*, Methuen, 1998.

Breton, André, *Mad Love*, tr. Mary Ann Caws, University of Nebraska Press, 1988.

Breton, André, *Arcanum 17*, tr. Zack Rogow, Green Integer, 2004.

Broyde, Stephen, *Osip Mandelstam and his Age: A Commentary on the Themes of War and Revolution in the Poetry (1913–1923)*, Harvard Slavic Monographs, Harvard University Press, 1975.

Celan, Paul, *Poems of Paul Celan*, tr. Michael Hamburger, Persea Books, 2002.

Eluard, Paul, 'Joseph Staline', in *Hommages*, included in *Œuvres complètes, 1913–1953*, Gallimard, 'La Pléiade' collection, 1968.

Foucault, Michel, *The Order of Things*, Routledge, 2001.

Freud, Sigmund, *The Standard Edition of the Complete Psychological Works of Sigmund Freud*, ed. James Strachey, Penguin, 2001. See vols 7

(Dora), 10 (The Rat Man, Little Hans), 12 (Judge Schreber) and 17 (The Wolf Man).

Genet, Jean, *The Blacks: A Clown Show*, tr. Bernard Frechtman, Faber and Faber, 1973.

Goethe, Johann Wolfgang von, *Faust I & II, The Collected Works, Vol. 2*, ed. and tr. Stuart Atkins, Princeton University Press, 1994.

Hegel, Georg Wilhelm Friedrich, *Phenomenology of Spirit*, tr. A. V. Miller, Oxford University Press, 1979.

Heidegger, Martin, *Poetry, Language, Thought*, tr. Albert Hofstadter, Harper, 2001.

Mandelstam, Osip, *Selected Poems*, tr. Clarence Brown and W. S. Merwin, Penguin, 1986.

Mao Tsetung, *Six Essays on Military Affairs*, Peking, Foreign Languages Press, 1972.

Perse, Saint-John, *Anabasis*, tr. and with a preface by T. S. Eliot, Harvest, 1970.

Pessoa, Fernando, *Maritime Ode*, in *Poems of Fernando Pessoa*, ed. and tr. Edwin Honig and Susan M. Brown, City Lights, 1998.

Sartre, Jean-Paul, *Search for a Method*, tr. Hazel E. Barnes, Vintage, 1968.

Valéry, Paul, 'The Graveyard by the Sea', tr. James R. Lawler, in *The Collected Works of Paul Valéry*, ed. Jackson Mathews, Princeton, 1956–75.

Vertov, Dziga, *Kino-Eye: The Writings of Dziga Vertov*, ed. and with an introduction by Annette Michelson, tr. Kevin O'Brien, University of California Press, 1984.

Index

CPSIA information can be obtained at www.ICGtesting.com
Printed in the USA
BVOW06s0608070616

450561BV00025B/183/P

9 780745 636320